Just Who Do We Think We A

Drawing upon diverse and specific examples of self-study, described here by the practitioners themselves, this unique book formulates a methodological framework for self-study in education.

This collection brings together an international range of self-studies carried out in teacher education, each of which has a different perspective to offer on issues of method and methodology, including:

- memory work
- fictional practice
- collaborative autobiography
- auto-ethnography
- phenomenology
- image-based approaches.

As method takes centre stage in educational and social scientific research, and self-study becomes a key tool for research, training, practice and professional development in education, *Just Who Do We Think We Are?* provides an invaluable resource for anyone undertaking this form of practitioner research.

Claudia Mitchell is Professor and Chair in the School of Education at KwaZulu-Natal University. **Sandra Weber** is Professor of Education and a Fellow at the Simone de Beauvoir Institute at Concordia University. **Kathleen O'Reilly-Scanlon** is Associate Professor and Chair of the Language arts/Reading/Literacy subject area at the University of Regina in western Canada.

Just Who Do We Think We Are?

Methodologies for autobiography and self-study in teaching

Edited by Claudia Mitchell,
Sandra Weber and
Kathleen O'Reilly-Scanlon

RoutledgeFalmer
Taylor & Francis Group

LONDON AND NEW YORK

First published 2005
by RoutledgeFalmer
2 Park Square, Milton Park, Abingdon, Oxon OX14 4RN

Simultaneously published in the USA and Canada
by RoutledgeFalmer
270 Madison Ave, New York, NY 100016

RoutledgeFalmer is an imprint of the Taylor & Francis Group

Typeset in Sabon by
Keystroke, Jacaranda Lodge, Wolverhampton
Printed and bound in Great Britain by
TJ International Ltd, Padstow, Cornwall

British Library Cataloguing in Publication Data
A catalogue record for this book is available from the British Library

Library of Congress Cataloging in Publication Data
A catalog record for this book has been requested

ISBN 0–415–29872–5 hbk
ISBN 0–415–29873–3 pbk

Contents

List of figures viii
List of contributors ix
Acknowledgements xvi

1 Just who do we think we are . . . and how do we know this?:
re-visioning pedagogical spaces for studying our teaching
selves 1
CLAUDIA MITCHELL AND SANDRA WEBER

PART I
Self-study through memory and the body 11

2 The pedagogy of shoes: clothing and the body in self-study 13
SANDRA WEBER

3 Heavy fuel: memoire, autobiography and narrative 22
VICTORIA PERSELLI

4 Drawings as a research tool for self-study: an embodied
method of exploring memories of childhood bullying 34
CATHERINE DERRY

PART 2
Self-study through literary and artistic inquiry 47

5 The monochrome frame: mural-making as a methodology
for understanding 'self' 49
MAX BIDDULPH

6 Using pictures at an exhibition to explore my teaching practices 58
MARY LYNN HAMILTON

7 Self-study through an exploration of artful and artless experiences 69
LINDA SZABAD-SMYTH

8 Apples of change: arts-based methodology as a poetic and visual
sixth sense 81
C.T. PATRICK DIAMOND AND CHRISTINE VAN HALEN-FABER

9 Inquiry through poetry: the genesis of self-study 95
LYNN BUTLER-KISBER

10 Truth in fiction: seeing our rural selves 111
TONY KELLY

PART 3
Reflection, life history and self-study 121

11 'It was good to find out why': teaching drama planning through
a self-study lens 123
LINDA L. LANG

12 Speak for yourselves: capturing the complexity of critical
reflection 131
VICKI KUBLER LABOSKEY

13 Just where do I think I'm going?: working with marginalized
and disaffected youths and their self-study 142
KATHARINE CHILDS

14 Pathlamp: a self-study guide for teacher research 154
CAROL A. MULLEN AND WILLIAM A. KEALY

15 Teaching about teaching: the role of self-study 168
AMANDA BERRY AND JOHN LOUGHRAN

PART 4
(Re)positioning the self in and through self-study   181

16 The sand diaries: visions, vulnerability and self-study   183
    ANASTASIA KAMANOS GAMELIN

17 A queer path across the straight furrows of my field: a series
    of reflections   193
    MARY PHILLIPS MANKE

18 Self-study through narrative interpretation: probing lived
    experiences of educational privilege   206
    KATHLEEN PITHOUSE

19 'White female teacher arrives in native community with trunk
    and cat': using self-study to investigate tales of traveling
    White teachers   218
    TERESA STRONG-WILSON

20 Starting with the self: reflexivity in studying women teachers'
    lives in development   231
    JACKIE KIRK

    Subject index   242
    Author index   245

Figures

4.1 Being excluded by my best friend in third grade   38
4.2 An incident of sexual assault by some older bullies   39
4.3 Seeing my self as two disconnected selves   40
4.4 Being the last one picked for teams in gym class   41
4.5 Taking part in the game of 'germs'   43
5.1 The image of the park railings   53
5.2 'It happened, it really happened'   55
8.1 Kerri's apple portrait   86
8.2 Kerri's apple batik   90
14.1 Pathlamp for planting   155

Contributors

About the editors

Claudia Mitchell is a Professor and Chair in the School of Education at the University of KwaZulu-Natal. Her research interests include youth and HIV/AIDS prevention, gender and development, gay and lesbian youth literature, South African young adult literature, teachers' professional identity, girlhood and popular culture. Methodologically, she is particularly interested in arts-based/image-based approaches to youth participation. Her most recent book (with Sandra Weber) is an edited book on dress studies, *Not Just Any Dress: Narratives of Dress, Identity, and the Body* (2004).

Kathleen O'Reilly Scanlon is an Associate Professor in the Faculty of Education, University of Regina. She is Chair of the Language arts/Reading/Literacy subject area. She completed her doctorate in the Department of Integrated Studies in Education, McGill University, where she focused on the role of memory-work in teachers' self-study. She is the author of *Tales Out of School*. Her research interests are in the areas of curriculum, memory work, arts-based research and Indigenous studies.

Sandra Weber is Professor of Education and a Fellow at the Simone de Beauvoir Institute at Concordia University where she teaches courses on gender, language, curriculum, image-based research methods and the popular culture of technology. Co-founder of the Image and Identity Research Collective (www.iirc.mcgill.ca), and the author of more than fifty articles and book chapters, Weber is currently directing one funded research project on body, dress, and identity and another on Digital Girls. Her most recent book (with Claudia Mitchell) is *Not Just Any Dress: Narratives of Dress, Identity, and the Body* (2004).

About the contributors

Amanda Berry taught general science and biology for ten years in high schools before joining Monash University as a science teacher educator. She is responsible for science teacher education in both pre-service and in-service programs. Berry has had a strong and continuing involvement in teacher research groups and has a keen interest in developing student-teachers' understandings of the complexities of teaching and learning. Her work in teacher education is highlighted in the *International Handbook of Self-study of Teaching and Teacher Education Practices* where her description of the tensions in teaching about teaching are a main focus for her chapter on self-study in teacher education.

Max Biddulph is a doctoral student at Nottingham Trent University and works as a lecturer in the Centre for the Study of Human Relations, School of Education, University of Nottingham, UK. His professional career in education spans twenty-seven years, during which time he has worked extensively in schools and higher education. A central interest throughout this period has been in the role of education as a vehicle for personal empowerment. Recently he has become interested in institutions, sexuality and identity in this respect, focusing on the experiences of staff and students in school communities. In 2001 he co-authored *Moving Goalposts: Setting a Training Agenda for Sexual Health Work with Boys and Young Men*, and he recently joined the editorial board of the *Journal of Pastoral Care in Education*.

Lynn Butler-Kisber is an Associate Professor in the Department of Integrated Studies in Education at McGill University, Montreal. She is currently the Director of the Centre for Educational Leadership, and of the Graduate Certificate Programs in Educational Leadership. She teaches courses on language arts, qualitative research, and teacher education. Her research and development activities have focused on classroom processes, literacy learning, student engagement, educational leadership, professional development, and qualitative methodologies. She is particularly interested in feminist/equity issues, and the role of arts-based analysis and representation in qualitative research.

Katharine Childs, a practicing adult educator and an academic mentor, is also a Ph.D. student in the Department of Integrated Studies in Education, McGill University, Montreal. Katharine uses much of the poetry she writes in combination with her own image texts to formulate theoretical statements that illustrate and support the work she does as a teacher researcher.

Catherine Derry is a doctoral student at McGill University, Montreal. Her research interests are in the areas of bullying, gender issues in education, arts-based research and social class issues. She has a chapter in *Not Just Any Dress: Narratives of Dress, Identity, and the Body* (Weber and Mitchell, 2004).

C.T. Patrick Diamond is Professor at the Center for Teacher Development, the Ontario Institute for Studies in Education, University of Toronto. He specializes in literary forms of arts-based narrative inquiry, mentorship, and teacher-educator-researcher development. He has led teacher educator institutes in Australia, Brazil, Canada, and Hong Kong. He is an associate editor of *Curriculum Inquiry* and has published over 180 works, including articles in the *Journal of Curriculum Studies* and *Teaching and Teacher Education*. He has co-edited special arts-based issues of the *Journal of Curriculum Theorizing* with Carol Mullen and of *Curriculum Inquiry* with Christine van Halen-Faber. Additionally, he is the author of *Teacher Education as Transformation* (1991), and co-author (with Carol Mullen) of *The Postmodern Educator: Arts-Based Inquiries and Teacher Development* (1999).

Mary Lynn Hamilton is Associate Professor in the Teaching and Leadership Department at the University of Kansas. Her current research combines her interests in the development of teachers' professional knowledge, issues of social justice, and the self-study of teaching practices. Some of her recent publications appear in *Teacher Education Quarterly* and the *Journal of Teacher Education*. She is one of the associate editors of the *International Handbook of Self-study of Teaching and Teacher Education Practices* and also edited the text *Reconceptualizing Teaching Practice: Self-study in Teacher Education* (1998). Currently, she serves as the Secretary for Division K and has been the Chair of the Self-Study of Teacher Education Practices Special Interest Group within the American Educational Research Association.

Anastasia Kamanos Gamelin obtained her Ph.D. from McGill University, Montreal, where she was also a lecturer. Her work has focused on language and literacy; multiculturalism, writing pedagogy, curriculum inquiry; qualitative methodologies, including narrative, feminist, arts-based and autobiographical inquiry and gender issues. Currently, she is an Assistant Professor in the Education Faculty of Effat College, Saudi Arabia's first private institution of higher learning for women. She holds a research fellowship from GREAPE (research in ethnicity and pluralism in education) at the University of Montreal's Center for Ethnic Studies and is an adjunct professor in the Liberals Arts Program at Union University, Ohio.

William A. Kealy is an Associate Professor of Instructional Technology in the Department of Secondary Education at the University of South Florida.

For over a decade, he has taught graduate courses on the design and development of instructional media such as digital video, interactive multi-media, and computer-based instruction. In addition to writing about the process of mentorship within educational contexts, Dr Kealy's primary research focus is on text learning with adjunct graphic displays as well as on the cognitive capacities of leading edge technologies. His numerous articles have appeared in such journals as *Contemporary Educational Psychology*, *Journal of Educational Psychology*, *Journal of Educational Computing Research*, and *Educational Technology Research and Development*. From 1997 to 2000 he co-chaired (with Carol Mullen) the Mentorship and Mentoring Practices Special Interest Group, American Educational Research Association.

Tony Kelly grew up and lives on a hill overlooking a little river in rural Nova Scotia. He teaches mid-elementary school in the same school where he set off along the road to learn forty-two years ago. Tony is currently pursuing doctoral studies in education at McGill University, Montreal. His research interests include the examination of rustic and literary landscapes as backdrops for teachers' lives. He is especially interested in documenting how particular teachers have been affected by the policy impacts of globalization.

Jackie Kirk has a doctorate from McGill University, Montreal, writing on women teachers in Pakistan. Her main area of interest is gender, education and development, and she acts as consultant to international agencies and organizations in this field. She is particularly interested in gender issues in conflict situations, and as a post-doctoral fellow at the University of Ulster will look in more depth at the experiences of women teachers in conflict-affected contexts.

Vicki Kubler LaBoskey is Professor of Education at Mills College in Oakland, CA where she co-directs the Teachers for Tomorrow's Schools Credential Program. She received her Ph.D. from Stanford University in curriculum and teacher education. She is President Elect of the California Council on Teacher Education and Chair of the American Education Research Association's Special Interest Group, Self-Study of Teacher Education Practices. LaBoskey is actively involved in many groups and projects intent on supporting both pre-service and in-service teachers in the trans-formation of their practice and their institutions according to the goals of equity and social justice. She has numerous publications on the topics of reflective teaching, narrative knowing and practice, and self-study, including the book, *Development of Reflective Practice* (1994) and, with Nona Lyons, *Narrative Inquiry in Practice: Advancing the Knowledge of Teaching* (2002).

Linda L. Lang is Associate Professor of Drama Education in the Arts Education Program, Faculty of Education, University of Regina. Her doctoral research at the University of Alberta utilized collaborative action research within the context of a school–university partnership to support and encourage classroom drama teachers to become innovative risk-takers. She is currently turning the research lens on herself to uncover and examine her own drama teaching practices – an initiative that supports her continuing interest in working with pre-service and in-service teachers to develop and refine drama education pedagogy.

John Loughran is the Foundation Chair in Curriculum and Professional Practice in the Faculty of Education at Monash University. His research interests include teacher-as-researcher, reflective practice and self-study. Recent publications include *Developing Reflective Practice*, *Opening the Classroom Door*, *Teaching about Teaching* and *Improving Teacher Education Practice through Self-study*. He is also a co-editor of the *International Handbook of Self-study of Teaching and Teacher Education Practices*.

Carol A. Mullen is an Assistant Professor in the Department of Educational Leadership and Policy Studies at the University of South Florida, and specializes in innovative mentoring approaches to research and leadership development. Mullen has published eleven guest-edited journal issues, most recently for *Teacher Development*, *Teacher Education Quarterly*, *Journal of Curriculum Theorizing*, and *Qualitative Inquiry*. She has also published many articles and five books, including *New Directions in Mentoring* (1999) and *The Postmodern Educator*, with C.T.P. Diamond (1999). *Breaking the Circle of One* (2000, 2nd edition) received the Exemplary Research in Teacher Education Award in 1998 from Division K of the American Educational Research Association. Forthcoming is *Backpacking with New Administrators Across the Himalayas of School Leadership*.

Victoria Perselli is a Senior Lecturer in education at Kingston University, UK, where she teaches courses in research methodology, special educational needs and inclusive education. Her prior work includes a five-year self-study investigating the role of the coordinator for special educational needs in mainstream education. Her particular interests include European high theory and the use of narrative and performance arts media as forms of representation and interpretation in qualitative research.

Mary Phillips Manke is Associate Dean in the College of Education and Professional Studies at the University of Wisconsin-River Falls. Earlier, she was a faculty member at National-Louis University and at Minnesota State University, Mankato. Her research interests include cultural diversity in education, self-study of teacher education practices, and action research.

She is currently working with her research partner, Jerome Allender of Temple University, on the development of a theoretical framework for self-study of teacher education practices. The focus of her current self-study research is on the maintenance of an integrated life in both professional and personal realms. She is a photographer, and uses her photography to elucidate her theoretical work.

Kathleen Pithouse is a doctoral student at the University of KwaZulu-Natal. She has taught English at primary and secondary school levels and has worked with learners with special educational needs. Her current research interests include collaborative teacher inquiry, curriculum and teaching, and HIV/AIDS in schools in South Africa.

Teresa Strong-Wilson is Assistant Professor in the Faculty of Education at McGill University, Montreal. She has been investigating the links between memory, imagination and learning for teacher education with educators from early childhood to the high school level. Because of her interest in memory and learning, she has been influenced by narrative inquiry and autobiographical approaches. The article in this book complements two others on narrative and self-study: Wilson, T., 2002, Excavation and relocation: landscapes of learning in a teacher's autobiography. *Journal of Curriculum Theorizing*, **18**(3), 75–88, and Wilson, T. and Oberg, A., 2002, Side by side: being in research autobiographically. *Educational Insights*, 7(2). She is currently working on a book called *Bitten by a Gadfly: Conversations with Teachers on Reflection and Difference* on how teachers' reflective practices inform their experiences with racial and cultural differences.

Linda Szabad-Smyth is Assistant Professor in the Department of Art Education at Concordia University in Montreal, Quebec. She received her Ph.D. in curriculum and instruction from McGill University, Montreal, in the area of life history research, looking at generalists' beliefs and attitudes about art and art education. Her experiences related to teaching are extensive and encompass a variety of contexts, settings and populations, both in schools and in the community. As an art teacher, she has taught art to elementary, secondary and college students, and as a teacher educator, she has taught art education to university pre-service art educators and pre-service early childhood educators. She has also developed numerous professional day art workshops for generalists in collaboration with the Quebec Ministry of Education. Her research interests include children's graphic development, life history research and memory work, arts-based research, and the role of art education in community settings.

Christine van Halen-Faber is a doctoral candidate at the Center for Teacher Development, the Ontario Institute for Studies in Education, University of Toronto. She is a lecturer at Covenant Canadian Reformed Teachers College in Hamilton, Ontario, Canada. Her research interests include visual and literary forms of arts-based narrative inquiry into self/other as artful pathways leading towards pre- and in-service teacher-educator-researcher development. She is a co-editor (with Patrick Diamond) of the Special Series on Arts-Based Educational Research in *Curriculum Inquiry*.

Acknowledgements

This story behind this book dates back to the 1990s. Between 1998 and 2002 an intense group of doctoral and masters students at McGill University in the Department of Integrated Studies all defended dissertations related to autobiography, self-study and teaching, and life-history research: Anna Rumin, Ruth Prescesky, Will Penny, Faith Butler, Linda Szabad-Smyth, Anastasia Kamonos Gamelin, Kathleen O'Reilly-Scanlon, Anna-Marie Klein, Susann Allnutt and Jo Visser. In the course of their studies at McGill some of them participated in the Language, Culture and Schooling Summer Institutes where they came in contact with a number of visiting academics from other parts of Canada, the UK, the USA and South Africa who, along with faculty from McGill and Concordia (including David Dillon, Nancy Jackson, Sandra Weber, Claudia Mitchell) each added something more to the breadth and depth of self-study: Gary Knowles, Ardra Cole, Jane Miller, David Buckingham, Anne-Louise Brookes, Jessie Lees, Henry Giroux, Ivor Goodson, Heather-Jane Robertson, Ann Smith. While not everyone from that group has a chapter in this particular collection, their contributions are nonetheless apparent, either implicitly or explicitly, and we would like to acknowledge the inspiration they (and their professors) provided for this book.

We are particularly grateful to Kathleen Pithouse of the University of KwaZulu-Natal in Durban, South Africa, not only for her own chapter in this collection which in and of itself has already expanded the boundaries of self-study both internationally and politically, and which has led to the development of what we believe is the first course on self-study in teaching in South Africa, but also for her careful and insightful editorial assistance, and her steadfast patience and vigilance in communicating back and forth between South Africa and Australia, Canada, the UK, and the USA with the various authors and editors, as well as with RoutledgeFalmer.

Thanks, too, to Catherine Derry, Anna-Marie Sellon, Shannon Walsh, Hourig Attarian, and Derek Buchler who have all taken their turn in keeping things running smoothly between Durban, Montreal and Regina.

We thank the reviewers of the original proposal for providing very useful feedback on the overall direction of the book, and we of course wish to acknowledge the many colleagues, some of whom are members of the Self-Study in Teacher Education Practice (S-STEP) and committed participants of 'the Castle conference', who responded so enthusiastically to the 'call for submissions'.

Finally, we gratefully acknowledge the Social Sciences and Humanities Research Council of Canada for its financial support.

Chapter 1

Just who do we think we are
. . . and how do we know this?

Re-visioning pedagogical spaces for studying our teaching selves

Claudia Mitchell and Sandra Weber

> *Just* who do we think we are?
> Just *who* do we think we are?
> Just who do *we* think we are?
> Just who do we *think* we are?

It should not be surprising that the opening chapter to a book on the 'how' of teachers' autobiography and self-study begins with questions. Repeating the same question but with different emphases offers a sense of a necessary uncertainty in the evolving field of teacher education wherein teachers and teacher educators (like other professionals) are questioning what they are doing and how this questioning might enhance professional practice. In the work over the last two decades or more on reflective practice, action research, teachers' personal and practical knowledge, teachers' stories, teachers' narratives of experience, teachers' oral histories, collective memory and auto-biography in teaching, and, of course, self-study, the focus of this book, the idea of questioning what happens in classrooms from the perspective of teachers and teacher educators, has been central. And while there is a great deal of overlap in the assumptions of these various areas – not the least of which is the valuing of experiential-based knowledge – it is important to acknowledge, too, that each of these areas has resulted in its own set of debates about veracity, quality, ethics, validity and so on, and its own set of questions about 'who', 'what', 'when', 'why' and, of course, 'how' in relation to subjectivity.

How do we 'study' self? What does method have to do with it? Increasingly, method is taking centre-stage in research in the social sciences. This book will thus be of interest to a wide range of scholars, graduate students, and practitioners who grapple with issues of method and 'doing.' Its unique contribution and appeal lies in the range of methods that are demonstrated (including memory work, fictional practice, life-histories, collaborative autobiography, image-based approaches) and the attention that is given to methodological issues. This edited volume brings together a wide range of self-studies in teacher education, each of which grapples in a different way with issues of method and methodology, and in so doing addresses some of the gaps in the existing professional literature, where the focus has been more 'about' self-study and less about the range of possibilities for 'doing' self-study or about determining a critical framework within which to examine self.

The 'how' of autobiography and self-study in teacher education high-lighted in this book comes out of work from the mid-1990s onward related to the idea of studying the 'self' of teaching as a specific activity of teachers focusing on their own teaching practices. This work is reflected in a Special Interest Group (SIG) of the American Educational Research Association (the S-STEP Self-Study in Teacher Education Practice http://www.usd.edu/aber/) and in a biannual conference held at the Castle in Herstmonceux, UK, on teachers' self-study, and is located within a larger body of research on self-study including the work of Hamilton (1998) and others, a two-volume *International Handbook of Self-study of Teaching and Teacher Education* (Loughran *et al.* 2004), and a newly established peer review journal, *Studying Teacher Education: Self-study of Teacher Education Practices*. Much of the work represented here comes out of a growing awareness of the need to explore a range of visual and arts-based methodologies, something that can also be seen in specific organizational groups such as the American Educational Research Association SIG for Arts-based Educational Research (http://www.usd.edu/aber/) or in local groups of scholars such as the Centre for Arts Informed Research (http://home.oise.utoronto.ca/~aresearch/airchome3.html), or the Concordia-McGill based Image and Identity Research Collective (www.iirc.mcgill.ca).

JUST WHO DO WE THINK WE ARE?

In *That's Funny You Don't look like a Teacher* (Weber and Mitchell 1995) and *Reinventing Ourselves as Teachers: Beyond Nostalgia* (Mitchell and Weber 1999) we highlight the significance of the political project of teachers and teacher educators taking on our own self-study. When we system-atically review films about teachers (*To Sir With Love, Mr Holland's Opus, The Prime of Miss Jean Brodie*) we conclude that too many outsiders – film makers, novelists, politicians – have made it their business to represent teachers and schools, and too rarely have we as teachers as insiders made it our business to 'write back' to the colonists of teachers' experience. Following Ashcroft *et al.*'s early model of postcolonial thinking (2002), we come to this book with a bit of 'attitude' which documents our writing back from a position of self-awareness. Indeed, the title *Just Who Do We Think We Are?* is meant to challenge the ways in which we as teacher educators are constantly 'under fire' – even, or especially – in our own universities, and the methodological issues that we are obliged to take on if we are to take seriously our work as teachers and with teachers.

JUST *WHO* DO WE THINK WE ARE?

The 'who' in *Just Who Do We Think We Are?* has a great deal to do with the self/selves in teaching, and we are reminded of the provocative installation of glass tunics created by the Canadian artist, Lyse Lemieux. Phantom-like and silent, the glass tunics are almost invisible, as teachers so often are ('*I'm just a teacher*'), and as students so often are when they are taken down in the presence of teachers ('*Just where do you think you're going?*'). Yet, grouped together these glass images seem to insist – but on what? Are they standing firm together in muted dignity to attest to their pedagogical convictions . . . to bear witness? Or are they reproaching us through silent protest – hard garments for hard times? Just who are the people who might wear or might have worn those tunics? Why choose the transparency of glass for a tunic, that traditional garment so often associated with school? Are we thus exposed, unable to hide, even from ourselves? Is it the rigidity that matters, or is it the fragility? How do we fashion ourselves? Do we see ourselves through a glass darkly or in light? Can we see *through* each other? Should self-study make our intentions and our actions transparent, or is it our souls that are *reflected*? And if so, how? It is questions such as these that underlie much of this book.

JUST WHO DO *WE* THINK WE ARE?

We are teachers and teacher educators from Canada, the UK, Australia, the United States and South Africa. Some of us are writing about work in our own university classrooms, while others are writing about our own elementary, secondary or adult education classrooms. Some of this work is with beginning teachers or experienced classroom teachers; others write of teaching and mentoring graduate students working on masters or doctoral dissertations, while still others are reflecting on our experiences in development contexts.

JUST WHO DO WE *THINK* WE ARE?

Who we think we are is, of course, related to the question 'Just how do we study ourselves?' and comes out of our previous work on methodology, including visual and arts-based approaches to teachers' self-study through the uses of performance, photography, art installation and video documentary (Weber and Mitchell 2004), methodologies such as photography and memory work in the study of childhood and popular culture (Mitchell and Reid-Walsh 2002; Mitchell and Weber 1999), dress stories as method (Weber and Mitchell, 2004), participatory arts-based methodologies such as narrative writing, photography and video documentary with youth in the study of gender and HIV/AIDS (Walsh *et al.* 2002) and particular girl-methods that recognize age and status (Mitchell and Reid-Walsh, in press). In posing such questions as 'what can a teacher do with a camera?' (Mitchell and Weber 1999), or 'What if teachers became documentary filmmakers?' (Mitchell and Weber 1999; Weber and Mitchell 2004) we have been interested in making practical the idea of teachers 'writing back.'

In editing this book, we recognize that the field of self-study in teaching, so rich in possibilities and yet so potentially fraught because of a lack of understanding of 'how' (and by association 'why'), warrants a specific focus on the methodologies themselves. Many of the doctoral studies with which we, the editors, had been involved at McGill and Concordia Universities since the mid-1990s have at their centre questions of 'how', and many of the sessions of the S-STEP of the AERA continue to lead to heated discussions of 'how' and 'who' and 'why'. But it is, as well, comments overheard in the hallways of conferences, voiced in small group sessions, or muttered over coffee or beer that have been telling clues as to how people *really* feel about autobiographic forms of self-study:

> 'His work is too touchy feely, too soft.'
> '*I* don't have time for the luxury of self-indulgence.'
> 'If *that's* self-study, I don't want any part of it!'
> 'Work like *that* can never be rigorous.'
> 'That's not scholarship, it's voyeurism.'
> 'That's not good scholarship, it's purely personal.'
> 'But this is just anecdotal evidence! How do we know that this is the truth?'
> 'How scholarly can it be to just study one's self?'
> 'Sounds like navel-gazing!'

Failing to grasp that looking inward can lead to a more intelligent and useful *outward gaze* is to seriously misunderstand the method and potential of narrative and autobiographical forms of inquiry. To pick up on the metaphor of navel-gazing, there is nothing about focusing inwards on the individual that necessarily precludes simultaneously pointing outwards and towards the political and social. Although narrative and autobiographical forms of self-study can make valuable contributions to scholarship, this in no way implies that this is the only form of self-study. Perhaps the expression 'navel-gazing' is sometimes meant as a criticism arising out of the fear that *we too* might be expected to follow suit; if some scholars are expected to reflect on the minutiae of their personal lives or to allow their bodies and emotions a place in their theorizing, others will *have to do so, as well.*

It is in our everyday language that we are most likely to lay bare our taken-for-granted assumptions, casually or unthinkingly revealing deep differences in the stances and values of our research, and perhaps of ourselves. In something akin to Hargreaves' (2001) notion of 'contrived congeniality,' we prefer to ignore or cover over the paradigmatic cracks that run through the self-study community, preferring to keep quiet so that we can get on with our work. Or, perhaps although *we are aware* of the many differences, we don't see these as problematic.

Are legitimate and important epistemological questions and concerns about quality and guidelines being disparaged as navel-gazing exercises? Is the self-indulgence of those particular papers and publications that do not evoke any commonality of experience, that do not resonate in some significant way with their audience, that bore rather than engage, that shut the reader out, that do not stimulate reflection, or that do not point, however obliquely, to broader social and theoretical concerns not being extrapolated to self-study in general?

Minutiae that brilliantly evoke the commonality of human experience in one piece may seem merely irrelevant in others. But these problems are not because the work is 'purely personal,' but rather have to do with the quality of the writing, the lack of transparency, or as Feldman (1997) or Mitchell and Weber (1999), or van Manen (1990) might charge, the failure to reflect on and critique broader political or social issues. A good example of this would be in relation to the ways that rural teachers with whom we are working in South Africa are beginning to explore their own personal responses to the HIV/AIDS crisis. A number of the teachers enrolled in an Honours course on Understanding Research at the University of KwaZulu-Natal, in carrying out research with other teachers on how well they are prepared to deal with HIV/ AIDS in their schools and communities, spoke of their own dilemmas in realizing that, as they interviewed their colleagues, they were in fact engaging in their own self-study. Their response conveys a sense of the autobiographical work highlighted in Ann Oakley's now famous article (1981) on feminist research methodology 'Interviewing women: a contradiction in terms.'

HOW THE BOOK IS ORGANIZED

As a review of the literature on self-study will attest, there are many different ways to address self-study. The accounts in this book by no means represent all the approaches and methodologies available, and in fact, as broad as they are, given the range of authors and locations, they are all approaches that have in common a number of features that may not characterize all forms of self-study: all fit within a qualitative framework; much of the work falls within the growing body of work on visual and arts-based methodologies and self-study (see also Weber and Mitchell 2004); there is a strong focus on personal subjectivity; and there is a great deal of overlap between methodologies (a point we take up in the final section of this chapter). Contributors all started with the same basic set of questions: How do you go about engaging in studying your own teaching? What was particular about the way that you went about doing self-study? What studies informed your work, and/or served as a kind of methodological foreshadowing? What aspects of your teaching were you involved in studying (or assisting others to study?) What challenges in terms of method did you encounter? Ethical concerns? Acceptability as a legitimate form of study? The unexpected?

The book is organized into four main sections: 'Self-study through memory and the body', 'Self-study through literary and artistic inquiry', 'Reflection, life history and self-study', and finally '(Re)positioning the self in and through self-study'. The first section of the book draws together methodologies for self-study that highlight some of the links between memory work and embodiment. Sandra Weber's work, for example, on the pedagogical possibilities of exploring issues related to clothing and footwear demonstrates how working within the space of memory, material culture and performance has contributed to understanding the roots of her own teaching curriculum. Does the shoe fit, she asks? How does my curriculum make room for the individual differences of my students? Vicki Perselli's text 'Heavy fuel: memoire, biography and narrative' draws attention to the arena within which to contest how we author our own self-studies by exploring the use of fictional memoire. Catherine Derry takes up methodological issues of working with memory and embodiment through the use of drawings. How do beginning teachers look back on bullying and peer rejection and how might the materiality of the drawings themselves provide an entry point to understanding ourselves now?

The six chapters that make up 'Self-study through literary and artistic inquiry' are all located within an emerging body of scholarship on arts-based methdodolgies and self-study. Max Biddulph, for example, explores the uses of mural making in examining his identity as an out gay teacher. Mary Lynn Hamilton takes the teacher out of the classroom and into artistic representations of teachers, students and schools in the art gallery by exploring the works of American artist Homer Winslow. Linda Szabad-Smyth follows up the theme of teachers and the artistic by exploring what she calls the 'artful' and 'artless' experiences of teachers. In so doing she highlights how the generalist elementary teachers in her study describe the art in their own homes and how their choices relate to how they see themselves as teachers of art. The chapters by Diamond and van Halen-Faber, Butler-Kisber, and Kelly each have a poetic or literary dimension to them. Diamond and van Halen-Faber, for example, describe their work with visual metaphors and batik as an art form with beginning teachers. Butler-Kisber demonstrates the way in which working with her own memories of schooling through poetry contributes now to understanding her work in supervising masters and doctoral studies. Tony Kelly writes about literary anthropology and the ways that a selection of novels all set in Nova Scotia might become central to the pedagogy of change for Nova Scotia teachers working with rural youth.

The selections in Part 3, 'Reflection, life history and self-study', all deal with issues of reflexivity and collaboration in one way or another. Two of these chapters (LaBoskey and Berry and Loughran) provide orientations to the significance of systematic reflection based on work with beginning teachers in the US and Australia, and these are followed by chapters that offer accounts that draw on a range of contexts: Linda Lang, for example, writes from the position of a teacher educator working in drama education; Katharine Childs describes her work with young people in an adult education program who themselves embrace the notion of self-study and reflection. The Pathlamp Project portrayed by Carol Mullen and William Kealy describes a partnership model for teacher researchers.

In the last section, '(Re)positioning the self in and through self-study', there is a deliberate questioning of the self within social, cultural and geographic contexts. Mary Phillips Manke engages in a series of reflections as a lesbian administrator and teacher educator about her sense of self and how she positions herself in the academy and within the work of the self-study community more specifically. Anastasia Kamanos Gamelin, while drawing on doctoral work in a Canadian context related to the position of the woman academic as artist in the academy, now finds herself teaching in a women's university in Saudi Arabia where she explores the notion of journey as quest. Finally, Kathleen Pithouse, Teresa Strong-Wilson and Jackie Kirk all write of white (and Western) privilege and the ways that this has taken them into a particular self-study. For Pithouse, it is the experience of being a white teacher working in a post-apartheid South Africa with adolescents in a teen writing project; for Strong-Wilson, it is the experience of being a white female teacher working in a first nations school in Canada, and in so doing she draws on the women travel writers of the late nineteenth and early twentieth centuries. Ironically, the book ends with a selection called 'Starting with the self'. In this selection, Jackie Kirk, a white woman writing of her work with women teachers in Pakistan and other development contexts, suggests the ways in which methodologies of reflexivity and feminist inquiry allow our work to go beyond our own classrooms and even beyond our own social and cultural contexts in our efforts to transform schooling globally.

AN ALTERNATE ORDER . . .

Clearly, there is a great deal of overlap between and amongst the chapters. While we have more or less grouped them according to specific methodological areas, there are some alternative groupings of these chapters that might be equally useful. For readers interested in the uses of literary memoire, it would be helpful to look at the ways that the writings of Perselli, Strong-Wilson, and Kamanos Gamelin, taken together, highlight this particular genre within autobiography and self-study. In extending this division as one on teachers and writing is Butler-Kisber's chapter on poetic inquiry. Visual approaches to self-study include Biddulph's use of murals, Diamond and van Halen-Faber's exploration of arts-based metaphors of teaching through batik and other visual forms, Hamilton's discussion on the pedagogy of the art gallery, Szabad-Smyth's exploration of teachers of artwork, Weber's work on clothing and the body, and Derry's chapter on the use of drawings. For those wishing to look specifically at how classroom teachers (as opposed to teacher educators) have used self-study methodologies in day-to-day teaching, one might look to the work of Childs and Pithouse, each of whom writes from a specific classroom context. The work of Biddulph, Phillips Manke, Derry and Kirk all highlight sex and gender which, given the increased emphasis on body and identity in teacher education, could constitute its own section, and within a further division of this, Biddulph and Phillips Manke write as gay teacher educators in a queer space. Finally, for those interested in the study of teachers, in relation to issues of geography and class, in particular, the chapters by Kelly and Derry provide a focus on rural teaching in the Canadian Maritimes.

AND A NEW ORDER IN SELF-STUDY . . .

These new groupings suggest that the study of 'who we are' and 'how we know it' as teachers has many dimensions to it. Clearly, the area of self-study and autobiography in teacher education is rich methodologically, conceptually and pedagogically. Each one of the new groupings, as with those we have already chosen, could be expanded into a whole book in and of itself. At the same time, as we note in a previous section, there are critical areas of methodology and self-study that remain to be explored. These areas range from concerns of ethical acceptability, confidentiality and anonymity, to addressing sensitive and critical issues such as the self-study of teacher educators and teachers in Southern Africa in relation to HIV/AIDS, to the need to expand the repertoire of possibilities for addressing class and culture; to the possibilities for sex and body to become more central to the project of self-study; and finally to the ways in which the study of self/selves can become more central to (and documented within) institutional change and transformation. Indeed, *that's* what we want our work to do and that's who we think we are!

REFERENCES

Ashcroft, B., Griffiths, G., Tiffin, H., Menin, S. and Ashcroft, E., 2002, *The Empire Writes Back: Theory and Practice in Post-Colonial Literatures* (London: Routledge).

Feldman, A., 1997, Varieties of wisdom in the practice of teachers. *Teaching and Teacher Education*, **13**(7), 757–73.

Hamilton, M.L. (Ed.), 1998, *Reconceptualizing Teaching Practice: Self-Study in Teacher Education* (London: Falmer Press).

Hargreaves, A., 2001, *Learning to Change: Teaching Beyond Subjects and Standards* (San Francisco: Jossey-Bass).

Loughran, J.J., Hamilton, M.L., Laboskey, V.K. and Russell, T.L. (Eds), 2004, *International Handbook of Self-study of Teaching and Teacher Education Practice* (New York and London: Kluwer Academic Publishers).

Mitchell, C. and Reid-Walsh, J., 2002, *Researching Children's Popular Culture. Cultural Spaces of Childhood* (London and New York: Routledge, Taylor & Francis).

Mitchell, C. and Reid-Walsh, J. (Eds) (in press), *Seven Going on Seventeen: Tween Studies in the Culture of Girlhood* (New York: Peter Lang).

Mitchell, C. and Weber, S.J., 1999, *Reinventing Ourselves as Teachers: Beyond Nostalgia* (London: Falmer Press).

Oakley, A., 1981, Interviewing women: a contradiction in terms. In Roberts (Ed.) *Doing Feminist Research* (London: Routledge & Kegan Paul).

Van Manen, M., 1990, *Researching Lived Experience: Human Science for an Action Sensitive Pedagogy* (London, Ontario: The Althouse Press).

Walsh, S., Mitchell, C. and Smith, A., 2002, The Soft Cover project: youth participation in HIV/AIDS interventions. *Agenda*, **53**, 106–12.

Weber, S. and Mitchell, C., 1995, *That's Funny You Don't Look Like a Teacher: Interrogating Images of Identity in Popular Culture* (London: Falmer Press).

Weber, S. and Mitchell, C., 2004, Visual and artistic modes of representation for self-study. In Loughran, Hamilton, LaBoskey and Russell (Eds) *International Handbook of Self-study of Teaching and Teacher Education Practices* (New York and London: Kluwer Academic Publishers).

Weber, S. and Mitchell, C. (Eds) (2004) *Not Just Any Dress: Narratives of Dress, Body and Identity* (New York: Peter Lang).

Part 1

Self-study through memory and the body

The pedagogy of shoes
Clothing and the body in self-study

Sandra Weber

If the shoe fits, wear it.
The shoe's on the other foot now.
Still waiting for the other shoe to drop.
If I were in your shoes . . .
What a heel!
Don't criticize a person unless you've walked 500 miles in her shoes.
Wear sensible shoes.
What a boot licker!
He's not good enough to lick my boots.
Put on your dancing shoes, we're going out.
He's got two left feet!
I've put my foot in it now . . .
Foot in mouth disease.
On an even footing.
Don't let him walk all over you.
Give him the boot.

Whatever can we learn about ourselves as teachers from studying our shoes? What relevance could these material objects have for self-study in education? Some might unthinkingly dismiss these questions as trivial or silly. That would be a mistake, as I intend to demonstrate. By sharing excerpts from memory work that centered on shoes in school staff photographs followed by excerpts from an autobiographic play that I wrote and performed, and by using a childhood encounter with one of Van Gogh's famous paintings of shoes to speculate on the role shoes can play in pedagogy, I will explore the use of shoes in self-study *as a narrative scaffolding device* for describing significant aspects of teaching identities and pedagogical practice, *as a mode of inquiry* into how both personal childhood experience and cultural codes shape who we are as teachers, and *as a metaphor for theorizing about teaching*.[1]

SHOES AS PHENOMENON AND METHOD

They just lie there in shop windows, taunting us and tempting us. We try them on, force our swollen feet into them, and walk a few steps back and forth trying to decide, trying to imagine wearing them to work. We scuff them, wear them out, polish them, have them re-heeled, abuse them, curse at them when they pinch or chafe, shove them in the back of cupboards, leave them in lockers, lose them, give them away, throw them out, or on occasion, cherish them, wrap them tenderly in tissue and boxes, collect them, bankrupt ourselves for them, renounce them. Shoes can denote status, wealth, and position, they can hint at a person's occupation, and enable or facilitate our work. On occasion, shoes are used as weapons or hammers. Shoes can be objects of desire (ruby red shoes like Dorothy's), subjects to be controlled (school shoe dress codes), or symbols of power (military boots, the latest 'in' runners or hiking boots, Gucci loafers or Prada sandals). Shoes can support, seduce, impede, shame, or even lame or injure us. In extreme cases, shoes can be the death of us (e.g. heel catching, falling off platforms . . .).

The wrong shoes can get you into trouble. A ridiculous but telling example of this was widely reported by the media at the Cannes festival in spring 2003. A young women dressed in a fancy evening gown, her invitation to the opening gala firmly in her hand, mounted the red carpeted steps only to be turned away at the door because her shoes were deemed unsuitable – not elegant or expensive enough. A more sobering example is how footwear such as top-of-the-line models of Nike become an object of desire for some youths who accost their weaker peers and threaten violence in order to steal their shoes, those coveted status symbols of conspicuous consumption.

Shoes are an example, par excellence, of how form and material can be mediated by function or purpose, and of how ordinary objects can take on incredible significance. Philosophers from Kant to Heidegger to Derrida use shoes as a metaphor to contemplate the nature of truth and knowledge, to explain how objects convey meaning, and even to speculate on the structure, function, and role of universities.[2]

Shoes are paradoxical: they are both rigid and flexible, and to get anywhere in them, one shoe (or rather, shod foot) must stay still (pushed against the ground), providing the resistance that permits the other one to be brought forward. Made on a last, shoes ultimately bear the imprints of both the last, the maker *and* the imprint of the wearer. The weight of the person and the way he or she walks wears the shoe out in a highly individual way. Shoes retain the evidence of our embodiment. Our shoe prints are unique, even if our shoes are not. As some of Van Gogh's famous paintings of muddied shoes so eloquently illustrate, empty shoes can evoke imagined wearers and imagined lives. What do teachers' shoes evoke? What do my shoes, the shoes of a teacher educator, say about me?

SHOES AND SOCIAL CONSTRUCTIONS OF GENDER

> Hobbling down the avenue, I became acutely aware of my body. My breasts jutted forward, while my back was severely arched. My ass felt bigger than a Buick, and my thighs, or rather my flanks, swung back and forth like a couple of sides of beef. Are these shoes disempowering? Do they enslave us? Are we rendered helpless by wearing them?
>
> *The answer is yes! Yes! Of course! What other point would there be in wearing them!*
>
> (Steele 1999, p. 21; italics added)

Yet, the heels mentioned by the woman interviewed in the above quote also made her feel 'mythically omnipotent.' Wearing spike heels, she reported, 'I felt a surge of power, knowing that I could lay waste to any man I chose to destroy.' She fantasized about being a dominatrix: 'Down on the floor, you worm! I said now, you worthless CEO!' (p. 21).

Lippert (1997) disapproves of the new trends in fashion and advertising, which she sees as 'the same old "woman as bitch" thing, dolled up in new rubber clothing.' Yet fetishist images may hold great appeal for some younger women, for whom high-heeled shoes – and stilettos, in particular – can carry connotations of rebellion against the established conventions of 'nice' femininity (p. 26).

Shoes play a significant role in the construction and performance of gender. For example, in one study by Susan Kaiser (1985), the respondents, who ranged in age from eighteen to seventy, regarded styles such as high-heeled pumps, strappy sandals, and women's high boots as being 'feminine and sexy.' In the popular imagination, it seems that 'feminine' shoes must be sexy and uncomfortable. By contrast, 'masculine' shoes are supposed to be comfortable and practical. On the 'masculine' side are shoes that men wear, such as Oxfords and loafers, which, of course, women have also appropriated, along with athletic shoes and various kinds of boots that were formerly regarded as masculine. On the 'feminine' side, we find shoe styles worn almost exclusively by women, such as pumps, sling-backs, and mules. Where does this leave female teachers? What does that mean about me?

TEACHING IN MY SHOES: A SERIES OF SELF-STUDIES

In the course of studying my practice, I have used shoes as *a narrative scaffolding device* for describing significant aspects of my teaching identity and pedagogical practice, *as a mode of inquiry* into how both personal childhood experiences and cultural codes shape the teacher I am, and as a *metaphor for theorizing about teaching.* I literally stumbled upon the potential value of shoes to exploring my teaching self. Although I had used more conventional approaches to self-study (self-video, for example, as reported in Mitchell and Weber 1999) to focus on things like how I use my voice in the classroom, I had remained unaware of my feet, my shoes, and the role they could play in self-study. Until, that is, I was on stage performing a self-study piece written by Claudia Mitchell about her mother (Mitchell 2000). As I stood there holding a shoe in my hand (as demanded by the script) – click – I realized all at once how important shoes could be as a method of inquiry into my teaching, how shoes would force me to confront things I was ignoring by other methods of self-study. Shoes would make me confront and reconsider my past. Thus began a series of self-studies using shoes.

Sandals and pedagogy: shoe as symbol

The first self-study I did using shoes involved looking at old photographs of myself as an elementary teacher, focusing on my footwear whose symbolic value became ever more apparent. There I am, at the end of a row of teachers in the staff photo in the early 1970s. I am the only one wearing corduroy pants, flat leather sandals, and bare feet. The sandals were favourites – handcrafted by a hippie who had an outdoor stall just down the street from where I rented a small room in a boarding house. Without giving them any special thought, I wore those sandals often to teach my grade three class. They were comfortable. Wearing them, I felt natural, I felt like myself, and I felt like a teacher. The other female teachers in the staff photograph, all older than me, are wearing stockings, dresses, and 'proper' low-heeled pumps or oxfords. The two men are wearing socks and rubber-soled, laced shoes. I did not realize how much I 'stood out' before scrutinizing this photograph. I did not consciously wear sandals to contest anything or to stand out from the crowd. And yet, the difference in shoes says a lot to me now about the kind of teacher I think I was then and perhaps still am now: Standing apart from the mainstream without particularly meaning to, but occasionally aware, out of the corner of my eye, of differences in pedagogical as well as sartorial styles. I was so 'into' the Dewey-inspired progressive movement, whole language models, and the British integrated day, cross-curricular project approach to teaching. Usually, I was too busy following my dreams to notice how much they differed from those of most of my colleagues. Looking around me now at the field of teacher education thirty years later, I feel much the same as I did back then, a bit on the fringe, swimming rather quietly upstream, not at the forefront of any great revolution, but doing my own thing in case it makes a difference to someone, if only to me. I notice I still wear sandals to work more often than my colleagues, although my current collection now includes a few high-heeled, high-fashion numbers, something I attribute more to a mid-life, wishing-I-were-young denial sort of nonsense than to a change in pedagogical values. Most significantly, the result of this shoe inquiry has been that in reading the research literature and attending conferences, I can now more eagerly and easily spot fellow 'sandal wearers,' many of whom do not ever wear actual sandals. I am no longer really looking at the physical shoe, which can be a decoy or camouflage, but am searching beyond to the inner pedagogical shoes, seeking other 'sandal thinkers' with whom I can share my educational aspirations and values.

Teaching in my father's shoes? Shoes as narrative structure for self-inquiry

The following is an excerpt from a piece that I wrote while working on a play, *When the shoe doesn't fit: death of a salesman* (Weber and Mitchell 2002):

> Shoes! Up until the day he died, my father simply adored them – especially women's shoes. He loved selling them, designing them, and handling them – laying them tenderly wrapped in tissue in their neatly stacked boxes, deeply inhaling the potent mixture of expensive leather, polish, and glue, or displaying them artistically in the shop window. A high school drop-out who had impulsively, perhaps defiantly started a family while still in his late teens, Avi had wandered from job to job, selling brushes or encyclopaedias, working as a short order cook, and so on until, he at last he found – shoes. Shoes didn't keep him in one job for long, but shoes did give him a specialty and a sense of continuity or even career, something he could continue with in one way or another from his mid twenties almost until he died.
>
> The proof, perhaps, that selling shoes was his true vocation is that he enjoyed fitting them on ladies' feet, no matter how swollen, tired or aged or calloused they might be. [Turn and look up towards Claudia on L3.] Finding the right fit was a particular point of pride to him.
>
> I can still hear him expounding on this in my head. It makes my blood boil – all those people out there walking around in poorly fitted shoes. You'd be surprised how many men and women don't even know their *true* shoe size. They *never* get measured. The young salesmen these days won't even take the time to properly measure a lady's foot – they just bring out whatever size the customer asks for, or if they don't have that size, try to talk them into a size larger or smaller, depending on what's in stock. And the women! They just slap on any size shoe, and if they think they're stylish or sexy or if the shoes are the same size they were told they wore as a girl, they buy them, even if they're limping! Not when I'm serving them, they don't. I always insist on measuring them properly: the length and the width, the shape of the heels, the size and angle of each bunion, the height of the arches, the bunions of corns. I won't let

a woman leave until we find a shoe that fits her right – something that's comfortable *and* fashionable . . .

Italians know how to make shoes. Ferragamo! Capezzio! Pappagali! Amalfi! They know grace and elegance, how to put a steel shank in for proper support, and finish a shoe with fine, even hand stitching. And the leather! So supple, and soft – like a fine kid glove. The vamps don't gape, but they don't cut your instep either. And the styling is so exquisite! A beautiful well-fitted shoe makes *such a difference* to how a lady looks and walks. It is a worthwhile investment, the final and finishing statement that pulls a look together. You can wear the most expensive and stylish dress, but if you don't have the right shoe, you just won't look classy.

One of my fondest childhood memories is watching Avi dye fabric shoes to match customers' evening gowns, a service he offered free of charge. He had a small wooden workbench set up for this purpose in the cramped stockroom in back of the shop.

I was allowed to sit quietly on a rickety wooden stool, sipping a grape soda through a straw as I watched the look of total absorption come over him.

I loved the way he would mix the dyes to get the color just right, confidently pouring a bit of murky liquid from one bottle and then a bit from another until he had what he wanted. Then, he would dip his flat brush into the shallow glass jar of mixed dye, carefully wiping off any excess against the rim before applying the color with short accurate stokes, first to a test swatch of the same white fabric as the shoe, and then, when he was satisfied that the match was perfect, to the shoe itself.

The swatches of both the dress fabrics and Avi's test swabs hung on a line just above his head, gaily bobbing misshapen squares of fuchsia, turquoise, emerald green, sapphire, and plum. I never ceased marvelling at how my father could match up a shoe color so exactly working from so *tiny* a sample of dress fabric. I would try to imagine what the dress itself might look like; conjuring up designs in my head, which for some reason, I always imagined, would be worn by my beloved teacher, Mrs. Galley. Mrs. Galley wore soft fabrics and her skirts swished as she walked. She smelled of flowers, and most importantly, her shoes were graceful and stylish, not scuffed and shabby like the drab footwear most of the other teachers wore. I thought she was so beautiful.

Avi never thought much of my decision to be a teacher. Actually, I'm not sure if he was even aware that I had become one until I was already planning to move on to graduate school and a university career in Teacher Education. We were estranged for over a decade after he abandoned the family and moved, first to Toronto, and then to Florida, establishing another family along the way, and leaving a trail of women swooning after him.

When we eventually reconciled, I told him about my teaching career, and he made all the right noises about being proud of me, but really, besides noticing when I gained or lost weight, or commenting on my long hair with approval, much of his attention seemed directed towards my shoes. Shoes were the way he best expressed his care or love or concern.

I remember, for example, visiting him as a young girl to be fitted for new shoes. This was when he worked in a shoe store with a large selection of children's shoes. I was hoping for something red and shiny, like Dorothy's shoes in *The Wizard of Oz*. Avi had other ideas in mind. He was more concerned with giving my growing foot bones room and support. I walked out of there with a pair of plain navy blue leather Oxfords, not the strappy Mary Jane's or ruby coloured patent pumps I coveted. NO, *my* new shoes had five lace-holes, not three holes like the white buckskins that were all the rage and that I would have happily worn. But Avi said they provided less support for growing feet. His general rule that shoes should not only be serviceable but beautiful didn't seem to apply to *me*, much to my chagrin . . .

I think I have always been relieved that Avi had so little to say on the subject of my teaching or university career. Worrying about whether or not my shoes fit was just about all the fatherly attention from him that I could handle. Indeed, all this worry about fit still spills over to my adult life and work. Is there enough room and support? Is the material fine? Am I comfortable? Are my students? Is the curriculum made for walking and running, or just for show? And is it beautiful? Is my sense of aesthetics offended or pleased?

Not long after Avi died, a relative commented on how similar my job is to Avi's. I was taken aback. Me – a salesman? Yes – she replied – But instead of loving, designing and selling shoes, you love, design and peddle ideas.

Initially, I was insulted at the comparison – is *that* what I spent 9 years studying at university for? But then, I began wondering if there is not a certain truth to her words. Do I notice and comment on delicate high arches, charming my students while caring for, and even loving, their feet, looking for something that suits them, that fits . . . hmmm . . . Sometimes, though, when I am trying to squeeze myself into someone else's curriculum, or research paradigm, or struggling to convince others that my ideas are worth considering, I find myself despairing that nothing in Education will ever fit me perfectly. And then I wonder – couldn't we all just go barefoot?

The connection of the last line to the bare-footed sandal inquiry reported earlier eluded me until writing this chapter. The love–hate relationship that I have with shoes could be used to symbolize my ambivalences about power and authority – both my own, wielded as a professor of education (not consciously enough, I think) – and that of the structures of education, both as a field and as a bureaucratic structure, that I find confining and stifling without knowing quite what to do to loosen them. This self-study is forcing me to reconsider my role as a teacher educator in ways I had not anticipated.

A Van Gogh memory: shoe meanings

This last memory piece returns to my childhood where I uncover the reason why shoes work so well for me as both a mode of inquiry and representation.

> My lovely art teacher, Mrs. Petts, has been regaling us at school with stories and photographs of the work of Van Gogh. He cut his own ear off. Imagine! And here I am in the Montreal Museum of Fine Arts viewing an amazing travelling exhibit of his original paintings; I am mesmerized and touched, returning again and again to my favourite paintings, reluctant to leave. And then I see the close-up still life of the well-worn leather boots or work shoes painted on a small canvas. Just shoes and laces, lying on a nondescript floor as if the wearer had just removed them and tossed them there. All dark browns, beiges, and black. So unlike most of the other paintings in the exhibit. And I don't know why, but I start to cry, silent tears welling unbidden from the corner of my heart. The shoes look so tired, so lonely, so patiently and acceptingly evoking suffering and loneliness. I move on, but go back again and again. And I think, 'so that's what art can do, what a great artist does.' And ever since, when I see that painting reproduced, I feel a special bond of recognition, a secret 'I saw it for real' sort of thing, almost as though Van Gogh painted it just for me.

My interest in 'reading' shoes can thus be traced back a long way to an art teacher and an artist. So imagine the impact when almost forty years later, I stumbled across a series of essays and learn that those very same shoes, or at least the series of paintings Van Gogh did of the shoes (I have to admit to an initial disappointment bordering on outrage that he did more than one painting of 'my' shoes), have been the subject of a series of debates and scholarship by philosophers such as Heidegger and Derrida on the nature of reality and how we interpret objects. They argue about whose shoes were the subjects of the paintings and about whether or not the shoes were really from a single matched pair or from two different pairs. They use shoes to argue about how or even whether we read objects differently depending on social context or whether meaning is built into the shoe by virtue of its 'thingness.' They use shoes and walking in shoes as metaphors for learning, embodiment, and sense making. Somehow, it no longer seems far-fetched to speak of a pedagogy of shoes, does it?

NOTES

1 For an elaboration of work on dress studies, see Weber and Mitchell's chapter, 'Theorizing dress stories,' in Weber and Mitchell (Eds) *Not Just Any Dress: Narratives of Dress, Body, and Identity* (New York: Peter Lang), 2004, pp. 251–72.'
2 See Derrida's fascinating essay, 'Mochlos,' in Rand (Ed.) *Logomachia: The Conflict of the Faculties* (Lincoln and London: University of Nebraska Press), pp.1–34.

REFERENCES

Derrida, J., 1992, Mochlos. In Rand (Ed.) *Logomachia: The Conflict of the Faculties* (Lincoln and London: University of Nebraska Press), pp. 1–34.

Kaiser, S., 1985, *The Social Psychology of Clothing* (New York: Macmillan), pp. 242–43.

Lippert, B., 1997, Sexual heeling. *The New Yorker.* 24 November, pp. 30–32.

Mitchell, C., 2000, Accessorizing death: Elsie never had a prom dress. The Third International Conference on Self-study of Teacher Education Practices. Herstmonceux Castle, East Sussex, England, July.

Mitchell, C. and Weber, S.J., 1999, *Reinventing Ourselves as Teachers: Beyond Nostalgia* (London: Falmer Press).

Steele, V., 1999, *Shoes: A Lexicon of Style* (New York: Rizzoli).

Weber, S.J. and Mitchell, C., 2002, Accessorizing death: a monologue for two voices. Act 2. *When the shoe doesn't fit: death of a salesman.* The Fourth International Conference on Self-study of Teacher Education Practices. Herstmonceux Castle, East Sussex, England, August.

Weber, S.J. and Mitchell, C. (2004) Theorizing dress stories. In Weber and Mitchell (Eds) *Not Just Any Dress: Narratives of Dress, Body, and Identity* (New York: Peter Lang), pp. 251–72.

Chapter 3

Heavy fuel

Memoire, autobiography and narrative

Victoria Perselli

HEAVY FUEL: **A CASE STORY**

When I was a child, and even after I was grown up, I never thought of my grandfather as disabled. He had a 'Disabled' sticker he put on the windscreen when he went to see the specialist at Freedom Fields in Plymouth. But I guess words have different meanings in your own family; or maybe there are words you never use. The sticker was so that my grandfather could park outside the specialist's office. He went there once or maybe twice a year and generally my grandmother went with him. Afterwards they would have lunch on the Barbican, at the Intercontinental Hotel. They were smart dressers, both of them, and Jack always wore a nice suit and good shoes. My grandfather was tall and walked with a stoop – but that was because my grandmother was very short. He had bright blue eyes that were always laughing. My eyes are not blue, they're brown-black, with whites like used porcelain; when I smile it's more from the mouth. My grandfather had a big Devonian face. A picture of the poet Ted Hughes in a field comes to mind, but of course that's not it. Those trips to Plymouth to collect his new leg were a real occasion.

It surprises me to realize that years can pass without thinking about someone, after they're dead. Only recently, when we exchanged my old Ford Sierra for a new Toyota Carina – after I changed my job and started commuting to work – something thudded in my brain and I made the connection. I was really fond of that Sierra, but it had no power steering, so it was heavy to drive, difficult to park. On long journeys it smelt bad and was getting to be seriously unreliable. Back in 1994 my partner was involved in a pile-up – unhurt, luckily – but the Sierra was written off. I persuaded the Ford garage to get the assessor out anyway. As it turned out, the assessor was a friend of the proprietor. A bottle of good whiskey was involved somewhere along the line and the car got fixed on the insurance – rebuilt practically – which was just as well, because back then I wouldn't have had the money to turn it in for scrap and buy a new one.

I've always been good with garages; that's where I spent my childhood. My grandfather had a Ford dealership, so you get to know how things are done. Before he got the Ford franchise he traded in executive models: Daimlers, Jaguars and Rolls. I used to play with the catalogues, putting them in rank order, least favourite to favourite. I was allowed to play in the cars in the showroom, too; pretend driving, fiddling with things on the dashboard. For ages afterwards I wasn't interested in cars at all but now recently that's what I enjoy the most, heading off into the distance in the Carina – or a hire car, when I'm in Canada or the States, where the roads are really wide. I like the glamour of it: the retro feeling. I like driving automatics, too. Until we got the Carina, I hadn't realized how good it feels to be rid of the gear shift.

Before he became a dealer, most of my grandfather's trade was in crash recovery and bodywork, and before that he contracted out farm machinery. He began his business mending bicycles, in a shack next door to the caravan where he lived with my grandmother. She ran a café for GIs and British servicemen on their way to training exercises at Slapton Ley. People said the Yanks used live ammunition down there on the beach, and a good number of US soldiers were killed who never saw active service. At the time it was all hushed up, but there's a memorial there now to commemorate them, and a tank preserved in black paint that they hauled up out of the sea. During the Blitz, if my grandparents went to the top of the hill at Marley Cross, they could watch Plymouth burning on the horizon. At one time my grandmother drove taxis from the city centre, to get people out.

For a while, until the repair was finished, I drove around in the Sierra with its doors all staved in. To get to the driver's seat you had to climb in through the hatchback, and that takes some practice – especially in a skirt. It was a good car, left-hand drive, twelve years old but without a speck of rust; built in Scandinavia (they have serious weather up there) and brought to the UK by a diplomat who was coming up for retirement, so he needed to get shot of it quickly. But even after the Sierra business, I never once thought about my grandfather, and how he used to swing his artificial leg into the foot-well; how he always drove an automatic. Sometimes, like with the trips to Freedom Fields, there would be a spare prosthesis on the back seat in a long cardboard box; the rest of the time it lived under his bed. Prosthesis, Grampy's artificial leg. I never heard anyone say 'prosthesis'.

So for some reason this morning (clear, blue sky, chilly), setting off for work in the Carina, it was that sound of his leg dropping into the foot-well I remembered. And the indescribable sound of his walk, so familiar suddenly I could practically touch it. My grandfather's leg was amputated at the thigh after an accident with a threshing machine. The story – unfolded, you under-stand, during an era of war veterans and medals for acts of bravery – ran like this. The young Jack Soper was contracted to a remote farm on the moor and was working a notoriously steep field, hurrying to get finished before nightfall. He slipped into the threshing machine and his leg was severed. It happened that Mrs Brockington – the new pharmacist (recently married) – was driving past the place on the way home from her rounds to the farms, as luck would have it. Realizing what needed to be done, she quickly applied tourniquets to the wound and drove hell-for-leather to the hospital, saving my grandfather's life. Jack Soper remained conscious throughout, and from time to time the story would re-emerge of their bravery, both. A true story of hero and rescue. Some years later, after a traumatic event in my own life, a well-meaning doctor – recognizing my maiden name – recalled that he had known my grandfather from his days at Freedom Fields; how courageous he was and how generous, making large donations to the police federation and the Foundation for Invalids. Which cut me up, actually; I guess it destroyed my coping mechanisms.

Thinking about it, running a garage wasn't the easiest way to earn a living for someone with an artificial leg. But at the time when I was little I can see my grandfather jumping in and out of vehicles; moving them from the fore-court to the body shop or on to the ramps, up from the compound to the back of the field, where the old bangers and write-offs were left to rust out. This was by far the best place to play. Me, Colin and Deborah from next door would climb the two huge pear trees in my grandmother's garden, then slide down the branches over the fence on to the bonnets of the old cars. One day another boy came around to play who didn't quite have the knack; he slid straight on to the edge of the bumper, gouging a chunk out of his buttocks and worst of all his school trousers. After that we weren't allowed to play there for a while. But every so often crash vehicles would come in and the broken glass and snarled up metal would lure us back. Sometimes, if you were lucky, there would be spatterings of blood on the fascia. There were always cars that needed moving and my grandfather used his good leg to slide from one peddle to another in a complicated manoeuvre involving the hand brake and gear shift. Once I was tall enough to reach the pedals I was allowed to move cars too: it was private property, you could do what you like. 'One day,' he told me, 'all this will be yours.' He had my initials carved in the concrete: S. R. J. L. S. My grandfather held the opinion that people of my generation were being overeducated, so no one would want to do proper work any more. 'What are you learning at school?' he would ask, but I could never think of anything to say, and the question made me feel awkward and stupid.

The centre of power in our family wasn't the garage, though; it was my grandparents' kitchen. This was where my father went to eat dinner when he first knew my mother, when he was an apprentice to the firm, and it was my grandfather who provided us with pocket money on Sunday morn-ings, not my parents. Jack and Joyce's house was a typical Devon farmhouse, long and narrow. Like most of the older part of the village – including the Victorian villa where my family eventually went to live – it was built out of the same massive river stones they used to build the Avon Dam, which is where we all learned to swim. Upstairs there were four bedrooms on the street side, opening off a narrow corridor on the garage side. Joyce Soper slept at one end, in the room above the forecourt, Jack slept at the back, over what must once have been the stables, but was now the paint shed. Whenever I stayed the night at their house I had the pink room directly over the street. I used to love sleeping there, when I was very young. You could hear the sounds of the drunks going home from the pub at closing time and every so often the roar of a motorbike. I loved the lights of the bike travelling across the ceiling; it was like being at the movies. In the morning sometimes there would be vomit on the pavement. My mother had the lilac room when she lived at home, but after our bungalow was built Joyce kept this room for her needlework and sewing things. My grandmother went to bed with an elaborate arrangement of women's magazines (*Women's Weekly*, *Women's Realm*, *Woman and Home*), cigarettes (Benson and Hedges usually) and a tumbler of whiskey. Both my grandparents were heavy smokers, although Jack cut down a lot when he got older. Jack's bedroom was pale blue; it was cold and musty; it smelled remote. At night the artificial leg was propped in the far corner beside the chest of drawers. I remember the feel of the leather straps and the shiny pink Bakelite material that the foot was made from. I remember his profile in bed; my grandfather looked much smaller asleep (like most people, I guess), the clotted cream rolls of stockinette for his stump on the dressing table (ordered specially from Mrs Brockington's), alongside a photo of my mother with long red hair in a ponytail, taken when she was about twelve. The chest of drawers in this room was full of other things belonging to Joyce: clothes and accessories, hats, gloves, wedding outfits, negligees and silk nightdresses, household goods like tea towels and soap from the Cleaneezy man, prizes from the Green Shield Stamp catalogue; nearly all of them unused.

Everyone in the firm worked incredibly long hours, especially through the summer months. During the school holidays if I was by myself I played with the new electric ramps in the body shop, or watched re-sprays being done in the paint shed. The men's room had urinals and calendars of naked women – from Pirelli Tyres. At dinnertime I used to go and sit with Douggie Linzel and Günther Schwarz, who were a bit older than the others; not quite so sarky. Günther had been a prisoner of war, but he liked it at Soper's so he decided to stay. The men used to give me jam sandwiches out of their lunch boxes: I was a mascot – and an illegitimate child. I was also the boss's grand-daughter – I was always self-conscious about that. In the offices up above the showroom there was my grandmother and my mother who did the accounts. There was Sid, who got teased a lot because he had a dodgy ticker, and Richard, 'Dickie Bird', who lived at home with his mum (even though he was in his thirties). Once a year, Dickie went off to exotic places for his holidays, like Thailand. They said he had girls out there. When Sid died my father cried like a woman, slopping his early morning cup of tea all over the bed sheets.

The franchise grew, and as a consequence Ford rewarded Jack and Joyce with trophies and holidays abroad. My grandparents bought several other smaller businesses in the area. These were the boom years; we had the first colour TV in the village (in the corner of the kitchen opposite the Aga, the old black and white set went in the drawing room), my grandparents took holidays on jet planes and discovered the high life. Joyce had the old wooden cupboards taken out of the kitchen and a modern fitted kitchen installed, with Formica work surfaces and tall taps. My grandmother was not at all domestically inclined but she did her housework rigorously every morning; a cold cup of coffee – then later Sanatogen or Buckfast Tonic Wine, Harvey's Bristol Cream or a tumbler of Johnny Walker – unfinished by the sink. I never saw my grandmother finish the drink; I think she liked the smell. It was around this time that Jack began to develop his empire in other directions, first doing property conversions and then building small housing estates, which he mostly designed himself. The Ford garage has long since gone but of course the houses are still there. They were popular because they were so nicely landscaped; they had little trees and shrubs that looked soft when they filled out their spaces. They upstaged the three council estates in the village (Courtney Park, Crowder Park and Corn Park; Avondale House for families – well, mothers and children – if you couldn't pay the rent or if your husband was in jail), although once, when I was at secondary school, I remember driving past Jack's latest project with one of our teachers: 'Gosh, look at those houses,' he said, 'they're no bigger than the width of my living room.'

As a wedding present, my grandparents gave my mother and father a piece of land behind the compound to build their bungalow on, but apart from that no one drew much in the way of wages from the business, and the post-Ford era – after Jack's death – was challenging for my dad, who must have found it difficult enough already, living in the shadow of the big man. He's OK now I guess. He and mum have a great place down in the South Hams; a split-level arrangement with rolling tides on three sides (they always said they hated being so close to the moor; they said they hated the rain). It's nice, no – it's sexy – a neat arrangement of slate, glass, bleached wood, red shellet, hand-riddled by my dad to make paths and a patio, little solar lights in among the aloes. 'Bloody hell, Dad,' I say, 'this place looks like something out of the Hollywood Hills.' Which pleases him no end, and that's what I really like these days: saying something unexpected that makes somebody smile.

My grandfather rewarded me with money for doing well at school: passing exams or getting a good report, but as I recall, he never came to the prize giving or any of my concerts. His absorption in his drawings and plans for his projects, his deep conversations with his architect took over his life, so that apart from visiting the sites he spent most of his time in the office, hardly stopping to eat or sleep even. Was there physical discomfort in movement, some awkwardness? Or something else? What impression management was going on, for me or for the rest of the world, that my grandfather's disability was so obviously there, yet not there? There was a magnet that bonded my grandparents in business – 'a formidable pair' – and a different force that circumscribed every other part of their lives. Worst of all was the way they fought at mealtimes. How the receiving and withholding of food was manipulated (his terrible temper, her slyness), and how, when my grandfather's health began to go (he was diagnosed with diabetes), it all got so much worse. Jack had always been a heavy man but gradually the weight fell away. I learned to cook at an early age; I bought my first Elizabeth David, *French Country Cooking*, when I was twelve, and on Saturdays I always did the lunch. That way, I knew that once a week he got something decent to eat.

Throughout my teenage years I spent a lot more time away from home. I was busy with projects of my own, breathing heavy fuel:

> Solzhenitsyn, *August 1914*, Publisher's Note: 'In the "screen" sequences in this book, the four different margins are used to represent four sets of technical instructions for shooting a film: 1. Sound effects; 2. Camera direction; 3. Action; 4. Dialogue. The symbol = indicates "cut to".'

At eighteen I got married. My grandparents offered us a house on the Clobells estate, but we turned it down, even though my fiancé had worked on the site in the months leading up to our wedding. I think that, at eighteen, bricks and mortar signified something more confining than marriage. Besides, we were students – a car would have been more useful. As my grandfather's health deteriorated I remember coaxing him, pleading even, to come and live with us, or at least have a meal and stop over the night, but he never took up the offer. He died just after Sam and I started our divorce proceedings. My grandmother said he wasn't angry that the marriage hadn't lasted, just hurt that I didn't tell him myself. It was grief that killed him, she said, not cancer.

After Jack's death, wealth trickled away like water. It became clear to us – me, my brother and sisters – that we were out on our own: *Every man for himself.* Which I guess characterized the era we were moving into, although of course we didn't know it at the time.

How do I take after my grandfather? Well, there's some machismo, that's for sure, some temperament. There's the Pioneering Spirit: wanting always to be the provider, the person who fixes things. There's the love of architecting, by which I mean the ability to invent elaborate projects (like this story!) to hold oneself at a distance from the sources of pain. Curiosity about cruelty, how it repeats itself, how it is done. And driving. There's this section of the dual carriageway, just before our house, where it loops under the Portsmouth Road and quits the gyratory – it makes a great chicane, especially when you do it in the dark.

Where is my centre of power located? At the kitchen sink? No! At the dining table? I hope not. On the podium? Not really. I think my centre of power lies in my hands, descending from the plane, clutching this little bag of wares to sell, unknowing and unknown, thinking: Who is out there? Who will buy this? Why might they want it?

My good friend – Carol Shields – dislikes this kind of writing. She says: 'Memoirs, journals, diaries. Works of the bio-imagination are as biodegradable as orange peels. Out they go. Psst – they blast themselves to vapour, cleaner and blonder than the steam from a spotless kettle. Nothing sticks but the impulse to get it down.' I take the point, she's right as usual, and to begin with I felt terrible writing about my grandfather, as though it were dishonest, a clumsy act of betrayal. But now I just say, we biographers have different agendas. And things get mixed up; until today I had forgotten everything, obliterated the lot from sight, sound, taste, smell – no linkage. 'Disability', 'Inclusion', words I never encountered as a child, but then again, how often do you come across *shellet* or *Hollywood Hills* in an academic text?

Until suddenly this morning, on this sharp October day: what was it exactly? A dull thump in a foot-well, a whiff of engine oil, a cramp in the left leg, and biography is all there, in the ether; so thick and urgent, that even breathing becomes a labour of love.

Stevie Soper 19 October 2002

HEAVY FUEL: A THEORIZATION

In the story *Heavy Fuel*, Stevie Soper says her 'centre of power' lies in her hands, 'clutching this little bag of wares to sell, unknowing and unknown'. For Stevie, the hand is the instrument through which the story is told, not the head or the heart, even though biography becomes 'an act of love' by being 'all there . . . in the ether'. And although the body delivers the story text – and its narration – the body is also, eventually, negated: the person, as author and performer, is 'unknowing and unknown'.

For sure there is, or was, a body/person in the story: 'My eyes are not blue, they're brown-black' . . . 'To get to the driver's seat you had to climb in through the hatchback, which takes some practice in a skirt', but just as Stevie's grandfather's disability was simultaneously present yet not present, there is a sense of the person/body appearing and disappearing: in descriptions of the body and its sensations and in self-disclosures (such as the story itself) which also act as masks: 'to hold oneself at a distance from the sources of pain'.

Stevie – teacher, academic, feminist, Marxist, filmmaker – has been reading Roland Barthes; she is interested in Barthes' (1968; 1977) argument concerning the *removal* of the author from the text.

According to Barthes,

writing is the destruction of every voice, of every point of origin. Writing is that neutral, composite, oblique space where our subject slips away, the negative where all identity is lost, starting with the very identity of the body writing.

(p. 143)

For those of us whose research concerns are centred precisely on issues of 'identity', 'representation', 'the body', 'voice', explored through auto/ biography, Stevie's accounting ('things get mixed up; until today I had forgotten everything') and Barthes' ideas generate a kind of representational crisis; blurring the distinctions we perhaps believed we could make (as author and therefore arbiter) between 'reality' presented as the world of lived experience, and 'truth' created through fiction.

The removal of the author, Barthes says,

transforms the modern text . . . the text is henceforth made and read in such a way that at all levels the author is absent. The temporality is different. The Author, when believed in, is always conceived of as the past of his own book . . . he exists before it, thinks, suffers, lives for it . . . as a father to his child. [Whereas] the modern scripter is born simultaneously with the text, is in no way equipped with a being preceding or exceeding the writing, is not the subject with the book as predicate; there is no other time than that of the enunciation and every text is eternally written *here and now*.

(p. 145)

For the biographer, one might have thought, body, person, time and space are vitally important. The biographer, as in this story, strives to situate persons and actions very precisely within both a location and a temporality which is knowable to self and others, and which seeks to explain 'psychologically' the protagonist's actions, character, beliefs, in these terms: 'it was private property, you could do what you like'; 'the post-Ford era . . . was challenging for my dad'; identifying the self within the social, the personal in relations and in tension with the political. In autobiography, especially, where protagonist and author are the same person, it would seem as though the opportunity to stabilize these elements and make them knowable is being maximized, so that the act of writing becomes the opportunity eventually for greater *self-knowledge*: 'I was also the boss's granddaughter – I was always self-conscious about that'; 'that's what I really like these days: saying something unexpected that makes somebody smile' – successful or not according to how the reader then receives the autobiographical tale; that is, as confirmation or disconfirmation of the 'self' that the tale is portraying.

Traditionally speaking, the auto/biographer seeks both an interiority (self knowledge) and an exteriority (recognition), achieved within a more or less chronological account of real-time events. In a self-study text she or he is also aspiring to reflexivity: the story is loaded with opportunities for the story teller to deconstruct according to gender, sexuality, social class, (dis)ability; and can function very well at that level. But here is Barthes' commentary – on literature in general, and of particular interest to the auto/biographer:

> The author is a modern figure, a product of our society insofar as, emerging from the Middle Ages with English empiricism, French rationalism and the personal faith of the reformation, it discovered the prestige of the individual . . . the 'human person' . . . the epitome and culmination of capitalist ideology, which has attached the greatest importance to the 'person' of the author . . . The image of literature to be found in ordinary culture is tyrannically centred on the author, his person, his life, his tastes, his passions. The *explanation* of a work is always sought in the man or woman who produced it, as if it were always in the end, through the more or less transparent allegory of the fiction, the voice of a single person, the *author* 'confiding' in us.
>
> (p. 143)

This is in complete contrast to the ancient literary forms. Greek tragedy, for example, is '[by nature] constitutively ambivalent . . . its texts being woven from words with double meanings that each character understands uni-laterally [which constitutes the 'Tragic' because the characters themselves cannot see this duality] (p. 148). However,

> [T]here is someone who understands each word in its duplicity and who, in addition, hears the very deafness of the characters speaking in front of him – this someone being precisely the reader (or here, the listener). Thus is revealed the total existence of writing; a text is made of multiple writings, drawn from many cultures and entering into mutual relations of dialogue, parody, contestation, but there is one place where this multiplicity is focused and that place is the reader, not, as was hitherto said, the author. The reader is the space on which all the quotations that make up a writing are inscribed without any of them being lost; a text's unity lies not in its origin but in its destination.
>
> (p. 148)

Stevie Soper has been reading Roland Barthes, and although her story ostensibly deals with 'the past' her major interest is in *what is going to happen next*. Stevie knows that it is the reader who sees what the child/woman telling the tale cannot see from their unilateral positions as actors in the drama. Whilst the style of writing may be naïve and confessorial, Stevie assumes (creates) an audience whose capability is to see more than and see differ-ently what the narrative is apparently saying 'through' its characters. [See also Barthes 1966; 1977, p. 114): 'Today, writing is not "telling" but saying that one is telling . . . contemporary literature is no longer descriptive, but transitive.']

Structurally, Stevie brings the reader/listener/viewer to the point at which the *story of this chapter*, in this book, is about to begin: '"Disability", "Inclusion", words I never encountered as a child, but then again, how often do you come across *shellet* or *Hollywood Hills* in an academic text?' – questions which self-study refuses to leave standing. Stevie cites her 'good friend' the author Carol Shields to disavow her own (modernist) faith in biography, equivocally claiming 'a different agenda', which is both to remember and to forget, but never to 'recreate', since:

> [W]riting can no longer designate an operation of recording, notation, representation, 'depiction' . . . rather, it designates exactly what linguists . . . call a performative . . . in which the enunciation has no other content than the act by which it is uttered . . . Having buried the author, the modern scripter can thus no longer believe . . . that his hand is too slow for his thought or passion . . . the hand, cut off from any voice . . . traces a field without origin . . . other than language itself, which ceaselessly calls into question all origins.
>
> (Barthes 1966; 1977, pp. 145–46)

These ideas are conflictual and difficult for auto/biographers because they upset the locations and temporalities that we have struggled to secure in order to establish our psychological identities – in this story, the modernist author/hero, poised at the outer edge of advanced capitalism 'descending from the plane' – our sense of agency and (subsequently) our moral positionings and actions: Stevie's observations on the apparently circumscribed nature of relationships, for example, or her 'Curiosity about cruelty, how it repeats itself, how it is done'.

Furthermore, Barthes actively discourages 'analysis': 'Once the Author is removed, the claim to decipher a text becomes quite futile. To give a text an Author is to impose a limit on that text, to furnish it with a final signified, to close the writing' (p. 147), presenting a radical alternative:

> In the multiplicity of writing, everything is to be *disentangled*, nothing *deciphered*; the structure can be followed, 'run' . . . at every point and at every level, but there is nothing beneath: the space of writing is to be ranged over, not pierced . . . *writing*, by refusing to assign a 'secret', an ultimate meaning, to the text . . . liberates what may be called antitheological activity, an activity that is truly revolutionary since to refuse to fix meaning is, in the end, to refuse God [the author] and his hypostases – reason, science, law.
>
> (p. 147)

which view challenges not only the Author: Stevie the child-woman-testifier who (ingenuously and unilaterally) clocks events: 'I never saw [her] finish the drink', but also the Auditor: Victoria the listener-interpreter-witness, who must reject her prior assumptions since – outside of language itself – none of these 'exists'.

However, for me the impression gained from reading Barthes for the first, second, third time is one of plenitude, not bereavement. Once text is no longer viewed as a transparent allegory of fiction: modernistic, heroic, self-mythologizing still (the 'persona' of Stevie implying a body of work 'this little bag of wares to sell' and therefore a more or less amenable market 'Who will buy this?), but simultaneously self-effacing (we have no way of knowing, finally, who Stevie is; neither does it matter) and psychologically/linguistically (self) contradictory (that is, released from 'the superstition of our interiority': 'illegitimate child'), text opens itself to a new lightness of touch.

> Succeeding the Author, the scripter no longer bears within him passions, humours, feelings, impressions, but rather this immense dictionary from which he draws a writing that can know no halt: life never does more than imitate the book, and the book itself is only a tissue of signs, an imitation that is lost, infinitely deferred.
>
> (p. 147)

Seeing ourselves, as self-study artists and teachers, drawing from this amazing dictionary of our lives as represented in text, aleatorically mixing writings to produce more writings, is a brave departure. Barthes seems to be saying that whilst lives may be circumscribed through language: 'I could never think of anything to say, and the question made me feel awkward and stupid'; 'There was a magnet that bonded my grandparents in business – 'a formidable pair' – and a different force that circumscribed every other part of their lives'; text is not: Text throws all responsibility back to us, the readers of our life texts, *to continue living our lives*; the libratory factor being what will happen next after 'writing' has happened.

Furthermore, neither writing nor reading is the lonely activity of our predecessors in modernity. (And nowhere, incidentally, does Barthes (or Foucault (1969; 1984) see *What is an Author?*) offer anonymity as an option.) Barthes draws from the Surrealists, whom he says '[accepted] *the principle and experience of several people writing together*' [p. 144, italics added].

Many self-study texts are written collaboratively, and all self-study texts are written to be worked on (rather than recognized as 'art': 'we appreciate "performance" not "genius"'). They become a democratically organized, collaborative project which permits us both to query once and for all the givenness of the linguistic material we work with in practice (curriculum, assessment, identification, differentiation) and the standpoint taken in autobiography; what MacLure (1993, p. 331) calls 'autobiography-as-knowledge'; whereby the autobiography appears as 'revelations of the honest or unbiased self' (Weiner 1994, p. 11).

Our writing, rather than our history, writes us, and our more relaxed theories of literature enable us to dispose of some well-established myths: 'disability', 'inclusion'; mixing these aleatorically and interminably with other languages that don't belong: 'shellet', 'Hollywood Hills', perhaps to produce a surprise or a question, at best a positive shift in the course of events. Whilst traditional auto/biography may have sought truth or identity, a good self-study text today looks for subjects. These subjects, depersonalized and distanced from the hand that wrote them, invite new readings that are neither 'literary' nor 'scientific'. They belong to the person who is reading them, in the moment of reading.

REFERENCES

Barthes, R., 1966, Introduction to the structural analysis of narratives (Trans. S. Heath, 1977) *Image, Music, Text* (London: Fontana), pp. 79–124.

Barthes, R., 1968, The death of the author (Trans. S. Heath, 1977) *Image, Music, Text* (London: Fontana), pp. 142–48.

David, E., 1951, *French Country Cooking* (Reprinted 1972) (Harmondsworth: Penguin).

Foucault, M., 1969, What is an author? In Rabinow (Ed.), 1984, *The Foucault Reader* (Harmondsworth: Penguin), pp. 101–20.

MacLure, M., 1993, Arguing for your self: identity as an organising principle in teachers' jobs and lives. *British Educational Research Journal*, **19**(4), 311–22.

Shields, C., 1989, *The Orange Fish* (Harmondsworth: Penguin).

Solzhenitsyn, A., 1971, *August 1914* (Trans. M. Glenny) (London: Bodley Head).

Weiner, G., 1994, *Feminisms in Education: An Introduction* (Buckingham and Philadelphia: Open University Press).

Chapter 4

Drawings as a research tool for self-study

An embodied method of exploring memories of childhood bullying

Catherine Derry

> It is time, however, to acknowledge that human experience cannot be completely understood through the scientific method and to apply the discipline, rigor and intelligence, that we commonly associate with science, to the process of aesthetic inquiry.
>
> (McNiff 1998, p. 15)

INTRODUCTION

A very important issue that teachers are dealing with on a daily basis is bullying in the classroom and in the schoolyard. As the media have reported, these incidences of bullying can have quite dire consequences (Weaver 2001; Vaughan and Clark 1999). Many teachers feel they do not know how to handle these situations and many others are not sure whether it is something that teachers should be worried about (Barone 1997). I discovered, while conducting my own self-study of memories of being bullied in childhood and while helping other teachers explore theirs, that a good way to connect to and understand the experience of being bullied is through one's own memories of it. Encouraging teachers to conduct self-studies of their memories of bullying may thus be a useful starting point to develop the empathy and understanding needed to deal with such a difficult and volatile problem in their classrooms. An effective point of entry for this kind of self-study is to draw a memory of bullying, something I found helpful for remembering and interpreting my memories of being bullied in childhood.

When I started my self-study, it was not my intention to have an art-based component. It was to be a study of my childhood memories of being the victim of bullying. I wanted to produce a study that would make teachers and teacher educators think about bullying, without intellectually detaching. I wanted them to connect with my experience on an emotional level, to understand how it feels to be bullied. This embodied knowing was important to me because traditionally social science research in this area has discussed the victims of bullying in a cold and impersonal way, one that usually blames the victim for having some sort of social deficit (Bagswell *et al.* 1998; Coie and Cillessen 1993; White and Kisner 1992; Asher 1990; Reisman 1985). Drawing was a tool that helped give my study that emotional aspect I was seeking. Drawings helped me access memories, write in a more embodied way and gave the readers that multi-layered intellectual/emotional connection to my experience.

Before I go on to describe the use of drawings in my self-study, I will explain what I mean by embodiment, because the term will be used throughout this chapter.

EMBODIMENT

Embodiment has become a popular word in academic writing, with the term appearing in the title of many academic articles and books. What differs from one text to another is the meaning of that term. Some authors use it to describe a well-thought out idea; some use it to describe an all-encompassing kind of knowledge, while still others use it to specifically refer to the body.

What most authors agree on is that embodiment is an inclusive term that does not include one way of knowing, being or experiencing (Satina and Hultgren 2001; Emig 2001; Matthews 1998; Williams and Bendelow 1998; Glenblow 1991). This lack of a clear definition has left many academics struggling to pin down a commonly understood meaning. Williams and Bendelow (1998) describe the term as uncontainable and ambiguous because of its inclusive nature. Although many researchers want to come from an embodied perspective, most are at a loss to give a clear definition of just what that is.

In light of all this confusion, it would be foolish to try to give a definition of embodiment but, for the purpose of this chapter, I view embodiment as a way of knowing that goes beyond the intellectual, logical and rational mode of thinking that has traditionally been defined as knowledge. It includes emotions, culture, physical sensation and life experiences.

Traditionally, knowledge has been seen as the domain of the mind, with experiences such as emotion, intuition, and life experience relegated to experiences of the body (Williams and Bendelow 1998). Learning experiences were considered those that came from the intellectual mind, which was thought to be disembodied from the emotionally laden subjective experiences of the body (Matthews 1998). This kind of theory is based on the Cartesian model that asserts that the mind and body work separately, and that the mind's functions are more important (Satina and Hultgren 2001). Many scholars disagree with these notions and want to put bodily experiences back into knowing (Weber and Mitchell 2004; Satina and Hultgren 2001; Emig 2001; Matthews 1998; Williams and Bendelow 1998; Glenblow 1991). This kind of knowing, one that puts bodily experience back into knowledge and learning has been loosely referred to as embodied knowledge. 'It is an experiential knowing that involves sense, precept, and mind/body action and reaction – a knowing, feeling, and acting that includes more of the broad range of human experience than that delimited within the traditionally privileged, distanced, disembodied range of discursive conceptualization' (Matthews 1998, p. 236).

To me this kind of research is not just about body. It is about including those experiences that were once considered the domain of the body to intellectual engagement. According to Csordas: 'If embodiment is an existential condition in which the body is the subjective source or intersubjective ground of experience, then studies under the rubric of embodiment are not "about" the body per se. Instead they are about culture and experience insofar as these can be understood from the standpoint of bodily being-in-the-world' (cited in Satina and Hultgren 2001, p. 529).

In my own work, I have experienced many types of knowing that fall outside the traditional notion of intellectual learning. My research has been influenced by my intuition, my emotions and my life experience. These qualities are the essence of what embodied knowing is about for me. Sometimes, writing and traditional inquiry do not completely convey this sense of embodiment in the same way an image does: 'visual forms – maps, pictures, bar charts, for example – which are synchronic in character afford us an "all-at-onceness" in perception that reveals what would be hard to grasp in diachronic forms such as language and number' (Eisner 1995, p. 1). Artistic modes of representation have helped me understand and express my findings in an embodied way that touches those 'bodily' experiences described earlier. According to McNiff (1998), 'If we stay closely attuned to the images and processes of creative expression, they will suggest frontiers of understanding' (p. 47).

USING DRAWINGS IN MY RESEARCH

A few years ago, I was scared to draw. You could not have paid me to do it. My third grade teacher told me my drawings were horrible and I believed that. When I started to write my self-study, using drawings was the furthest thing from my mind; these words of my third grade teacher echoed in my heart and soul. However, I encountered a problem as I started to write narrative descriptions of being bullied. I realized that something was missing in the reading and writing. My descriptions were dull, flat and the detail was sparse. What was missing was something that would help me to write fuller descriptions and would give the reader a multi-layered perspective of my experience. The research literature I had been reading seemed to indicate that an arts-based exploration would give my data that embodied perspective I was seeking.

Art can make aspects of the world vivid, as it awakens people from their stock responses (Eisner 1995). McNiff (1992) believes that artistic images can expand communication and offer insight outside the scope of the reasoning mind. And van Manen (1984) sees the intellectual value of artistic forms of inquiry: 'The phenomenologist knows the value of having read widely and deeply and having an insatiable interest in the ways in which sensitive artists are providing us vicariously with expressive examples of fundamental truth experiences. There exists a hermeneutic dialectic between lived life and art: art interprets life and life interprets art' (p. 51).

The biggest influences for me in this area were Weber and Mitchell's (1995) study of teacher's stereotypes of teachers and Ganim's (1999) writing on art therapy. These works helped me put aside my fear of art and experiment with creating my own images. Therefore, with much trepidation and the encouragement of my supervisor I decided to try my hand at drawing. I use drawings in two ways in my self-study: to elicit data, and for the presentation of material.

ELICITING DATA

I have used drawings along with writing and interviews to elicit a more detailed, fuller account of my experience as a bullied child. I have used drawing to elicit memories, emotionally difficult information, and perception of self.

Memory

I first used drawings when I was trying to write a description of being excluded by my best friend in third grade. I had trouble remembering exactly what happened. I sat down with a sheet of paper and some pencil crayons and I drew my memory of that incident. This drawing made all the feelings and details of the situation flood back and I was able to draw the picture (see Figure 4.1) and write my narrative. According to Ganim (1999), art can allow us to experience for the first time feelings and thoughts that may have been repressed or forgotten. I found this to be the case; my drawing helped me elicit more detailed and embodied description. The positive results of this drawing experience encouraged me to continue to use drawings as a research tool for this study.

Emotionally difficult information

I found drawing useful in eliciting emotionally difficult information. 'Using art to express what your body-mind is saying will enable you to connect, perhaps for the first time, with your deepest feelings and emotions' (Ganim

Figure 4.1 Being excluded by my best friend in third grade.

1999, p. 21). Weber and Mitchell (1995) point out that things we have repressed or things we might censor in our verbal and written speech often slip into our drawings.

Many of the memories I recalled of being bullied were emotionally upsetting. I found it difficult to put the emotions that these memories contained into words. For instance, I had difficulty remembering all the details and feelings I experienced during an incident of sexual assault by some older bullies that took place in fifth grade. Whirling images of the incident were floating through my head. I decided to sit down and draw one of those images (see Figure 4.2). While looking at this image, I recalled this memory in detail. As the memory and emotions accompanying it unfolded in my head, I wrote the text to describe them.

In this case, my drawing was an object used to remember an emotionally difficult situation. Others have used visual cues in their memory work. Mitchell and Weber (1999), for example, used photos and Ash (1996) used clothes to facilitate memory. Art therapists often have their clients draw to uncover emotionally difficult memories that they may have repressed (Ganim 1999). Even though self-study is not a therapy situation, the same principles can be applied to unlock difficult memories. Sometimes we repress painful

Figure 4.2 An incident of sexual assault by some older bullies.

memories. An embodied research tool such as drawing can be an effective method for uncovering these memories.

Perception of self

Drawings can show us how we perceive others. Weber and Mitchell (1995) revealed pre-service teachers' stereotypes by having them draw pictures of a teacher. Bryson and de Castell (1996) used drawing to survey students' stereotypes of gender and technology. Drawing can also be a mirror to view our perceptions of ourselves. Richards (1998) used self-portraits to evaluate her teaching practices. She also had pre-service teachers do self-portraits for the same reason.

I have used drawings as a self-study method for examining my perception of self. I wanted to explain how my experiences with bullying had left me (at that point in time) with a fragmented sense of self, divided into two very distinct personas. Figure 4.3 illustrates how I experienced this divide. This drawing gave both me and my audience a clear vision of the experience of this split in a way that text alone could not. It provided an embodied perspective that showed that being bullied was something I had experienced emotionally and bodily. And yet, as the drawing shows, I myself was quite disembodied – seeing my self as two disconnected selves. This drawing invoked in me an emotional connection that I did not feel when writing.

Figure 4.3 Seeing my self as two disconnected selves.

PRESENTATION

> The artistic treatment of any form of representation is a way of creating
> an impact, of making ideas and images clear, of having an effect on those
> who 'read' the form.
>
> (Eisner 1995, p. 1)

Drawings became more than just a tool to elicit data. I decided to include
them to help represent the findings of my research. When drawings and text
combine, they have the potential to give the audience a multi-layered look
at a phenomenon and may help foster an embodied understanding. Drawing
gives the audience an alternative mode of knowing, a perspective that text
alone cannot. 'As the work of art opens the door for bodily engagement, it
allows for a broader understanding of how we come to know the world
through the body' (Glenblow 1991, p. 10).

   Artistic forms of representations have been seen as a challenge to prevailing
modes of discourse, 'Indeed, it is this emphasis on "embodied praxis" (i.e.
performance art) and "visual narratives" (i.e. autobiographical art) that, we
have argued, provides an important counterweight to the predominantly

textual forms of representation' (Williams and Bendelow 1998, p. 206). It is very important to me that my work engages my audience emotionally. In my own academic experience, lines of black and white text may help me intellectually to understand feelings and emotions, but I do not emotionally connect with them.

My drawings have provoked strong reactions from their audience. The drawing in Figure 4.4 is my representation of being the last one picked for teams in gym class. I used this image in my thesis along with a written description. This one image can represent something that it could take many pages to describe. Teachers who have seen this and some of my other drawings have told me they were moved. This particular image, when recently presented to a group of teachers and teacher educators, initiated a dialogue about their memories of gym class and opened up a discussion about physical education in schools. I achieve my goal with these kinds of drawings; they evoke personal memory and emotion and make educators think about how to deal with these issues, with their whole, embodied selves.

Figure 4.4 Being the last one picked for teams in gym class.

TEACHING DRAWING AS A SELF-STUDY METHODOLOGY TO TEACHERS

> [A]rt, in its manifold forms, opens up wider possibilities for a critical celebration of embodied sensuality – one in which reason is no longer prioritized over emotion, and new ways of 'being', 'seeing' and 'relating' to the world . . . can freely evolve.
>
> (Williams and Bendelow 1998, p. 206)

Many victims of bullying note that the teacher is not often around when bullying occurs. They perceive the teacher as not being too concerned with the problem (Derry 2001). Barone (1997) points out that many teachers see bullying as just a normal part of growing up, and not something to be concerned about. In my work in teacher education programs, I often have the opportunity to speak to teachers and pre-service teachers about the topic of bullying. I present my self-study and notice that my drawings often get a more powerful response then my narrative. These responses made me recall something that a teacher who had been bullied as a child told me; she said that the experience of being bullied made her more empathetic and understanding of bullied children in her classroom. This made me believe that the best way to give teachers the embodied understanding of bullying, that would affect their practice, was to engage them in 'mini' self-studies of their own experiences with bullying. My own research experience with drawing, coupled with teachers' powerful reactions to my drawings, convinced me that drawings were a tool I would use with this group.

Recently, while speaking to a graduate class of experienced teachers, I asked them to talk about bullying, to tell me what they know and what they think can help to prevent bullying in classrooms. The students gave me the facts and figures they had read in educational literature. Their words were connected to books and journals, but not to experience, and they did not seem particularly enthused about the topic. Then I started reading them narrative excerpts from my self-study, which I presented along with my drawings. The room became quieter and the students seemed to be feeling emotion. They seemed, perhaps, to be a bit uncomfortable with feeling such emotion in the context of a university classroom and with knowing such vulnerable secrets about an instructor.

It was at this point that I handed out the paper, crayons and colored pencils. I asked the students to 'draw a picture of an incident in your childhood involving bullying. Either you were bullied or witnessed bullying or you were the bully'. They all set to work with intense passion. When they were finished, I asked them to share their drawings with me. The drawings displayed children who were bullied in school or on the playground. With emotion in their voices, the students told the class about the incidents and the roles they played in them.

One student showed us her drawing (Figure 4.5) and recounted a time when she took part in bullying. She told us that she used to love taking part in the game of 'germs', a game where all the children chased each other trying to give each other a particular 'picked on' child's germs. She explained that, reflecting back on this as an adult, she felt very guilty because she could imagine how bad that targeted child must have felt.

Figure 4.5 Taking part in the game of 'germs'.

This drawing exercise got students in touch with their own feelings about and experiences with bullying. The dialogue that ensued was more personally and emotionally tinged. Students (future teachers) talked about the victims of bullying as human beings instead of as stats from a study and they seemed to care much more about the topic after this exercise. They were enthusiastic about the kind of changes they felt needed to happen in classrooms. These 'mini' self-studies seemed to have helped them to learn about bullying from an embodied perspective, one that valued personal experience as a tool of knowing. These teachers learned that their own personal experiences could help them to better understand their own students' problems.

CONCLUSION

> Objects of art are visual, tactile, auditory, kinetic texts – texts consisting of not a verbal language but a language nevertheless, and a language with its own grammar. Because artists are involved in giving shape to their lived experience, the products of art are, in a sense, lived experiences transformed into transcended configurations.
>
> (van Manen 1990, p. 74)

The use of drawing in my self-study taught me many uses for this methodology. I discovered that drawing can be used as a memory prompt, to elicit emotionally difficult information, to understand perceptions of self and to present data. My self-study also gave me the tools to instruct teachers on how to conduct their own arts-based self-inquiries.

Personal experience is a form of knowledge that gets researchers involved with their research in an embodied way. Just writing my memories did not convey the full essence of my experience. Drawing gave my self-study that embodied kind of knowing I wanted to achieve for my reader and myself.

This study has convinced me that art-based self-studies of our own childhood can give us rich information that can help us understand the experiences of children today. In their day-to-day lives, teachers are often somewhat removed from their own childhood experiences. If, as teachers, we learn how to conduct these kinds of self-studies, we can acquire the tools to understand our students better. The teachers I have worked with have told me that doing 'mini' self-studies of their memories of bullying has convinced them of the importance of bullying in children's lives and has given a better understanding of what these children are dealing with.

Since using drawing in this initial self-study, I have gone on to use it as a research method for many other projects. I have used drawings to brainstorm research ideas, to understand thoughts that are not clear and to elicit data from others. I have also used them to further my understanding of myself as an embodied researcher. I understand that I must become embodied if I want teachers and teacher educators to experience my work in an embodied way. To this end, since finishing my initial self-study, I have done a series of drawing that have helped me find my embodied selves.

REFERENCES

Ash, J., 1996, Memory and objects. In Kirkham (Ed.) *The Gendered Object* (Manchester and New York: Manchester University Press), pp. 219–24.

Asher, S.R., 1990, Recent advances in the study of peer rejection. In Asher and Coie (Eds) *Peer Rejection in Childhood* (New York: Cambridge University Press), pp. 3–14.

Bagswell, C.L., Newcomb, A.F. and Bukowski, W.M., 1998, Preadolescent friendship and peer rejection as predictors of adult adjustment. *Child Development*, **69**(1), 140–53.

Barone, F.J., 1997, Bullying in school: it doesn't have to happen. *Phi Delta Kappan*, **79**(1), 80–82.

Bryson, M. and De Castell, S., 1996, Learning to make a difference: gender, new technologies, and in/equity. *Mind, Culture and Activity*, **2**(1), 3–21.

Coie, J.D. and Cillessen, A.H., 1993, Peer rejection: origins and effects on children's development. *Current Directions in Psychological Science*, **2**(3), 89–92.

Derry, C., 2001, Women's recollections of childhood peer rejection in school. Unpublished Master's Thesis, Concordia University.

Eisner, E.W., 1995, What artistically crafted research can help us understand about schools. *Educational Theory*, **45**(1), 1–6.

Emig, J., 2001, Embodied learning. *English Education*, **33**(4), 271–80.

Ganim, B., 1999, *Art and Healing: Using Expressive Art to Heal Your Body, Mind and Spirit* (New York: Three Rivers Press).

Glenbow, V.L., 1991, *The Embodied Viewer* (Calgary: Glenbow Museum).

Matthews, J.C., 1998, Somatic knowing and education. *The Educational Forum*, **62**(3), 236–42.

McNiff, S., 1992, *Art as Medicine: Creating a Therapy of the Imagination* (Boston and London: Shamhala).

McNiff, S., 1998, *Art-Based Research* (London and Philadelphia: Jessica Kingsley Publishers).

Mitchell C. and Weber, S., 1999, *Reinventing Ourselves as Teachers: Beyond Nostalgia* (London: Falmer Press).

Reisman, J.M., 1985, Friendship and its implications for mental health and social competence. *Journal of Early Adolescence*, **5**(3) 383–91.

Richards, J.C., 1998, Turning to the artistic: developing an enlightened eye by creating teaching self-portraits. In Hamilton (Ed.) *Reconceptualizing Teaching Practice: Self-Study in Teacher Education* (London: Falmer Press), pp. 34–44.

Satina, B. and Hultgren, F., 2001, The absent body of girls made visible: embodiment as the focus of education. *Studies in Philosophy and Education*, **20**, 521–24.

Van Manen, M., 1984, Practicing phenomenological writing. *Phenomenology and Pedagogy*, **2**(1), 36–39.

Van Manen, M., 1990, *Researching Lived Experience: Human Science for an Action Sensitive Pedagogy* (London, Ontario: The Althouse Press).

Vaughan, K. and Clark, N., 1999, Note blames victims. *Rocky Mountain News.Com*, retrieved 22 February 2001, http://denver.rockymountainnews.com/shooting/0424scho0.shtml

Weaver, M., 2001, Bullied 11-year-old seeks royal assist. *The Gazette*, 17 February, 21.

Weber, S. and Mitchell, C., 1995, *'That's funny, you don't look like a teacher': Interrogating Images and Identity in Popular Culture* (London: The Falmer Press).

Weber, S.J. and Mitchell, C.A. (2004) Using visual and artistic modes of representation for self-study. In Loughran, Hamilton, LaBoskey and Russell (Eds), *International Handbook of Self-study of Teaching and Teacher Education Practices* (London: Kluwer Academic Publishers).

White, K.J. and Kisner, J., 1992, The influences of teacher feedback on young children's peer preferences and peer perceptions. *Developmental Psychology*, **28**(5), 933–40.

Williams, S.J. and Bendelow, G., 1998, *The Lived Body: Sociological Themes, Embodied Issues* (London and New York: Routledge).

Part 2

Self-study through literary and artistic inquiry

The monochrome frame

Mural-making as a methodology
for understanding 'self'

Max Biddulph

On reaching a fortieth birthday, many people look forward to their entry into mid-life with positive expectations, the personal and professional domains of life taking on an air of stability, progress and consolidation after the exertions of youth. My own experience of this transition was quite different – I remember entering this phase with a distinct feeling of unease. I seemed to be heading for the classic mid-life crisis in which the central question really was 'who am I?'. The question centred on sexual orientation – I thought I had understood this, being comfortable in a heterosexual personal and professional identity. How wrong could I be? I gradually realized that my gayness matters to me – not just in terms of personal integrity, but from a professional point of view as a secondary school educator of twenty-four years.

Being a gay/bisexual man or a man who is questioning his sexuality in an education environment actually means something – it became clear that the changes taking place in my personal life were also impacting at the interface with my professional role. On the face of it this sounds a rather predictable, obvious thing to say. In reality, gaining a greater understanding of this complex relationship has been enormously challenging. In this chapter I aim to share some of my experiences of working with this challenge, specifically in terms of how it is possible to use visual imagery in conjunction with written text as a methodology for clarifying understandings of the 'self'.

THE TRIGGERS OF REFLEXIVITY

Any reader of this book who has experienced a period of profound personal change will know how demanding this is in terms of physical, intellectual and emotional energy. A positive byproduct of my own reflexive process has been a profound curiosity in the experiences of others who may find themselves in a similar situation. This has been formalized in my doctoral research in which I am striving to gain a better sense of the experiences of gay/bisexual men who are educators, specifically in relation to how identity is managed in education environments. Having acquired a number of narratives from my research participants, I set about the task of analyzing the text and writing up my observations. I soon encountered a significant block to my progress. I felt resistant to putting pen to paper – on reflection I think this has something to do with the enormous weight of responsibility that I feel in representing my participants' stories with any degree of accuracy. At some level I am aware of a risk that I may massage or misrepresent their story to meet my own political needs as well as any academic requirement.

I am also aware that some of my phenomenological view remains hidden, even to me. I started to wonder how my unconscious process was influencing the texts that I write and what the implications might be for questions of rigor and validity. Ely *et al.* (1991, p. 179) note that 'qualitative research is by nature a reflexive and recursive process' and during the last decade much attention has been devoted to role of the researcher in the research process (Ellis and Bochner 2000; Ellis and Berger 2002). An important insight came when I realized that I had never really articulated my own experience beyond my personal journal. I had no idea of the visual appearance of this territory in terms of its imagery. Clearly a piece of the jigsaw was missing and I decided to construct a 'visual text' or mural.

DEVELOPING A VISUAL METHODOLOGY TO REVIEW 'SELF'

Two main methods were employed in the construction of the mural. The first method involved the acquisition and use of black and white photographs, a technique for which I am indebted to Mignot (2000). The photographic images were then enlarged on a photocopier to provide raw material for the design on the 'canvas', which consists of a 6 foot × 4 foot expanse of paper attached to a wooden frame. Another level of complexity was added when these images were augmented with written text recorded in my research journal. This text was distilled from experiences and interactions with colleagues and young people, and extracts from this were typed up in the form of a word-processed document, using different font sizes. The statements were then printed out and further enhanced visually by photocopying – this opens up the possibility of enlarging/reducing certain statements, thus placing emphasis on certain ideas.

ACQUIRING VISUAL TEXTS

I set off with a camera loaded with black and white film to photograph a series of sites and images that represented ideas that I had about the gay teacher experience. Some sites were chosen as the exact locations of my direct experience – others were chosen more for their representational or image potential. The sites representing education experience were fairly easy to locate, being mainly located in the secondary school in which I was then working. The sites representing gayness were more problematic. How was it possible to represent the gay aspect of my experience in terms of photo-graphic imagery? At this time I had become intrigued by the notion of how geographical space is delineated in terms of sexuality. Brent Ingram *et al.* (1997) argue that some geographical spaces function as sites of resistance for the 'queer community'. This is an important influence in the design of the mural and informed my thinking on how I used different areas of the canvas to reflect different discourses relating to sexuality and identity.

Arguably, a range of gay community spaces exist ranging from bars, pubs and clubs of the 'commercial gay scene' to more liminal spaces frequented by men who have sex with men, such as public parks and cruising areas. In selecting a representational space I chose the latter, photographing a cruising area located on a canal towpath that flanks a public park in an inner city area. The location is rich in imagery – the stark winter landscape produced some striking images that were powerfully captured by the black and white film.

THE PROCESS OF MURAL CONSTRUCTION AND RESPONSES FROM OTHERS

The actual physical construction of the mural, together with the acquisition of a purpose-built cardboard box for its transportation, brought some interesting learning about the intrinsic interest and curiosity that individuals have in visual imagery, 'story' and the contents of large cardboard boxes. The following anecdotes illustrate what I mean.

I began working at the photocopier at my university base and from the outset those around asked questions about what I was doing – the photo-graphs interested them as did the enlarging/reducing activity. The same phenomenon also manifested itself when I began to assemble the mural in an empty teaching room. Students with whom I had never had conversations came to look and ask questions about what I was doing. I can vividly recall the energy and strong feelings that the process generated. The power of the exercise gripped me like a drug and I became aware of a rising tide of anger triggered, I suspect, by the material that I was handling. I started at about 3 pm with the intention of going home at 5 pm. I was still there at 8:30 pm and the process seemed to take on a momentum of its own.

The level of interest did not stop there either. Some months later, I transported the mural in its box to the European Conference of Education Research held in Edinburgh in 2001. Again the questions came thick and fast from airline check-in staff and taxi drivers alike. What was in the box? What did I mean by my story? The experience was challenging. What should I disclose? What should I not disclose? In retrospect, the prominent labels on the box that read 'fragile' and 'passenger baggage' had more than a little irony.

IMMEDIATE LEARNING: SURFACING CONSCIOUS AWARENESS

In constructing the mural, I began by making a visual framework that surrounds the whole piece. At first glance the imagery is one of a fretwork – I created the image by photocopying and enlarging a photograph that I took of the winter sky as seen through the bare branches of trees. The effect gives the mural an enclosed, contained feel – this has metaphorical as well as visual significance, an issue I will return to later.

The main canvas of the mural consists of two main parts representing teacher experience and gay experience; I used the image of the park railings crossing diagonally from one corner to another to separate the two – see Figure 5.1. The use of the park railing photograph immediately struck me in terms of its potential for representing the interface between the two aspects of experience. The railings themselves in physical terms are a permeable barrier – it is easy to see through them to the environment on the other side. The implication of this in metaphorical terms is that 'permeability' suggests a sense of movement – this is an important conceptual notion that relates to the ways that identity and context interact. I will explore this further in due course.

I was interested in two other photographic images that I acquired on the canal towpath. Apart from maintenance of the railings, there was other evidence that the local authority had taken measures to deter the nocturnal activity of cruising men. Considerable remedial work was being undertaken on the towpath including the cutting back of trees and the installation of CCTV on the approach to the canal from a street nearby. Someone had sprayed the phrase 'crude cure' on a concrete wall adjacent to the towpath – this may or may not have a connection with the clean up campaign and it struck me as an interesting statement in that context. If I am honest, it quite appeals to my sense of the transgressive or subversive.

The gay domain in the mural also contains images of mainly affirming experiences in my personal/professional development. The swan photographed on the park lake nearby represents a gay men's assertiveness training association that I helped to co-found. The cover of the 1991 Pride march in London is a fond memory of a day out with a colleague from school.

On examining the mural again, I am struck that I seem to have reserved most of the space for the teacher experience domain. The use of different font sizes and bold enabled me to produce a variety of styles of text. The

Figure 5.1 The image of the park railings.

repeated questions communicate the wearying effect of continually being asked 'are you married?' or 'do you have any children?' or (from the more assertive students) 'are you gay?'. This happened so frequently that I wanted to include it as a significant aspect of my experience. I was also keen to include comments that I interpreted as affirming and positive as well – these came from colleagues and students.

The image of the television and video case is also significant here. In my journal I noted my vulnerability in the early days of questioning my sexuality as the following extract reveals:

> It was in 1988 that I really started to question my sexual orientation again. I remember teaching PSHE [Personal, Social and Health Education] at around this time in the secondary school in which I was working. One of the modules that I was teaching focused on Sex and Relationships Education and I received through the post one morning information about the BBC's drama adaptation of Leslie Stewart's novel *The Two of Us* which was broadcast in the schools TV series. The story centres on the relationship between two young teenage men, Matthew and Phil, who grow up in the suburbs in the south of England. Matthew identifies as a young gay man and Phil has a girlfriend whilst also being sexually and emotionally attracted to Matthew.
>
> Following the advice in the teacher's notes, I decided to preview the programme before using it with young people. Every lunch time for a week I remember retreating to the privacy of my classroom located on the top floor of the school, away from all the noise and bustle. I watched the programme again and again – it had a kind of fascination for me, tapping into a set of personal issues that I was only just becoming aware of.
>
> The image of me watching the TV in a classroom isolated from the rest of the school is a powerful metaphor for how I was seeing my sexual identity at that time in relation to my other selves. I can only describe this as being a very split off, separate aspect of my identity. Whilst I was increasingly aware of my feelings of isolation and desire for separateness, I was having to address the issue of sexuality on a day-to-day basis, in my interactions with other members of the school community.
>
> A very difficult aspect of these interactions was the feeling of rejection. In classes, I know that kids have not wanted to sit next to me because they think I am gay; I also know that kids have wanted to change groups because they think I am gay. I have also been verbally abused inside and outside of lessons.
>
> (Research Journal, 1995)

I note that the two statements that I pushed well to the fore via enlargement on the photocopier relate to this verbal abuse, i.e. 'fucking queer' and 'it happened, it really happened'. The first relates to verbal abuse that was delivered to me again not directly, but definitely for my consumption, by a student who shouted it to me three times while he was hidden out of sight. This had a profound effect on me, my sense of outrage was total, and the

Figure 5.2 'It happened, it really happened'.

incident consumed a great deal of time and energy in following it up. In foregrounding it I wanted to counter any attempt to 'hush the incident up'. The second phrase, 'it happened, it really happened' (see Figure 5.2), has haunted me ever since I heard it used in a paper given by Melanie Walker at the British Educational Research Association conference in Belfast 1998. The inclusion of it here immediately brought into my awareness that not only do I not feel heard as a gay man in a school environment, but I worry that I may not even be believed.

SUBSEQUENT LEARNING: SURFACING UNCONSCIOUS AWARENESS

In the weeks following the mural construction I entered a period of doubt and guilt – had I been unfair, unduly negative, disloyal, inappropriate . . . vengeful even in my use of imagery on the mural? Perhaps I should just accept the words of Scott Peck (1978, p. 1) that 'life is difficult' and get on with it. I started to re-frame my perception of the environment and made a conscious effort to think that how others perceived 'my difference' might not matter in that situation. For a couple of months life proceeded on a very ordinary footing but one day I was brought back to reality when I experienced more homophobic abuse (delivered in the usual 'hidden way' from a male in a group of young people on a crowded stairwell). A week later I encountered homophobia again, this time in the staff room. This makes me think that the social/political landscape of school environments is complex and shifting by nature.

Despite these rather depressing and at times distressing reflections on both of the domains, the one constant image on the mural is the fretwork effect that surrounds the whole piece. In my perception this represents some boundary or containing structure, some kind of common denominator to all this experience. Another way of looking at the whole is that it represents some kind of human system, where relationships and behaviours, values and attitudes are simultaneously separate and yet connected (no matter how distantly). For me this raises an interesting question of how individual teachers and students manage aspects of their identity in educational environments. The image of the railings permits movement because of their permeability. If the metaphor is translated into the context of social and political interactions, a great range of personae and identities could be displayed in any given situation. What is fore-grounded one day may be back-grounded the next. What is disclosed in one situation may be withheld in another. The notion of monitoring or screening can be connected to the CCTV imagery on the mural. The complexity of these processes is both obvious and mind-boggling at the same time – I am hypothesizing that identities have the potential to be fluid and changing.

CONCLUDING THOUGHTS

I am aware that I could have constructed any number of murals, which could have told many different stories. I have become very protective of this mural; it resides wrapped in plastic, delicate and parchment-like in its box. Some of this protectiveness is related to the risks that I took in revealing my emotional fragility and its physical fragility. I am continually surprised at the interest that is shown in it as a medium in its own right – I think that the monochrome frame conveys some powerful messages. In retrospect I was naïve to think that I might be able to purge myself of subjectivity into some more clinical, objective place and I am reassured by the view of Russell and Kelly (2002, p. 1) who note that subjectivity in the post-modern approach 'is both assumed and appreciated'. The phenomenological lens that I am bringing to the project in terms of my own experience is in itself part of the data in my research.

REFERENCES

Brent Ingram, G., Bouthilette, A. and Retter, Y., 1997, *Queers in Space: Communities, Public Places, Sites of Resistance* (Seattle: Bay Press).

Ellis, C. and Berger, L., 2002, Their story/my story/our story: including the researchers' experience in interview research. In Gubrium and Holstein (Eds) *Handbook of Interview Research* (London: Sage), pp. 849–75.

Ellis, C. and Bochner, A., 2000, Autoethnography, personal narrative, reflexivity: researcher as subject. In Denzin and Lincoln (Eds) *Handbook of Qualitative Research* (London: Sage), pp. 733–68.

Ely, M., Anzul, M., Friedman, T., Garner, D. and McCormack Steinmetz, A. 1991, *Doing Qualitative Research: Circles within Circles* (London: Falmer Press).

Mignot, P., 2000, Using visual methods in careers education and guidance. *Pastoral Care in Education*, June 2000.

Russell, G. and Kelly, N., 2002, Research as interacting dialogue processes: implications for reflexivity. *Forum: Qualitative Social Research* [online], 3(3). Available at: http: www.qualitative-research.net/fqs-texte/3-02/3-02russellkelly-e.pdf [6 June 2003].

Scott Peck, M., 1978, *The Road Less Travelled* (New York: Simon & Schuster).

Walker, M., 1998, Mrs Palmer gave me a scholarship to Sterkfontein. Presented in the symposium on *Narrative Fiction and the Art of Educational Research* at the British Educational Research Association conference. August 1998, Queens University, Belfast.

Chapter 6

Using pictures at an exhibition to explore my teaching practices

Mary Lynn Hamilton

MUSING AT THE BEGINNING

Within the recent literature on teacher education research, there are competing frameworks of teacher preparation. Each frame has a knowledge base that supports it. Widely cited examples include a range from Gage's 'effective teaching practice' that lead to the 'process-product research' (Gage 1972, 1994; Good and Brophy 1986) to Shulman's (1987) notion of 'the wisdom of practice' captured in the Carnegie work. Further examples extend from Cochran-Smith and Lytle's (1993) idea of local knowledge produced by communities of teachers who adopt an inquiry-as-stance to Clandinin (1992) and Clandinin and Connelly's (1999, 2000) theory of personal practical knowledge that employs narrative inquiry. Additionally Eisner's (1991, 1993, 1995) understanding of educational practice and educational research as aesthetic endeavors and Ladson-Billings' (1995) culturally responsive teaching supported by cultural funds of knowledge (Gonzalez 1995; Gonzalez *et al.* 1993, 1995) contribute to the work recognized as the foundational knowledge within these frames. Zeichner's (1993a, 1993b) image of teachers as agents of social transformation engaged in action research and Giroux's (1997) formulation of teachers as cultural workers informed by consciousness-raising 'critical theory and cultural studies' research also contribute to this foundation of knowledge.

Much of this work can be located within one of two major theoretical frameworks – a modernist framework that offers 'the' way and a post-modernist framework that calls for a multi-faceted view. These two frameworks provide an uncomfortable relation for much of the recent research on teachers' practical knowledge. Alleviating this discomfort requires an understanding of the methodology used to present the work. While the modernist frame has numerous methodological strategies associated with it, strategies of the post-modern sort – specifically relevant for the work of researchers engaged in self-study – have been delineated less frequently.

The writer's intention

This paper examines one element of the self-study of my teaching practices undertaken in my advanced qualitative research class taught during one semester. In this paper, I describe in word and with example some strategies for exploring my teaching in ways that allow for a multi-faceted view. I pay particularly close attention to describing these strategies because self-study work is frequently critiqued for paying less than ample attention to methodology. I am often without critical friends and colleagues in my surrounding area with whom I can discuss my work, so I must be inventive. Using Winslow Homer's art and my journals, I hoped to explore the use of artistic works as a way to look at self-study and as a way to help think about teaching. In the next section, I engage in a conversation about the methodology of self-study and the implications for post-modern research. To do this, I will demonstrate and provide evidence for the way I used this selected strategy to undertake my self-study. One of the hallmarks of self-study research is our willingness to hold our work up for others to examine (Hamilton and Pinnegar 1998, p. 240). This, in a sense, is what makes self-study a specific area of teacher research. We both 'do' and 'show'. Where we need to develop our expertise is in relation to representation and the ways in which we portray our work to others (Hamilton and LaBoskey 2002, p. 7). Because our work is innovative and often on the fringe of acceptability, we need to find ways that clearly represent our work and we need to find ways that represent that work so others can clearly understand it. With this work, I attempt to do that.

Providing a context

When you involve yourself in a self-study while teaching a research class, you have an opportunity to refract ideas in many directions. That is where I found myself – teaching an advanced qualitative research class while asking questions about how to better address course content in ways that my students' understandings might deepen and their writings would strengthen. Simple, you might say, just try this or that strategy. However, I had tried a variety of teaching strategies and we were proceeding in ways that satisfied neither my students nor me. Specifically, I was looking for better ways to talk with my students about the power and the value of qualitative research in order to support them in the design of their theoretical/conceptual frameworks for their dissertations or research studies. The students were having difficulty in fully understanding the distinctions I attempted to make (they expressed this and I could read about it in their journals) and I was not having an easy time.

As I proceeded through the semester, I tried to explore the best practices for presenting information about research to students who were steeped in the positivist tradition. Some could easily see and operationalize ideas presented, while others could not. From my perspective, the difficulty was students' ways of listening and understanding rather than their intellectual capabilities. The students were smart enough, so what was happening? This was the study in progress when this particular segment of the fieldwork at an art gallery began.

A critical friend?

Over the years as I have come to understand self-study, I have used a variety of methods. To document my experiences throughout the semester, I used my teaching journal, conversations with an artist as a critical friend, student journals, informal interviews with students (in the form of discussions), student documents, and collected documents to explore my work. This information was collected for delineating what occurred in our class and how these occurrences affected the students. I also engaged in a variety of critically reflective practices to consider ways to improve my practice for the purposes of increasing my students' learning and writing. For their part, my students also kept weekly research journals that I read.

I present this work not as a completed project, but rather as an example of how one researcher engages in the methodological aspects of her study. Usually in self-study work, the researcher has a critical friend or a colleague to support the thoughtful process of the self-study. Missing that at my institution, I have previously used collage as a tool for my reflective analysis and engagement. For this study, I extended the idea of 'other', and I invited Winslow Homer, or should I say his spirit, to engage with me in the analytic consideration of my teaching. He seemed like an appropriate selection because during his time (1836–1910) he was considered by many to be at the cutting edge of the art world. Of him, critics wrote, 'Homer's paintings of American life inspired his audiences to reassess our national art, but his compelling images were caught in the crossfire of aesthetic battles that raged as our country and its art matured together' (Nelson-Atkins 2001, p. 1). These critics suggested that Homer pushed the art of the time beyond the limits found to be acceptable. While self-study work might not be quite so far-reaching, it has been considered by some (Zeichner 1999, p. 8, for example) to be a significant contribution to teacher education. At the time, it seemed right to select Homer as a critical friend.

Regarding research, I believe that research is contextual and deals with values. Furthermore, good research requires that researchers know themselves and see that knowing themselves is related to change. According to Hamilton and LaBoskey:

> we are not yet . . . expert at portraying [our work] to others, since it seems to require new ways of doing so. . . . [To engage in this work, the aim] is

more personalization than generalization. The knowledge generated by self-study is not decontextualized. We are teachers engaged in an on-going process of personalizing what we are coming to know with the people with whom we work – our student teachers and colleagues, the primary audience, if you will, for the work. We have developed considerable expertise with regard to this personalization of knowledge.

(Hamilton and LaBoskey 2002, p. 7)

For the full self-study, all data collected – journals, interviews, and documents – were triangulated to provide the most complete picture of the teaching and learning experiences within my classroom. In this way, each piece of information or conclusion was validated by the other collected information (Borman *et al.* 1986; Denzin 1978) and helped me avoid presenting unexamined assumptions. In this way, I insured the best representation of data as well as the strongest interpretation of the information gathered.

SETTING THE SCENE: VISITING THE NELSON-ATKINS ART MUSEUM

Winslow Homer – the particular master who is the focus of this study – was a radical in his time. An advocate of the use of color and a sense of observation, he was controversial in his time because he stepped outside of convention. Critics of Homer's work sometimes focused on his depictions of the world. He did not glamorize what he saw. He also included many of the people – women and people of color – that were not ordinarily included in art of the time. His commitment to a sense of social justice appealed to me. I saw myself in some of the struggles that he had and some of his thoughts about the world. I had always appreciated his work and as I meandered through the museum halls, I found myself captured in thoughts about my own work and my own place within teacher education. I have been interested in visual and artistic symbols for some time. For the last Castle conference, I had addressed the use of collage as a tool for critical reflection (Arizona Group 2000). Using the symbols and ideas from pictures and words found in magazines, I constructed work that served as a 'critical friend' that pushed my thinking about my experiences forward as well as served a symbolic representation of my ideas. When academics are in a less-than-supportive environment, they may lack colleagues who support them in the development of ideas. Certainly, this was and is my experience. Consequently, the use of collage filled that lack of support because the act of selecting the pictures and the words for the creation as well as the design of the collage itself served to stimulate my reflective process. By the time I viewed Homer's work, I knew I had to publicly document the ways in which he served as 'the other' as a point of departure to explore the effects of this art exhibit on my thinking about my teaching and my self-study.

Who is this person?

Not being of the time of Homer, I cannot presume to interpret his experiences and his work through the eyes of his time. For those interpretations, I turned to the critics of his time. Even here, of course, we must assume bias. However, since this paper is using Homer as a tool and I am not worried about the 'fairest' interpretation of all, I use the voices of critics to provide a brief broad stroke to offer a picture of the artist.

Born in Boston, Massachusetts, in February 1836, Homer learned his art mostly on his own. Apprenticing with a Boston lithographic firm in his late teens, he rather quickly developed his sense of style and became a contributor to *Harper's Weekly*, a well-respected magazine in Homer's time. As he matured, he developed his skills with oils and moved along to watercolours, focusing on his observations of life he saw around him. Throughout his life, Winslow Homer was both lauded and critiqued in excess for his creations. People saw him as an artist who straddled a line between the approaches to art during his time – realism and impressionism. History sees him as one of the greatest American painters of the nineteenth century.[1]

Eventually, Winslow Homer was seen as a great American artist. When he first came to the attention of the public, however, he was seen as un-American because of the ways that his work resembled the work of the contemporary French painters as well as sloppy, crude, and loose (Conrads 2001). (During Homer's time, impressionism was not held in as high regard as it currently is.) According to one critic 'Art['s] . . . purpose is . . . to interpret the great truths of life and nature; not merely to please the optic nerve, but to elevate the soul' (Benjamin 1881, p. 23). Homer endeavored to do that with his work. Now, I do not think I have quite so lofty a goal with my work, but I do attempt to have an impact on the educational practices of my students for the purpose of graduating the best teachers and teacher educators from our program. Given that, Homer was a likely critical sounding board – he was a risk-taker who knew enough about his discipline to want to move beyond convention. His work evoked a story, a texture, an experience, and more. I hoped he would help me.

Pictures at the exhibition

As I prepared for my study, I decided to keep a journal about my experiences through a series of detailed notes. I also decided to prepare elaborate lesson plans and rationales for the work I did in class. Additionally I elected to keep records of student work, student conversation, and evidence of classroom engagement. At the point I invited Winslow Homer to be my critical friend,

I had collected some materials from my students and written some journal entries, but felt that I needed some deeper level of support. Winslow Homer seemed a wonderful choice. His controversial, provocative, and ground-breaking work offered an interesting instigation for critical reflection.

Homer was seen as a powerful storyteller who went beyond a simple story. To provide the best examples I explore these paintings by Homer: *The Country School, Taking Sunflower to Teacher (a Flower for the Teacher), The Cotton Pickers* and *A Visit from the Old Mistress* to demonstrate the ways that I interacted with the work. I selected these works as exemplars because they prompted the greatest breadth of response.

The Country School (1872)

My notes: *When I viewed 'The Country School' I identified with the school scene. Students are depicted attending to their work and ignoring the teacher, and the teacher, while central to the picture, is not central to the classroom action as presented in the scene. The canvas is large with a teacher centrally located on the canvas. Students are scattered around, mostly in groups of two or three. There are an equal number of male and female students. All of the students are white. The room has three windows that appear to look out upon an open hilly area. The colors in the painting are muted. The theme of the painting is quite 'American' in nature. There is an involvement in the work that also seems to represent the expectations of people at the time, even those of apparent lower social class.*

About this particular painting, critics addressed 'how subject and style might be strategically maneuvered.' Further, these critics 'recognized that an especially national subject [that] allowed him greater stylistic freedom, or conversely, that a more traditional technique could gain him latitude with thematic content' (Nelson-Atkins 2001, p. 1). As an artist, Homer hoped to inspire the participation of viewers in the construction of meaning about his work. From Homer's perspective, there was a multitude of possible meanings for the painting (Conrads 2001).

As I initiated my self-study in late winter, I asked myself – How could I push my thinking forward about my teaching practices? How do I keep myself conscious about my teaching? Or do I? Strolling in the gallery on this spring day, I asked myself these questions: In what ways is my class like the class in Homer's painting? How might the ideas expressed in this painting help me think more deeply about my classroom experiences? How might Homer and his willingness to be on the cutting edge push me along in my thinking about my teaching?

Beginning simply, I asserted that my class seemed similar in structure. Several students had acquaintance relationships with each other, whereas others had joined us from the larger University community (beyond the School of Education) and know no one at the beginning of the course. In this class, then, while there were loose links among students, there was no strong comradery – at least at the beginning. During the semester, I focused on the development of a learning community using certain exercises and through discussion. In qualitative research, the support of colleagues is critical and a learning community seems essential for the work. Although the students would talk together, their involvement in the class as community seemed less than satisfactory. In looking at the painting, there was a distance between most students and from the teacher that was striking.

Why, I asked, was that occurring? Homer did not answer. I looked again at the painting. Homer reminded me that the painting itself, the style, the texture, differed from the convention. The stark contrasts in the ways that the colors and the images conflicted with the status quo of the time suggested a possibility. Perhaps I thought, my students were mired in convention. Perhaps, they had not had courses where they were expected to engage in meaningful dialogue that might contribute to themselves and to others. If true, their discomfort would make sense. I explored this issue. In a review of journals and informal discussions students would say, 'I've never had a class like this before' and describe previous classes that followed a more formal lecture format. While Homer could not offer suggestions about possible strategies, he did help me think more carefully about my experience.

Although the teacher holds an open book and could be reading, it is not clear that the students are attending to her. The student that seems visually in front of her might be reading aloud – but may not be. All students, except the crying boy in the front of the canvas, seem engaged in work of some sort. And Homer asked about the ways in which my students engage in my classroom. I had to respond that my students engaged in the work – perhaps not as I might like them to engage. I wanted them to drink in all of this new information and be transformed in ways I could not predict. Homer giggled, or I thought he did. How, he seemed to say, could I expect my students to experience such an epiphany within such a short time span? Perhaps I expected too much.

At this point, I moved along in the exhibition.

Taking Sunflower to Teacher (a Flower for the Teacher) (1875)

My notes: *Of particular note with this picture and the others to follow is the subject matter. Few well-known artists of the time – who for the most part were white and male – selected people of color as a focal point. If they were the subjects of the artist's text, they were often portrayed in a derogatory manner. This is not true of Homer's work. Here we have a young boy carrying a sunflower for his teacher.*

Homer asked – what do you think I am telling you? I had to think for a moment. I saw the young boy's clothing, I saw his downcast face, I saw his innocence, and I thought I saw bewilderment. I also saw an engagement with nature, signified by the butterfly not dusted from his shoulder, but sitting there in comfort. I also supposed that Homer had this boy pose for hours and hours, which could have led to the bewildered look. I wondered about my students. I asked myself about their feelings of bewilderment. They were learning – or were being asked to learn – about ways of thinking with which they were unfamiliar. Did they experience bewilderment? Were they tired? They often wrote in their journals about the pressures of the class. How does this fit with ways I will have to write my dissertation? Does Dr So-and-So understand this sort of research? I could not always answer those questions.

The question of dealing with issues of difference followed me as I continued to walk through the exhibition.

The Cotton Pickers (1876)

My notes: *As I arrived in front of 'The Cotton Pickers', my breath was sucked away. This breath-taking canvas with a salmon-sandy sky imposing over a field of cotton sees two women walking – one focused on the current, immediate task at hand, and the other focused on the indefinable future. They are beautiful self-contained women. I found myself staring into the canvas for what seemed liked hours. I tried to imagine Homer's thinking, his motivation for the work. I could not.*

What I do know is that, at the time, his decision to undertake work focused on women of color in such a realistic and humane fashion must have been quite courageous. This work was completed within ten years of the end of the American Civil War. African-Americans had been freed from slavery, but not from the prejudices and attitudes of the times. Few artists followed his example. According to some historians, the exhibition of 'The Cotton Pickers' seemed unfathomable to the viewing public. The viewers could not understand his choice of subjects. However, the reviewers found his work to be critically worthy and centered on subjects that were distinctly American in nature.

I thought about Winslow Homer. I thought about the women in the picture. I asked myself how my work might be courageous. How could I encourage my students to critically analyze their work and question the 'modern' view with which they are most familiar? Winslow, I said, you have inspired me! Winslow smiled.

Not a showy person, Homer painted his pictures more for his interest in painting than to attain a label or receive recognition. I saw him as a model. I saw that I needed to focus on my students and my task at hand (not unlike the woman in the field) rather than focus on some future possibility. I needed to encourage my students to step away from the safety of the thinking they found so familiar.

I continued to stroll.

A Visit from the Old Mistress (1876)

My notes: *When I arrived at this painting, I immediately felt some recognition with the subjects. The most striking element in this picture for me is its darkness. This darkness suggests turmoil to me. What you see in the picture are the living quarters of former slaves, which do not seem much improved from the days before the American Civil War. There are few amenities. Their clothing is homespun and well worn. Looking more deeply into the picture, I see an interesting relation between the white woman and the black women. First, there is the quest status of the visiting white woman. While the white woman seems to have power, there is a reticence, and, perhaps, respectfulness. In the scene, the white woman is standing while one of the black women is standing. I also think I see some tension about how to 'be' in the scene among all of the women. The stance of each person in the picture seems to suggest wariness about how to behave. They seem frozen in the question of it. I felt that Homer captured that awkwardness.*

He asked me, so are your students awkward in your classroom? Interesting question. While I attempted to work with issues of power and ways of talking about issues, I imagined that awkwardness did exist there. How could that not be true? I am the person who gives the grade. I am also someone pushing on their ideas about how to think about important issues. And I am challenging the ways that they think about things. From my perspective, I might say that some of my students seemed frozen-in-the-headlights. That is, sometimes my students seemed frozen in the worry about how to behave in my classroom. Their behaviour did not mirror the images in the painting, but it came close. Art mirrors life/life mirrors art. They were learning how to stretch their minds and how to trust.

SELF-STUDY AND ISSUES OF METHODOLOGY

My work strives to explore ways in which methodologies used in self-study can support the development of teachers' ideas about teaching. Since there are not many examples of self-studies of teaching practices and fewer studies with details about methodology, it seemed appropriate to use this chapter to explore the ways that we talk about and think about the methodology of the self-study of teaching practices. I found that working with Winslow Homer served as a useful reflective tool that helped me unearth some of my notions about my teaching. In the give-and-take between the paintings and myself, I found myself pushing my thinking about ideas in deeper ways. I am, of course, not the first researcher in education to try to see the pedagogical possibilities of the art gallery for researching the shaping and mirroring of gender and literacy (see, for example, Cherland 1994; Mitchell 1994). As for the 'staging' of a self-reflexive artistic dialogue in relation to teaching,

Charlotte Hussey (2000) engages in a poetic self-study through imaginary letters and dialogues with a critical friend, as well, the poet HD.

I found this strategy useful in several ways and on several levels. As a researcher, I stretched my theoretical and creative possibilities for understanding ways to examine teaching. As a teacher, I modeled ways to step beyond conventions to develop the students' ideas. In turn, my students, over time, felt nudged (in a good way) to present their ideas and deepen their understandings. For example, one student created an interactive painting project of work and picture to explore her understandings of our class. From this encounter with Winslow Homer, I see grand potential for strengthening our work if we are willing to invite alternatives into our methodology.

NOTE

1   This brief summary of Winslow Homer's life represents a composite of information drawn from the websites of http://www.lacma.org/press/home rpr.htm; http://web.syr.edu/~ribond/homer.ltm; http://www.artcyclopedia.com/artists/homer-winslow/html; http://www.nga.gov; http://govschl.ndsu.nodak.edu/~rausch;homer.htm.

REFERENCES

Arizona Group, 2000, Myths and legends of teacher education reform in the 1990s. Symposium presented during the Castle Conference. July, East Sussex, England.

Benjamin, S.G.W., 1881, The exhibitions. VII – National Academy of Design – Fifty-sixth Exhibition. *American Art Review*, 2, 23.

Borman, K., Lecompte, M. and Goetz, J., 1986, Ethnographic and qualitative research design and why it doesn't work. *American Behavioral Scientist*, 30, 42–57.

Cherland, M., 1994, *Private Practices: Girls and Literacy* (New York and London: Routledge).

Clandinin, D.J., 1992, Narrative and story in teacher education. In Russell and Munby (Eds) *Teachers and Teaching: From Classroom to Reflection* (London: Falmer Press), pp. 124–37.

Clandinin, J. and Connelly, M., 1999, *Shaping a Professional Identity: Stories of Professional Practice* (New York: Teachers College Press).

Clandinin, J. and Connelly, M., 2000, *Narrative Inquiry: Experience and Story in Qualitative Research* (New York: Teachers College Press).

Cochran-Smith, M. and Lytle, S., 1993, *Inside Outside: Teacher Research and Knowledge* (New York: Teachers College Press).

Conrads, M., 2001, *Winslow Homer and the Critics* (Princeton: Princeton University Press).

Denzin, N.K., 1978, *The Research Act: A Theoretical Introduction to Sociological Methods* (New York: McGraw-Hill).

Eisner, E.W., 1991, *The Enlightened Eye* (New York: Macmillan Publishing Company).

Eisner, E.W., 1993, Forms of understanding and the future of educational research. *Educational Researcher*, **22**(7), 5–12.

Eisner, E.W., 1995, What artistically crafted research can help us to understand about schools. *Educational Theory*, **45**(1), 1–7.

Gage, N., 1972, *Teacher Effectiveness and Teacher Education: The Search for a Scientific Basis* (Palo Alto, CA: Pacific Books).

Gage, N.L., 1994, The scientific status of research on teaching. *Educational Theory*, **44**(4), 371–85.

Giroux, H., 1997, *Pedagogy and the Politics of Hope: Theory, Culture, and Schooling* (Boulder, CO: Westview Press).

Gonzalez, N., 1995, The funds of knowledge for teaching project. *Practicing Anthropology*, **17**(3), 3–6.

Gonzalez, N., Moll, L.C., Floyd-Tenery, M., Rivera, A., Rendon, P., Gonzales, R. and Amanti, C., 1993, *Teacher Research on Funds of Knowledge: Learning from Households* (Santa Cruz, CA: The National Center for Research on Cultural Diversity and Second Language Learning).

Gonzalez, N., Moll, L.C., Tenery, M.F., Rivera, A., Rendon, P., Gonzales, R. and Amanti, C., 1995, Funds of knowledge for teaching in Latino households. *Urban Education*, **29**(4), 443–70.

Good, T. and Brophy, J., 1986, Teacher behavior and student achievement. In Wittrock (Ed.) *Handbook of Research on Teaching* (3rd edn) (New York: Macmillan), pp. 328–75.

Hamilton, M.L. and LaBoskey, V., 2002, Delineating the territory: reclaiming and refining the self-study of teaching practices. Paper presented at the annual conference of the American Educational Research Association, New Orleans.

Hamilton, M.L. and Pinnegar, S., 1998, The value and promise of self-study. In Hamilton (Ed.) *Reconceptualizing Teaching Practice* (London: Falmer Press), pp. 235–46.

Hussey, C., 2000, Of swans, the wind and H.D.: an epistolary portrait of the poetic process. Unpublished doctoral dissertation, Faculty of Education, McGill University.

Ladson-Billings, G., 1995, Toward a theory of culturally relevant pedagogy. *American Educational Research Journal*, **32**(3), 465–93.

Mitchell, C., 1994, Reading reading in popular culture. *Textual Studies in Canada: Canadian Journal of Cultural Literacy*, **4**, 69–80.

Nelson-Atkins, 2001, Commentary about Winslow Homer's painting. Nelson-Atkins Museum.

Shulman, L., 1987, Knowledge and teaching: foundations of the new reform. *Harvard Education Review*, **57**, 1–22.

Zeichner, K.M., 1993a, Action research: personal renewal and social reconstruction. *Educational Action Research*, **1**, 199–219.

Zeichner, K.M., 1993b, Connecting genuine teacher development to the struggle for social justice. *Journal of Education for Teaching*, **17**(1), 5–20.

Zeichner, K., 1999, The new scholarship in teacher education. *Educational Researcher*, **28**(9), 4–15.

Chapter 7

Self-study through an exploration of artful and artless experiences

Linda Szabad-Smyth

I have fond and vivid memories of myself as a child, at home, enjoying many exciting moments of art-making, inviting my imagination to soar above and beyond my immediate time/space to other worlds where time stood still. I recall my silent adventures to the attic to rummage through the forgotten boxes of old musty books, where within the jackets of these books I would find pages on which I could draw. I remember building micro homes for my dolls within the crawl space beneath the living room sofa.

I remember the first day of school heralding the onset of the new school year with the distribution of supplies: pencils, erasers, rulers and, of course, crayons. The scent and the look of these crayons, brightly and deliciously coloured, sharply pointed, and neatly lined up in a fresh crisp box, stirred within me much excitement and anticipation.

(Personal recollection)

INITIATING A STUDY OF TEACHERS' BELIEFS ABOUT ART

These two snippets of autobiographical text represent glimpses into my 'lived experience' (van Manen 1992) as a child who loved to make art. As I 'relived' these experiences through reflection and from my perspective as artist and art educator, I recalled that the experience of art-making at home differed significantly from my art-making at school. While at home, I could experience imaginative flights into fantasy, magic moments of creating through art and play, experiences that were never replicated in my elementary years of schooling. The school year would start off well with the new box of crayons; unfortunately my artful memories of school ended there with the new boxes of crayons. Art was never 'taught,' it was never treated as a discipline but rather as a hands-on activity of drawing 'anything' or some form of holiday art, reserved for Friday afternoons, and as a reward for acceptable class behaviour during the week.

As a mother with two daughters, I collected the many works of art that my children made over the years both at home and at school and discovered that not much had changed with respect to visual arts education in the elementary schools. History was repeating itself. This reality led me to question the marginality of elementary visual arts education and to consider what could be done to improve the situation.

As a teacher educator in the area of visual arts education with in-service and pre-service generalists as well as art specialist student teachers, I observed that the needs of generalists differed significantly from those of specialists. I noticed that both pre-service and in-service generalists shared similar anxieties and uncertainties about making art as well as the teaching of art. I questioned whether past experiences or preconceived ideas about art and art education might have contributed to their insecurities, fears and in some cases apathy? More importantly, could there be a link between how teachers felt and thought about art and their own art-making abilities (disabilities) and how they taught art in their classrooms? How might teachers' beliefs and attitudes about art and art education contribute to the marginalization of art in the elementary classroom?

Growing out of my concern to find answers to these questions, I chose to look at generalist teachers' life experiences related to art and art-making. I initiated a study that asked teachers to tell me about their positive and negative experiences with art and to reflect on how their past might have influenced their current beliefs and philosophies about art and art education.[1]

I chose life history as my research model to frame my study of generalists' lived experiences related to visual arts. My study focused on the meaning of art throughout one's lifetime, from a variety of perspectives: the teacher as child, the teacher as student and the teacher as teacher. I wanted to understand the *lived experiences* of my teacher participants from their own perspective; I wanted to know what role art played in their lives. Ultimately, I wanted to understand how past experiences had influenced their beliefs about art and their teaching of art in their classrooms.

My study of teachers' lives supported the approach used by life history researchers to find answers to questions by looking closely and deeply into the individual's life and with the understanding that lifetime events influence beliefs, attitudes and choices. This study also introduced teachers to a form of self-study. With my guidance, the participants traveled into their pasts and began to discover for themselves the influence of past experiences.

RESEARCH PROCESS

To begin my study of life histories, I sought the participation of elementary school teachers who were currently teaching visual arts as part of their classroom curriculum. I was not looking for art specialists, nor was I seeking specifically those who were 'gifted' in the arts. My goal was to find individuals (male or female) with whom I could develop a *'research partnership'* (Cole and Knowles 1993, p. 477) that would be mutually beneficial and where the participant could feel 'a sense of ownership' (Cole 1991, p. 193). Life history research requires the participant to invest a substantial amount of time and emotional commitment both with the interview questions that represent in-depth and intrusive inquiries into one's personal life and with on-going negotiation throughout the research process. I quickly discovered that my biggest obstacle was finding teachers who would want to sacrifice time for me outside of their demanding and rigorous teaching commitments and on-going staff meetings.

Added to the inconvenience of fitting me into their busy schedules, I wondered, did generalists feel there was nothing in this for them and so why bother? I was approaching them with 'my' research questions and invit-ing them to participate in a study of my choosing, not theirs. Contrary to other studies of generalists, none of these teachers were my former students and none were involved in graduate work that might have paved the way for teacher reflection and self-study. I also thought that perhaps some teachers might not have been interested in the topic of study or might have felt inadequate talking about 'art' since they did not consider themselves 'artists.' The resounding theme from those teachers who refused to participate was that they were too busy both during the school year with teaching and in the summer months with their family plans. With the participants who did agree to go forward with the study, we negotiated for time, place and any special conditions relating to future meetings.

When I had first proposed to carry out this study, my focus was not aimed at the lives of women teachers. However, given the fact that I was working primarily with elementary school teachers, there was a greater likelihood that my participants would be women. What resulted was that four women teachers, all in their forties and with seven to twenty-six years' teaching experience, volunteered to participate; my final sample became a women only group. Although this group of participants represented a small sampling of women very close in age, and with similar cultural and educational back-grounds, the outcome of this study was nonetheless significant as it provided a very detailed look at the source of teachers' beliefs and their influence on the teaching of art.

DATA COLLECTION

Data for this study consisted of stories from the lived experiences of teachers as they related to a lifetime of artful and artless events. Data collection consisted of two phases. Phase one began with self-reflective writing, com-pleting a biographical data sheet and the choosing of a pseudonym. This was followed by two semi-structured interviews in the second phase.

Self-reflective writing

At the end of the first meeting, if a teacher agreed to participate, she was asked to write one and a half to two pages about two 'significant' art-related experiences from the past; one was to represent a positive or 'artful' experience, and the other was to represent a negative or 'artless' experience. These stories could be of experiences inside or outside of school and be representative of the teacher as child, adolescent or adult. An 'artful' experience could be any visual arts-related experience where the participant came away with a good feeling about making art, teaching art or of having had a memorable aesthetic experience. An 'artless' experience could signify a negative or painful encounter with visual arts; even a project that a teacher taught and viewed as a 'flop' would qualify. These short, written autobiographical texts of key events or '*protocol writing*' (van Manen 1992, p. 63) served as short initial glimpses into the lives of the teachers to be studied and provided themes or questions that could be pursued in the interviews to follow. I assumed that the teachers would be very selective in their choice of stories to write about as they were asked to write only one story from each of the artless and artful categories. Chances were that in choosing to write about unforgettable experiences, these same stories might resurface later in the interviews and for now would provide me with themes to consider.

The collected short stories from the teachers revealed 'key' art experiences as they related to classroom events. Although the experiences that the teachers wrote about did not reveal any major turning points in their lives, the events that they did experience had left significant impressions, which in turn had impacted on their ways of thinking about art and art-making. Denzin (1989) refers to these kinds of stories as representative of '*epiphanies*' or 'interactional moments and experiences that leave marks on people's lives' (p. 70). My teachers' written stories represented 'minor epiphanies' which as defined by Denzin 'symbolically represent a major, problematic moment in a relationship or a person's life' (p. 71).

The interviews

My intention was to space my interviews a week apart to allow for continuity as well as time for reflection. Again, the issue of being too busy or having other commitments interfered with this plan. I had never anticipated the delays, interruptions and postponements that ensued caused by sickness, travel plans, unexpected visitors, report card preparation, summer vacations and the weather.

Teachers were asked to commit to at least two interviews which would last approximately one and a half hours each and possible additional interviews if the need should arise. They all agreed to be tape-recorded and were given the option of seeing an outline of the questions before the interviews. None chose to see the questions beforehand and all chose to simply 'wing it.' A few teachers demonstrated feelings of anxiety prior to the interviews when they commented on their concerns about not having enough to say about art.

Finding suitable sites to carry out the interviews was critical. As a researcher, I had to consider the importance of securing an interview setting that would be physically and psychologically informal, comfortable and conducive to establishing 'rapport and trust' (Cole 1991, p. 198). Woods (1986) adds that giving the participants choice of time and place 'give[s] them a sense of control and confidence' (p. 70). When given their choice of location, three teachers chose their own homes and one a teachers' room at school. What is interesting to note is that, in the home locations, the first interview often took place in the kitchen; the second interview in the living room/den.

I arrived at all the interview sessions with cookie treats in hand. The ritual coffee and cookie chat before the 'research interview' provided us with time to get to know each other through the sharing of anecdotes not necessarily related to education. This essential 'ritual' helped to alleviate some tension and to establish rapport between 'strangers.'

Woods (1986) acknowledges the interviewer's responsibility to 'be natural' and not 'private and inaccessible' (pp. 66–67). He prefers to consider the interview as 'conversations or discussions, which indicate more of an open, democratic, two-way, informal, free-flowing process, and wherein people can be "themselves" and not feel bound by roles' (p. 67).

Glesne and Peshkin (1992) refer to a type of research relationship that is 'bilateral' where 'power' is shared and non-hierarchical (p. 83). As researcher, I assumed a somewhat dominant position by initiating and framing the study. The participants, on the other hand, exercised control in their choice to participate or not, and where and when the interviews would take place. They could withdraw from the study at any point, refuse to answer any questions, and were given control over the pause button during their interviews.

This study supported the type of collaborative research that Cole and Knowles (1993) refer to as 'partnership research' (p. 477), which challenges the traditional view that sees the 'researcher' as the sole controller of every aspect of the research process. Partnership research sees both participant and researcher as valuable contributors of 'expertise' (p. 478). Cole (1991) points out that this form of collaborative research which supports a 'researcher/ participant relationship' (p. 191) is well suited for life history research because it is more conducive to establishing a sense of trust, which in turn can significantly affect the 'quality and quantity of information gathered' (p. 194).

Collaborative research methods require the researcher to pay attention to a host of issues that define the research relationship between the researcher and the teacher/co-researcher, beginning with the planning stage right up to the point of reporting the research findings (Cole and Knowles 1993). At the start, teachers were consulted about meeting times and how they wanted to space their interviews. Throughout the course of this study, teachers were given the opportunity to read the transcripts that I had prepared and add, change or delete if they chose to do so. It was when teachers were asked to read their transcriptions after the interviews that their involvement as 'collaborators' began to dwindle. None of the transcripts was returned to me for changes, additions or deletions. One teacher, somewhat embarrassed, confessed that she had not even read the interview transcript. From this comment, I assumed that she was perhaps not that interested in the study nor concerned enough to ensure that she had not been misinterpreted. She gave me permission to go ahead with my analysis and I assured her that she would have another chance to make modifications.

In attempting to formulate a set of questions that would elicit stories of art experiences, I struggled with the types of questions I would ask and their sequencing. I considered context to be of great importance but questioned how deep I should delve, how far and wide into a life I should explore; what did I need to know? I chose art as my connecting thread and framework within which to work. I chose to follow a somewhat chronological structured and semi-structured line of questioning that looked at art experiences from early childhood to adult life. This multidimensional perspective encompassed the many selves and experiences contained in someone's lifetime within established boundaries. Art stories were not limited to art-making experiences, but rather included experiences related to play, aesthetics and other art forms as they defined the self and observations of others in an art context. I did not want to focus on individuals' professional journeys of becoming teachers but on the role of art as lived experience and its consequent influence on the teacher's art instruction. The questions served only as 'general guidelines.' I also read the teachers' written reflective stories to pull out themes or questions that I felt needed further clarification. In this way, new questions were developed/customized to delve further into the personal themes that surfaced. At times, questions deviated from the chronological time sequence. As Yow (1994) points out: 'Chronology is indeed one of those areas where narrators are apt to depart from the expected answer because people often remember things according to significant life events rather than dates' (p. 75).

One question that ran through my mind at the onset of the interviews was whether these teachers would have any recall of art stories as far back as early childhood. None of them had pursued this line of study/interest in their lifetime and some had reminded me that they did not think they had that much to say about art. My concerns were realized once the interviews began; most teachers had had difficulty recalling experiences of making art as a young child. Subsequently, I expanded my line of questioning to include play, aesthetics and the other arts as areas to reflect upon for art stories. Questions remained open-ended and loosely structured to allow the participants to journey through key events in their lives. Sessions usually began with general questions and gradually became more personal, more intrusive. Personal questions had to be introduced carefully at the right moment, never at the start of a session. At times, I felt awkward asking participants to tell me about their relationships with their parents and found myself justifying this line of questioning by explaining that it might have some relevance to the type of teacher they had become. One teacher refused to discuss her relationship with her mother stating that 'you could write a whole thesis on my mother'. I respected her wishes and moved on.

Another aspect that was included in this study and had not been planned for was the inclusion of photographs of artworks that hung in the teachers' homes. The idea to include photographic documentation came about after the first interview I had with my first teacher participant, Molly. As I was preparing to leave for home, Molly began to reveal stories related to the artwork that hung on her hallway walls. The way she spoke of the artwork revealed something of her aesthetic. With her permission, I photographed the work upon my return for the second interview and for all the teacher interviews that followed I brought my camera along. In keeping with the 'emergent design' (Lincoln and Guba, 1985, p. 41) of this study, the use of visual text suddenly became part of my data collection. Most interesting were Priscilla's descriptions of the artwork that she had saved in boxes or that she had hung on her walls, which revealed a preference for art 'that tells a story.' What follows is a short excerpt from Priscilla's life history and her description of various art pieces from her collection.

Priscilla's story

Houses and home surface as significant themes throughout Priscilla's life story. She used the metaphor of house to signify her classroom/school/space that she occupied as teacher. This 'home' was the site where Priscilla chose to be interviewed, unlike the other teacher participants who chose their actual 'homes' away from school. We met in the small teachers' conference room for two consecutive days after school at the height of winter.

Priscilla's life story is about displacement, victimization and isolation, and her struggle to rise above the negative effects of these experiences. Priscilla, the youngest of three children, was born in the small rural village of Mille Roches in 1947 and lived there with her parents until 1955 when they were forced to vacate because of the expansion of the St Lawrence Seaway. Flooding was initiated and villages virtually disappeared under water. Only some houses were moved to create new villages and because Priscilla's house was too large, it was not one of them.

Priscilla remarked on being saddened by the move and having felt somewhat displaced. Accompanying these feelings, she was anxious about changing schools. She did not have many friends and was continuously teased for being overweight.

Priscilla had very few memories of making art as a young child. She recalled how she used to make things as part of her creative play. She told me about a 'wonderful place,' a huge field between school and home, where she would often play and construct 'houses' with her friends:

> Well, the first thing that comes to mind is taking leaves in the fall and making them into rows of walls for houses – and leaving openings for doors and then we designed furniture with leaves and then we got even more adventurous and went and got twigs and – oh, bushes and tall weeds that are stiff and stuff. We made furniture and accessories for the rooms – then we made paths from one house to the other so we could visit each other.

In these early years, art-making was part of play and served to transform and construct props that occupied her play space.

Shortly after the move from Mille Roches, around the time when Priscilla was in grade four, she used to spend time with her family at the cottage where she would write poetry and construct little poetry books complete with illustrations:

> I used to write a lot of poetry and I thought I was a real poet and I would write short little poems and then draw pictures to go with them and make little poetry books and that kind of stuff.

Years later, for both grades six and seven, Priscilla had an inspiring teacher whom she called 'the light at the end of the tunnel.' He aroused in her a lasting interest in literature and sustained her appetite for writing. She claimed that he 'turned her right around.' Reflecting on this time, she shared her memories:

> I do remember the enthusiasm – that I would go home and I would write poetry for hours or I would read books – because I had been such a lonesome lonely kid. I was now into reading, swallowing, inhaling books from the library.

This teacher strongly influenced Priscilla's choice to pursue an English major in university and to eventually become a teacher.

This short excerpt from Priscilla's life history highlights key experiences that show how art, writing and dramatic play were interconnected and that in later years she developed an interest in literature. When asked to describe works of art from her personal collection and to elaborate on her own aesthetic, Priscilla's response reiterated her passion for literature and writing.

It did not surprise me when Priscilla revealed a preference for 'art that tells a story.'

Art that tells a story

The most memorable art object that Priscilla recalled growing up with was a mother-of-pearl image of a Japanese-style bridge situated over a pond, with the moon shining overhead. Her mother always had it hanging on the wall, regardless of where she lived.

Priscilla described it as being huge, measuring four feet by two and a half feet and surrounded by 'a beautiful carved wooden frame with gold leaf on it.' She recalled how she would stare at it for hours because of its beauty and its story potential:

> I love things that tell stories – any kind of art that you can look at and there's a story there – that you can look at all the different pieces and make up stories to go – with the names of the people and what they've been doing yesterday, what they're going to do tomorrow, and what's happening. That was one of the things I could look at for ages because not only did it reflect and the light bounced off it and everything, but I thought it was just beautiful. I thought it was made by fairies, you know, it was gorgeous and it just sort of was my treasure.

Priscilla now owns this work of art and has it 'in protective storage' in her basement.

Priscilla told me about an oil painting that she and her husband acquired after many visits to galleries in search of a work of art to decorate their home. The painting tells a story of a man riding a horse through a blizzard. Priscilla's account of the story brought life to the painting and once again showed the importance that Priscilla placed on story:

> It doesn't look like much but this guy on a horse in the middle of a blizzard – that's all it looks like. But there's a story to it and the story is that this fellow was in a concentration camp and he escaped in the middle of a raging blizzard. No one saw him go. He faded into the blizzard and just about when he had given up and thought 'I might as well die because I can't walk another inch,' this horse is there. This horse is just standing in a field, and he pulled himself up, and he got onto the horse and I guess he passed out and the next thing he knew this horse had taken him to a farmhouse where the people hid him and saved his life and so on. And so this picture is of this passed-out kind of figure on a horse in the middle of this raging blizzard but it's the story behind –

Another art piece from her home, a ceramic image glued onto barn board, also had a story to tell. According to Priscilla, this piece depicted 'an old house with a tree and a tire hanging from the tree and a little 'for sale' sign out front. She imagined this might be a story of a young family with children who had outgrown their home.

The interconnectedness of art and story from childhood followed Priscilla into adulthood. She explained to me that it is not enough that a work of art be just a pretty picture, 'I want something to tell me stories.'

Priscilla as teacher of art

Priscilla approaches art education with the belief that art should be fun and a diversion from pencil and paper bookwork. Her training in art education was minimal and teaching art is a constant struggle. Because her skills and knowledge in visual arts are limited, she relies on project 'ideas' to make up her curriculum content. The emphasis is primarily on 'product,' fed by ideas she has gathered from magazines, occasional workshops and teachers' bulletin boards. Over the years, she has developed a repertoire of project ideas that are quick, easy, fun but lacking in thematic connection or academic rigor.

At the time of the interviews, Priscilla was teaching English to grade seven and eight students who were on rotational schedules. Although she was not required to teach art as such, she did incorporate art-making into drama by way of set design and in the making of props. She mentioned that drama provides a *raison d'être* for doing art. Priscilla added that she felt art projects done for drama had a more '*laissez-faire* kind of freedom' to them compared to art projects assigned in a regular art lesson where art is viewed as a discipline. The play or special event becomes the source for ideas and the artwork produced is less individualized and more collaborative by nature.

Priscilla views her classroom as her 'house' where her guests (her students) must obey certain rules. She is very demanding and sometimes strict; however, there is room for fun as long as teacher and students are having fun 'together.' Conducting art sessions in this 'house' ushers in the potential for chaos or, according to Priscilla, 'loss of control' where noise levels and messes get out of hand. Although Priscilla firmly believes that art should be fun, she continuously struggles with making art in her classroom a positive experience for all.

FINAL REFLECTIONS

At the end of my study, I asked the teacher participants to voluntarily reflect in writing on the experience of having participated in life history research. None chose to do so. Nonetheless, during the interviews when I asked them to comment on the process of reflecting on their pasts and whether they had discovered anything new about themselves, the following comments implied that the experience had been both insightful and meaningful:

> I think it's been really good. You don't ever sit down and reflect, you really don't have the time in your life to do that. You might sit down immediately after a fact and analyze why something went wrong or why something went right, but very rarely do you look back ten years or fifteen years or twenty-five years and think about what experiences you had. I think I discovered why I approach my kids, my students the way I do.
>
> (Molly, 1996)

> Actually, it was really fun to do all this. I hadn't spent much time even wondering about how art affected me – I guess it kind of explains why I'm so off the wall a little bit with art now and people think I'm artistic.
>
> (Josephine, 1997)

> Well, it's made me think about art in terms of the fact that up until grade three I thought it was wonderful, exciting, and terrific. I ran home with my stuff. And now I'm doing to kids exactly what was done to me as of what I feel was grade four. And I'm not allowing kids that opportunity to fly and experience and have fun with and enjoy stuff – in an artistic way.
>
> (Priscilla, 1996)

When asked to comment on what she had learned through the process of reflective practice, Krystle stated that the experience made her aware of how different we all are with our own individual preferences and strengths.

I was most grateful to and appreciative of the teachers who allowed me to study their personal lives in such depth so that I might learn about the meaning of art in their lives and the impact that their positive and negative experiences had upon their current beliefs and attitudes about art and art education. As I guided these teachers through a self-reflective process, a study of self, they learned about themselves as 'makers of art' and as 'teachers of art.' They discovered how and why they teach art by reflecting on past experiences, and on their beliefs about art.

Because of this study, issues related to methodology come to mind. How could a study of this sort be set up as self-study? How might the teachers who were involved in this study undertake the kind of work that Hamilton (1998) and Mitchell and Weber (1999) suggest, as well as others, to study one's own teaching practice? What new insight might a study of the 'teacher' self give us related to the teaching of art? How different might a self-study look from a study done by an outside researcher such as myself? I am reminded of Priscilla's comment that touching art was like 'pulling teeth.'

How might a self-study reveal the source of her pain when viewed in the context of her 'teaching self'? Might the teaching of art become more meaningful and less painful for Priscilla if she were to teach art in the context of 'art that tells a story'?

This study began with a concern about the marginalization of art in the elementary school and a felt need to examine how art is taught by generalists and, most importantly, their reasons for teaching art. By inviting teachers to participate in this life history study, I was able to follow the threads of experience that created their tapestry of beliefs about art and the teaching of art. Continued research into the beliefs of generalists, and the influence of these beliefs on the teaching of art, can inform teacher educators of ways they can provide worthwhile learning experiences for teachers. As a result, maybe teachers will eventually cease to carry on the tradition of teaching art only on Friday afternoons and as a reward for good behavior.

NOTE

1   I titled my dissertation 'Artful and artless experiences: teachers tell their stories' (Szabad-Smyth 2002).

REFERENCES

Cole, A.L., 1991, Interviewing for life history: a process of ongoing negotiation. *RUCCUS Occasional Papers*, **1**, 185–208.

Cole, A.L. and Knowles, J.G., 1993, Teacher development partnership research: a focus on methods and issues. *American Educational Research Journal*, **30**(3), 473–95.

Denzin, N.K., 1989, *Interpretive Biography (Qualitative Research Methods, Vol. 17)* (Newbury Park, CA: Sage Publications).

Glesne, C. and Peshkin, A., 1992, *Becoming Qualitative Researchers* (White Plains, NY: Longman).

Hamilton, M.L. (Ed.), 1998, *Reconceptualizing Teaching Practice: Self-study in Teacher Education* (London: Falmer Press).

Lincoln, Y.S. and Guba, E.G., 1985, *Naturalistic Inquiry* (Beverly Hills, CA: Sage Publications).

Mitchell, C. and Weber, S., 1999, *Reinventing Ourselves as Teachers: Beyond Nostalgia* (London and New York: Falmer Press).

Szabad-Smyth, L., 2002, Artful and artless experiences: teachers tell their stories. Unpublished doctoral dissertation, McGill University, Montreal.

Van Manen, M., 1992, *Researching Lived Experience: Human Science for an Action Sensitive Pedagogy* (London, Ontario: The Althouse Press, University of Western Ontario).

Woods, P., 1986, *Ethnography in Educational Research* (New York: Routledge & Kegan Paul Inc.).

Yow, V.R., 1994, *Recording Oral History* (Thousand Oaks: Sage Publications).

Chapter 8

Apples of change

Arts-based methodology as a poetic and visual sixth sense

C.T. Patrick Diamond and
Christine van Halen-Faber

FORMS OF ARTS-BASED TEACHER-SELF CHANGE

Arts-based educational research is inspired by and borrows its methods from the humanities, literature, and the visual and dramatic arts. Like Byatt (1995) we argue that 'what literature can and should do is change the people who teach' (cited in Kemp 1999, p. 230). What arts-based educational research can and should do is change the people who teach and who teach teachers. We (Patrick and Christine) use the term 'teacher development' to refer to how individual teachers *choose* change for themselves over the course of their careers. Development is thus reserved for teacher change that is self-directed rather than externally imitated or imposed. What develops is neither a hoard of treasured 'tips' nor a collection of guarded self-deceptions, but rather a working theory of an artistic teacher-self that is constantly being 'put to the test' and changing as richer explanations of on-going practice are being reconstrued. But even a teacher's own self-movement is seldom so straight-forward. Rather it includes pauses, time-outs, and cyclic returns. Self-change cannot be mandated or 'measured' by using simple, linear, and so-called scientific tools.

Arts-based change means that teachers choose to explore personally relevant issues by intuitively following their own 'poetic [and visual] sixth sense' (Heaney 1995, p. xiii). They then plot 'a reliable critical course,' drawing on and representing their personal experience, enjoying the wisdom and companionship of their inquiry topic, which particularly includes their teacher-self. Arts-based approaches allow them then to reflect on and thus renew experience. Change is an active process whereby teachers learn to make more public (if even more problematic) the intuitions and meanings that they make out of a lifetime of teaching, especially those involving their own developing teacher-selves.

STORIED ACCOUNTS OF SOME OF OUR OWN
SELF- AND OTHER-STUDIES

Changes in artful meaning-making are often promoted by changes in the forms that the inquiry takes. And so we (Patrick and Christine) begin by looking backwards to some of Patrick's former shape-changing metaphors of arts-based educational research and teacher development that he has used alone and in collaboration with others. These ways of seeking to grapple with the developmental and dynamic qualities of arts-based method and myth-based methodology in teacher education include the uses of the Frankenstein creature, Proteus, and the spiral of the Whirlpool galaxy (Diamond and Mullen 1999; Buttignol and Diamond 2000; van Halen-Faber and Diamond 2002).

These instances of change and development in self- and other-study were provoked by and metaphorically represented as shaping and making, replacing and remodeling, and even as grafting and growing. We need to remember that words and language are the original metaphors that allow us to name and place what we experience in the world for reconsideration. As the biblical Book of Proverbs has it, 'a word aptly spoken is like apples of gold in settings of silver.' Words and metaphors help us form and develop the inner and outer reaches of experience. These literary devices are no longer to be dismissed as in social science in general but are now to be explored and delighted in as in arts-based work.

We can rescue the way we think and feel about arts-based change and methodology ('the heart of the matter') by using *primary* metaphors like 'raw material' and apple growing. They remind us of the organic nature and basic physicality (Lakoff and Johnson 1980) of educational research and teacher development. We are reweaving fabric fragments into new forms. Thus, in arts-based educational research and teacher development, we are constantly refabricating and sewing together isolated shreds of experience into new bodies of experienced knowledge of events, including those relating to the self. We can then galvanize this mass/mess of fragments first into life and then into concerted action by using arts-based modes like palimpsest and overlay (Diamond and Mullen 1999). We can further dramatize this process of change and composition by drawing on, for example, the *secondary* or literary metaphor of the Baron and his creature that was appropriated from Mary Shelley's (1818/1998) *Frankenstein or The Modern Prometheus* (Diamond and Mullen 1999).

We are not introducing literary or arts-based turns for their own sake or to pretend to any 'arty' turn. Rather, we are following our own development through invoking a poetic or visual sixth sense, trusting that it will lead us to renewed understandings and further outer reaches. As teacher educator-researchers, we (Diamond and Mullen; Buttignol and Diamond; van Halen-Faber and Diamond) are using a metaphorical and figurative methodology.

We do this also to illustrate how the humanities, literature, and art help further our inquiries, particularly into the complex matter of self- and other-change. We use evocative images to access, formulate, and embody our position on artful method. In arts-based educational research and teacher development, metaphor, as a central and inciting device, helps to flesh our thinking and commitments, helping to reanimate their dynamic qualities. But such use of metaphor for aiding thinking and feeling is normal and every-day, not just 'artistic.' As Dewey (1934/1980) wrote, aesthetic experience integrates all the different elements of experience, making a new whole (however temporary) out of their common elements while also retaining their differences. Grumet (1988) agrees that: 'The aesthetic is distinguished from the flow of daily experience, the phone conversations, the walk to the corner store, only by the intensity, completeness, and unity of its elements and by a *form that calls forth a level of perception* that is, in itself, satisfying' (p. 88; our emphasis). As self-studying researcher-artists interested in arts-based teacher development, we rely on metaphor as the main source of our methodology.

Arts-based educational research and teacher development then allow us to draw on multiplicity, transience, temporality, and change all as rich resources. Unlike traditional educational research that is non-metaphorical, disembodied, literal, and so limited, arts-based educational research and development enable us to get our inquiries off the ground and to take them to previously unimagined places. Sometimes it may seem that our central conceits (research and development as artworks in progress) are too far-fetched and run the risk of seeming to be distractingly paradoxical and even of entailing a pseudo-logic (see Drabble 2000, p. 665). But what better way can there be of reanimating traditional and even stagnating forms of empirical research and teacher education?

Buttignol and Diamond (2000) thus used the Proteus myth with its metaphor of morphing and shape-shifting to illustrate the forms of self-deception that may be forced upon beginning teachers. Forced to comply to survive. During their pre-service preparation, they initially sought just to appear as and so pass for the 'good' teacher who then gets the job. But the real job for teachers involves a lifelong commitment to further change, refashioning themselves many times over a career devoted to learning to teach. In artful development, enforced conformity is reclaimed by self-chosen, experienced and embodied change. As teachers explore change as feeling and form, they intuitively, imaginatively, and confidently come to trust themselves as their own reliable agents of change.

Most recently, in van Halen-Faber and Diamond (2001, 2002) and van Halen-Faber (in progress), we are using the spiral (of the Whirlpool galaxy) and apple-making to explore our collaborative work together, as well as that with six pre-service/beginning teachers. The latter apple image provides an evocative metaphor of artful method, having long served as the symbol of the very best ('the apple of one's eye'), good health ('an apple a day'), and immortality (the Edenic tree of knowledge). Teachers' pets are known as 'apple polishers.' And gifts for a 'Special Teacher' frequently bear the hallmark of the apple image.

Extending the relevance of the apple as a metaphor into the realm of educational research requires an imaginative leap on the part of the researcher, the researched, and the viewer/reader. It requires being comfortable with ambiguity rather than relying on pre-cast paradigms and predictable methods. '[A]rt-centered experiences . . . involve feelings and thoughts of a transcendental nature. What is transcended in such situations are the boundaries of custom. The experiencer undergoes an altered sensibility, achieves a novel way of looking at things' (Jackson 1998, p. 96). As shown below, we embrace the fluid form of metaphor as a medium that allows for shaping and reshaping. Such changes in metaphor and meaning-making serve to illuminate the layering that lies at the core of change. These shifts authorize and illustrate an organic methodology for our pursuing such development.

Plants like the apple tree are universal symbols of growth and vitality, but the impermanence of their fruit (and flowers) also warns of the fragility and vulnerability that attend development. Each of us as an educator-researcher provides the initial stock for the further budding growth of self and others. We seek to support our/their storytelling and artistic inquiries even as a graft promotes new life while retaining the best of previous forms. The term *graft* derives from the Greek *graphion*, for writing instrument. Art-inspired poetic writing and visual strategies are particularly well suited to describe and promote shifting forms. Inquirers then become morphographers (from the Greek *morphe*, for form) or educational artists who portray changing forms by using text and image when reconsidering the past and projecting out of the present to imagine the future.

By trying out graphic, evocative, and poetic forms such as elaborated metaphorical accounts and the multi-text forms of palimpsest, we can relate differently to ourselves, others and to our shared experience of these experiences. We can combine intuition and imagination, and then seek a metaphor that links without submerging two seemingly unconnected concepts, and so create a new field of play. Through art-centered inquiry, 'we find ourselves attending to feelings, ambiguities, temporal sequences, blurred experiences [as] we struggle to find a textual [or visual] place for ourselves and our doubts and uncertainties' (Richardson 1994, p. 521).

CHANGING APPLES AS APPLES OF CHANGE

We (Christine and Patrick) here present an extended example of shape-changing using the symbol of the apple. This exemplar is drawn from Christine's present doctoral inquiry into the knowledge-generating experience of 'beginnings and change' in teacher development as seen through her eyes as a teacher educator and, for now, through those of one of her six pre-service students, Kerri. In this inquiry into self/other, and teacher development, the focus is especially on a method embodied in a medium of arts-based methodology. The method that we highlight here involves the use first of a fragmented apple shape as a form of self-representation, and then realized as and changing into a stylized apple batik panel.

Setting I: *My college classroom*

My (Christine's) inquiry into the ethics and aesthetics in the experience of self/other as a beginning arts-based inquirer, and as a teacher educator working with six pre-service students, began inconspicuously enough in my own classroom, with what I only later recognized as an intuitive leap. Like much of our teaching, learning begins with the pursuit of personal knowledge, when individuals begin to look for understanding within their own classrooms, institutions, and neighbourhoods (Greene 1995).

Playing with the apple metaphor

'Metaphors are not just the concern of the poet or the literary critic [or the visual artist] . . . They represent one of the ways in which many kinds of discourse are structured and powerfully influence how we conceive things' (Sarup 1993, p. 48).

One rainy afternoon, we (a group of six pre-service students and myself) discussed the 'practicum as a form of action research.' We spoke about the messiness of 'doing field-based research' and touched on the challenges of 'living research' as a finding and seeking without quite knowing what we are looking for when we begin. I shared with my students a favourite metaphor from Lakoff and Johnson (1999) that has guided so much of my thinking about doing artful inquiry: that is, as we trace the contours of our inquiry, we often do so with 'a hidden hand that shapes conscious thought' (p. 12).

Rather than following a carefully pre-planned lesson outline, I then acted on a playful sixth sense: I distributed scissors, glue sticks, large sheets of white paper, and six 8.5 × 11 inch sheets of green paper outlined by me with a very basic shape of an apple with a stem and one leaf. I invited the students to cut the apple along its edge, to segment it into smaller pieces, and then to glue (reassemble) the parts onto the larger sheet of paper, leaving spaces between the fragments. Immediately, a busy kind of silence took over the room. From the sidelines, I watched how each student approached this simple task, each in his or her own unique way. As the 'cutting and pasting' pro-gressed, I asked the students to think about ways in which their apples might represent them as student-teachers in a practice teaching setting. The sharing of insights that resulted from these acts of metaphoric self-representation began then, and now continues with you, the reader. Kerri's apple was one of the six self-portraits that we shaped that afternoon.

Kerri's apple

Without hesitation, Kerri guided her scissors to cut flowing lines to section her apple. Quickly at first, she began to paste the pieces back together – following the instructions, leaving spaces between her fragments. She began at the top, with leaving the stem and the leaf intact, and then tried to maintain the original apple image. She soon discovered this was not quite working. Somehow, her apple had been left with a gaping hole in the center, and the leftover pieces had transformed the round apple into an asymmetrical oval shape. It no longer looked just like an apple. When asked to describe her practice-teaching experience, Kerri hesitated for only a moment, and then began to speak,

> Well, it's quite like this apple really. From the outside, it looks like I've got it altogether. Then, suddenly, at some point during my practicum it's as if the bottom falls out of it! So far, I've been able to pick up the pieces, and fit them back together somehow.
>
> (Kerri, *Journal* 2000)

Figure 8.1 Kerri's apple portrait.

As a representational shape produced by Kerri, her apple offers an evocative self-study artefact. Its contours are scissored pathways traced and travelled by the hand of the teacher-candidate herself. Its fragments and spaces present intuitive and incisive parings. The apple that began as a representational symbol has changed into a metaphor of her thinking about practice teaching. As image and text, it honours a visual and poetic sixth sense so that gaps become places where uncertainties and questions may be voiced and shape-shifting is accepted. Kerri's apple fragments and spaces become the body and margins of the expressive and interpretive personal text of her changing teacher-yet-to-be self.

I had come to know Kerri as an open, even transparent individual. Outspoken. Outgoing. Often, our class discussions would gravitate toward layering our own understanding of our learning about teaching, and our learning about learning. Kerri was very vocal about her learning in courses during her undergraduate studies at a university in her hometown.

There we just had to memorize 'stuff.' Most of our exams were multiple-choice. We never had to write essays or papers. I now think I never really thought back then. I just learned. It's different now. You get us to think, and to ask our own questions. Sometimes it feels as if I'm not really learning, but yet I think I know so much more now. I am beginning to think it is how I want to teach, so my students will learn – their way.

(Kerri, *Journal* 2000)

Changed setting II: *My inquiry into self/other*

Variations on a batik metaphor

'A metaphor is not merely a linguistic expression, it is the process of human understanding by which we achieve meaningful experience that we can make sense of' (Johnson 1987, p. 15).

I had increasingly been interested in examining aspects of my own work as a teacher educator who interacts with small groups of pre-service students in the setting of a Christian college that offers a teacher education program. I was intrigued by the interactive effects of teaching and learning in the development of both the students (as individuals and as a cohort group) and myself, their instructor who is now taking her own first steps into the field of arts-based inquiry. I had been seeking a representational activity that would allow me to look at aspects of absorption and resistance in relation to personal and professional development. Intuitively, I chose to pursue a batik technique, with its own interplay of dye and resist, as my medium and method, as my metaphor for meaningful experiences. But why batik?

As I now reflect on my lived experience of my own teaching, and my own arts-centered inquiry in educational research and teacher development, I become more consciously aware of the deeply personal approach that I often take in my work and my life. I act intuitively, but not impulsively. Somehow, I 'know' it is what I need to do. Often, I first 'do,' and only then reason why I did what I just did. Often, these intuitive moments arrive quite unexpectedly. Out of nowhere and at the most unpredictable times. They are my significant or inciting incidents. Once brought into consciousness, these intuitive experiences are transformed into conscious thought. They become crystallizing moments, followed by an introspective second round of inquiry. I hear my own thoughts in conversation: 'This approach works. I know it does. But why? How can I extend it, apply it, and justify it? I know it's a detail that belongs to a bigger picture. But how does it fit? Are there limitations to the idea? If there are, what might these be?' The responses to the questions then pour out of 'no-where,' out of a deep well of self, a bubbling spring. My poetic and visual sixth sense asserts itself, and plots its own reliable course.

So, why batik? Batik is an ancient Javanese art of wax-writing derived from painting. Along with music and dance, I later read that batik holds strong symbolic meaning as it was also considered to be a way or method to develop spiritual discipline. According to the Indonesian tradition, each time the batik artisan executes an intricate pattern, the design is not only fixed to the cloth, but the meaning of the design is engraved ever more deeply in the soul of the maker. I recognize and honour the longstanding and rich provenance of batik, the contributions of Dutch traders to it, and to my own family background. I now celebrate the vitality and presence batik lends to my inquiry. The essence of the process is to produce a design on textiles through the use of a dye-resist. The resist, usually wax (but other materials such as rice paste are also used), prevents the dye from penetrating the covered areas of the fabric, thus creating a pattern. Additional wax is added to embellish the design or preserve areas in the color of the initial dye bath. Once I had decided to use the batik process to represent my learning about my students as teacher-candidates and their learning, I knew I needed fabric to work with. I also knew that I could not use just one large piece of material. I wanted to capture both 'sameness' (by using the same batiking process) and 'difference' (by using a different fabric for each one of my six students/co-participants). I knew that not all are cut of the same cloth. The combination of fabric and the absorption and resist in the batik process became the medium, the form, the process and the product of our self-study.

As I navigated my way through the heavy morning flow of highway traffic on my way to class, I thought about where and how my six student-teachers/co-participants might fit. By the time I turned onto the exit ramp, I 'knew how I had to do it.' I knew that I wanted all six fabrics to be the same white. So, what six different fabrics might I use? Taking fibre content as my starting point, I mentally divided fabrics into two categories: those made of natural fibres and those made of 'other' or synthetic fibres.

I wanted three natural fabrics. I found linen, cotton, and silk. I also had to search for three 'other' fabrics made of a blended, an unknown, and a polyester-type of fibre. Before I reached the parking lot a mere eight minutes later, I had matched each fabric with a name . . . It seemed almost too easy. Was I too impulsive? Too judgmental? But I knew I had uncovered a way of using arts-based inquiry to aid development. My batik way of thinking became 'the sympathy by which one is transported into the interiors of [six persons] in order to coincide with what there is unique and consequently inexpressible in [them]' (Bergson 1946/1992, p. 161). For me, the intuitive process by which I selected the six fabrics also resonates with the 'personal coefficient' present in tacit knowing, a knowing more than we can tell (Polanyi 1958). It was a heartfelt intuition as when 'one sees clearly only with the heart, [and as when as yet anything] essential is invisible to the eyes' (de Saint-Exupéry 1943/2000, p. 63). Intuitive introspection then became a knowing that was open to change. This imaginative grasp is expressed next in the form of a prose poem.

Confirmation of a batik metaphor

Following a sixth sense gives form to feeling, as 'it is not discursive . . . but it formulates a new conception for our direct imaginative grasp' (Langer 1957, p. 23).

> Yet, then, it was not 'quite good' enough for me.
> I felt I needed to make my seeing with the heart visible to my
>   participants.
> But without 'telling' them.
> Somehow, I needed my seeing to be confirmed by theirs.
> I was looking to hear a sounding board in their perception of my
>   intuition.
> I was seeking to justify
> what I feared to be a form of impulsive interpretation, on my part.
> I still needed to learn to trust myself as an arts-based inquirer.
> I went to my classroom, and sought out my 'Group of Six.'
> Without giving away the specifics,
> I described the appearance of six different fabrics.
> I described what I had done.
> How I had 'labeled' six persons in terms of fibre and fabric.
> I then invited them to label themselves and each other . . .
> After filling in a chart, a matrix of six names and six fabric labels,
> the students asked if we could now share our choices.
> I asked whether all felt comfortable with the idea,
> and, in a spirit of unanimity and trust, an intense discussion followed.
> There were some variations, honouring differences and similarities.
> Feeling was given form.
> Choices were explained and justified.
> There was overwhelming agreement, in this
> Intuitive introspection, in this
> Impromptu vocalization of thought
> Of self and other.
> My own fabric choice for Kerri was silk.
> I chose it first of all for its natural quality, its translucence and
>   transparency.
> I also chose it for its provenance.
> Silk is an ancient fabric.
> Threads-stronger-than-steel,
> Spun by the industrious silkworm,
> Woven by patient hands into intricate designs.
>
> (van Halen-Faber, in progress)

Encouraged, I next embarked on the actual batiking process itself as an echo of the lived experience of my inquiry process: a 'tracing of contours.'

For each of the participants, I decided to use their own original 'fragmented paper apple shape' as the basis of their batik image. Perched on a stool, I now found myself carefully tracing (again in pencil) the outlines of Kerri's apple onto the silk fabric. I repeated this process with each of the six panels of different fabric. Using 'fabric dye for ALL fabrics, even the undye-able,' I filled the apple segments with color, and then protected them by covering the apple shapes entirely with wax. I then dipped all six panels into the same (first) dye bath, for the same length of time. I took them out, rinsed them with cold water, and hung them to dry. With large brush strokes, I then applied more wax to each panel. I traced another, shadowy contour along the outside of each apple. I then applied additional wax strokes in random patterns. My reliable mediating course meant that I chose curved lines for some, straight ones for others. Layering the wax on the fabrics, I then repeated the dyeing process, using a different coloured dye bath this time. But the same for all. Again I rinsed the panels in cold water, and dried them. This time I placed the panels between thick layers of newspapers, and used a hot iron to remove all the layers of wax. The results were astounding: each fabric had absorbed the dyes in different ways. As in the following second prose poem, each panel was now distinct from the other:

> Kerri's silk batik panel shimmers, rich with vibrant colour.
> It has an organic quality, as it pulsates with life.
> Her 'apple with a hole' now appears in the form of a human heart,
> Complete with aorta, arteries, veins, and even capillaries and blood
>   vessels,
> Like spidery varicose veins left behind in places where the wax had
>   cracked,
> and dyes were absorbed deeply into the fabric.
>
> (van Halen-Faber, in progress)

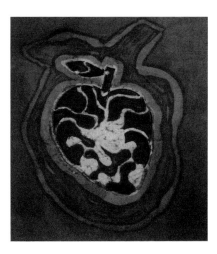

Figure 8.2 Kerri's apple batik.

Kerri's interaction with the metaphor of morphing (apple batiks)

'One feature of a medium is that it mediates and anything that mediates changes what it conveys; the map is not the territory and the text is not the event. We learn to write and to draw, to dance and to sing, [and to batik] in order to *re*-present the world as we know it' (Eisner 1991, p. 27).

Like art, arts-based inquiry 'breaks open a dimension inaccessible to other experience' (Marcuse 1977, p. 72). Likewise, as I found, arts-based teacher development may unexpectedly break open a dimension of self to the self/other of the teacher, making 'perceptible, visible, and audible that which is no longer, or not yet, perceived, said, and heard in everyday life' (Marcuse 1977, p. 72). Like 'the children in the apple tree, Not known, because not looked for/But heard, half-heard in the stillness between two waves of the sea' (T.S. Eliot, *Little Gidding* 1942/2001).

In my arts-based inquiry, I have learned to listen for the stillness between two successive turns in my research, traditional forms (like batik-as-art) and their post-modern metamorphoses (like batik-as-representation). Even when not looked for, the apple batik panels continue to evoke reactions. In their stillness, they are seen as images of possibility that bring about new levels of consciousness. Their shapes morph and merge into a deeper level of understanding. As representations, each of the six apple batik panels becomes an object with a rightful existence in itself. As forms that each call forth a level of perception, the fragmented apple images become portents that lead us to perceive each teacher-self and other in new ways. Each batiked fabric panel tells stories, introduces challenges, reveals perceptions, and invites reflection. Like works of art, the panels refresh and renew us every time they are encountered. In Kerri's words:

> I have to tell you that the finished products hanging on the wall in your classroom are so much more than just apples. They really are us! The other day, you said how I was always sitting on the same side of the table now . . . Well, I love facing the apple batiks. Every time I notice something new about each image. It's like getting to know my classmates better by the day!
>
> (Kerri, *Reflections* August 2000)

Changed setting III: *My apple text* . . .

For me, dissertation writing is like leaving contours of thought so that they can then be traced by others. Developmentally, when such traces touch areas of intuitive introspection, what was invisible now becomes visible. Intuitive introspection is bathed in an analytical light. In Bergson's (1946/1992) terms, such analysis becomes 'the operation which reduces the objects to elements already known' (p. 161). From the interior of self, we are now transported to the exterior of other.

As one of six artful batik images on fabric panels, Kerri's apple image has become a presentational form. As an arts-based researcher, I render her apple as an artistic symbol. I secure from it the meanings that it displays. To the viewer (or the reader), Kerri's apple image may appear opaque, even when its silk fabric lends it a translucent quality. Through writing about my self-thought conversations and interactions with my co-participants, I gradually reshape the meanings of our experiences. I peel back the layers of self/other. I then express my experience in a text that transforms the apple batik panels into 'symbols that *point to* the meanings they are intended to convey' (Eisner 1991, p. 31; italics in original). In this writing process, Kerri's paper apple shape now turned into a heart-like apple batik, transforming into a morphing form that aids my understanding of my own change and development.

My artful approaches to inquiry into self/other as teacher development are anchored in the values and aesthetics of what Greene (2001) calls wide-awakeness. 'Connectedness, responsibility, attentiveness . . . seem more and more significant when considering teaching. [It is] the kind of caring that sustains others' desires to become what they chose to be' (p. 82). I, too, consider these core values in my own work as a teacher educator. An intense self-study or inquiry into my own practice has allowed me to re-view that practice, and to re-search myself.

My apple batik experience confirms once again that, as a teacher-of-teachers and a learner-of-my-own-learning, I need to be involved in research projects that emerge from my practice. I discover the many ways in which my work resonates strongly with Kerri's matters of the heart. I know that my arts-based inquiry practice will be affirmed when my 'imagination, more than any other capacity, breaks through the "inertia of habit"' (Dewey 1934/1980, p. 272), and I am open to possibility and change.

MORPHOGRAPHY: REVISITING SHAPE-SHIFTING ART FORMS AS OUR OWN STORY OF CHANGE

Revisiting our work allows us to see that in arts-based forms of inquiry, there is no 'one and only way.' There is no formula. No step-by-step, foolproof methodological recipe to be followed. Arts-based forms look for and are enhanced by methodologies that allow for intuitive folding and conscious unfolding. By means of enfolding one layer of understanding into another, our play with intuition and thought in turn takes on a poetic and visual sixth sense that trans-forms us.

As we now place our artful exemplars in the context of an arts-based form of storied accounts of self- and other-study before you, the reader, we sense more clearly the elusive elements in the forms that we use to shape our work.

Metaphors change, evolve, and shift shape as forms morph and mesh. Making sense of such chaos in inquiry is not casual or easy. We find that arts-based inquiry leads us to a place of agitation, not of acquiescence. We discover that 'it is not possible to create without serious intellectual discipline; likewise it is not possible to create within a system of fixed, rigid, or imposed rules' (Freire 1996, p. 169). Just 'who we think we are' will always be a shape-shifting artwork in progress that requires both on-going self-invention and negotiated collaboration with others. Then self- and other-study in teacher education becomes morphography and an artful matter of the heart: we see ourselves, our students, and our readers as (he)artworks-in-progress.

As two researcher-artists we accept that it is the 'hidden hand' of metaphor that shapes changes in our understanding of the central role of imagination and aesthetics in teacher development. As our collaborations deepen, we are learning to trust that 'a reliable critical course [will] be plotted by following a poetic [and visual] sixth sense' (Heaney 1995, p. xiii).

REFERENCES

Bergson, H., 1946/1992, *The Creative Mind* (New York: Carol Publishing Group).

Buttignol, M. and Diamond, C.T.P., 2000, Preservice teachers as Proteus. Paper presented at the annual meeting of the American Educational Research Association, New Orleans, April.

De Saint-Exupéry, A., 1943/2000, *The Little Prince* (Trans. R. Howard) (San Diego, CA: Harcourt).

Dewey, J., 1934/1980, *Art as Experience* (New York: Putnam's).

Diamond, C.T.P. and Mullen, C.A. (Eds), 1999, *The Postmodern Educator: Arts-Based Inquiries and Teacher Development* (New York: Peter Lang).

Drabble, M. (Ed.), 2000, *The Oxford Companion to English Literature* (6th edn) (Oxford, UK: Oxford University Press).

Eisner, E.W., 1991, *The Enlightened Eye: Qualitative Inquiry and the Enhancement of Educational Practice* (New York: Macmillan Publishing).

Eliot, T.S., 1942/2001, Little Gidding. In Abrams (General Ed.) *The Norton Anthology of English Literature* (7th edn) (New York: W.W. Norton), pp. 2632–39.

Freire, P., 1996, *Letters to Cristina. Reflections on My Life and Work* (New York: Routledge).

Greene, M., 1995, *Releasing the Imagination. Essays on Education, the Arts, and Social Change* (San Francisco, CA: Jossey-Bass).

Greene, M., 2001, Reflections on teaching. In Richardson (Ed.) *Handbook of Research on Teaching* (4th edn) (Washington, DC: American Educational Research Association), pp. 82–89.

Grumet, M.R., 1988, *Bitter Milk: Women and Teaching* (Amherst: University of Massachusetts Press).

Heaney, S., 1995, *The Redress of Poetry. Oxford Lectures* (London, UK: Faber & Faber).

Jackson, P.W., 1998, *John Dewey and the Lessons of Art* (New Haven, NY: Yale University Press).

Johnson, M., 1987, *The Body in the Mind: The Bodily Basis of Meaning, Imagination, and Reason* (Chicago: University of Chicago Press).

Kemp, P., 1999, (citing A.S. Byatt interview in *Newsweek*, 5 June 1995) *Oxford Dictionary of Literary Quotations* (Oxford: Oxford University Press).

Lakoff, G. and Johnson, M., 1980, *Metaphors We Live By* (Chicago: University of Chicago Press).

Lakoff, G. and Johnson, M., 1999, *Philosophy in the Flesh. The Embodied Mind and its Challenge to Western Thought* (New York: Basic Books).

Langer, S.K., 1957, *Problems of Art. Ten Philosophical Lectures* (New York: Charles Scribner's).

Marcuse, H., 1977, *The Aesthetic Dimension. Toward a Critique of Marxist Aesthetics* (Boston, MA: Beacon Press).

Polanyi, M., 1958, *Personal Knowledge* (Chicago: University of Chicago Press).

Richardson, L., 1994, Writing. A method of inquiry. In Denzin and Lincoln (Eds) *Handbook of Qualitative Research* (Thousand Oaks, CA: Sage), pp. 516–29.

Sarup, M., 1993, *An Introductory Guide to Post-Structuralism and Postmodernism* (2nd edn) (Athens, GA: University of Georgia Press).

Shelley, M., 1818/1998, *Frankenstein or The Modern Prometheus* (Oxford: Oxford University Press).

Van Halen-Faber, C., in progress, Seeing through apples: an exploration into the ethics and aesthetics of a teacher-educator-researcher's arts-based beginnings. Unpublished doctoral thesis, University of Toronto, Toronto.

Van Halen-Faber, C. and Diamond, C.T.P., 2001, A gallery exhibit of inquiry artifacts: an inclusive nebula of spiraling pebbles. Presentation at the Curriculum and Pedagogy/ABER Conference, Victoria, BC.

Van Halen-Faber, C. and Diamond, C.T.P., 2002, Doing an arts-based dissertation inquiry: an inclusive nebula of spiraling pebbles. In Poetter, Haerr, Hays, Higgins and Wilson Baptist (Eds) *In(Ex)clusion: (Re)Visioning the Democratic Idea: Selected Papers from the Second Annual Curriculum and Pedagogy Conference, University of Victoria, Canada* (Troy, NY: Educator's International Press), pp. 47–63.

Chapter 9

Inquiry through poetry

The genesis of self-study

Lynn Butler-Kisber

In this chapter, I examine the theoretical waves that have moved my work in qualitative inquiry into the exciting contemporary 'seventh moment' (Lincoln and Denzin 2000) in which traditional studies and representational texts are being replaced by and/or augmented with alternative, more expressive, and (frequently touted) more authentic ways to report research findings (Richardson 2000). The chapter illustrates how my experimentation with found poetry, my ensuing dialogue with students, my exposure to poetry workshops, and my resulting exploration of autobiographical poetry have heightened my awareness of how much our research reflects our interests and experiences, as well as contributed to my work with graduate students, both in my qualitative research courses and in my supervision. Furthermore, it suggests an avenue of self-study using poetry as the vehicle.

METHODOLOGICAL EVOLUTION

The work that I describe in this chapter has been informed and influenced by a number of qualitative approaches and researchers, as well as by the students with whom I work. My early ethnographic research heightened my awareness of the power in narrative and the advantages of examining the particular in context. In my study of peer collaboration in a primary classroom (Butler-Kisber 1988), which resulted in a long-time friendship and on-going research with an exemplary teacher, I became poignantly aware of the importance of relationship in the research process, and of accessibility in the research product (Berger 2001; Bolster 1983). Feminist voices concerned with issues of power, reflexivity, and the marginalization of voices in research (Personal Narratives Group 1989) challenged me to seek alternative ways of representing my work to avoid the hegemony that is inherent in more traditional texts, to situate myself in the process, and portray what otherwise might have been silenced stories (Butler-Kisber 2002a). Arts-based research and post-modern thought opened up these possibilities, and illustrated how form and function mediate each other. I discovered how alternative representational forms provide new ways of seeing, understanding, and connecting (Eisner 1991; Diamond and Mullen 1999). In addition, permission to use these forms allowed me to choose from a range of expressive modalities those that best suited my communicative propensities (Gardner 1999). As a result, I am able to argue for the worth of 'particularizing', that is, examining the particular to take away from it what may be useful in another context (Donmoyer 1993), rather than attempting to generalize research findings, or apologizing for not being able to do so. When the essence of the particular is expressed in an artful form, it evokes an embodied response and a different kind of interpretation and understanding.

Most recently, I have become interested in participatory, artful inquiry that requires retrospective or memory work (Onyx and Small 2001) in order to collaborate and tease out important insights (Butler-Kisber *et al.* 2003). This type of research illustrates the complexity of the process, and highlights the need to examine the self in relation to others. It 'fosters relationship formation and exchange, and develops rapport' among participants (Berger 2001, p. 507). All of these research orientations have contributed to the evolution of my work and how I think about it. I have been influenced significantly by teaching qualitative research courses and by working with graduate students. In order to encourage risk-taking, the use of alternative methodologies, and to acknowledge the need to situate oneself in the research process, I have felt compelled to explore and mirror these dimensions in my own work so that I can share them with students. I have found that student involvement in this type of work encourages experimentation and helps students to delve into unfamiliar territory such as poetry and other arts-based approaches. This fosters a sense of empathy and collaboration among peers in the course, and produces a very trusting and safe environment (Butler-Kisber *et al.* 2003).

FOUND POETRY

When I became interested in arts-based qualitative research in the early 1990s, I was attracted first to the use of found poetry, which takes words distilled from field texts and shapes them into poetic form (Richardson 1992), as a way to represent a particular narrative or interpretation. In retrospect, I believe this alternative form provided me with a certain measure of comfort because it remains very close to the data/transcripts, and, as a result, limits the scope and choice of words. It is a close cousin to narrative form, and because it is textual in the traditional sense, it does not require the same kind of shift in communicative skills that visual art forms demand. It was in my exploration of found poetry that I ultimately moved to autobiographical forms of poetic representation. This move sparked my interest in the use of poetry as an approach to self-study.

Found poetry made its debut in the qualitative research scene when Laurel Richardson transformed a sociological interview into poetry that represented the life story of her participant (Richardson 1992). As researchers have explored the art form of found poetry, it has become apparent that it gets at the essence of a narrative, yet permits multiple interpretations. It is more evocative than the typical, linear kinds of research writing because of the embodied and melodic nature of the text. At the same time, found poetry retains the signature of the creator, countering the criticism of more traditional research in which authors write in a 'scientific, all-knowing voice' (Berger 2001, p. 513).

I have explained in some detail elsewhere (Butler-Kisber 2002a) how I first used found poetry to describe a story that emerged as the subtext of a study I was conducting on the collaboration between two graduate students in a course I was teaching (Butler-Kisber, in press). It was a story of how Ann, a graduate student, discovered the ability to use her own ideas and voice in her work as a result of her collaboration on a qualitative inquiry assignment with Debbie, a peer in the course. I pieced the story together from transcripts that spanned many months. I believe that this story would have been lost if not for the close relationship that developed among the three of us and allowed the story to emerge during our discussions, and the videotaped data to which I could return to get at the nuances of Ann's speech and interactions. I needed Ann's words and voice to make the poem evocative. In this first experience with found poetry, I attributed my interest in getting Ann's story told in this form to the fact that it reminded me of some of my own earlier experiences as a woman student, and my expectation that it would resonate (Conle 1996) with those of other women.

The process of creating found poetry is not a linear one. First, it requires distilling the narrative from the transcript; Mishler (2000) and Reissman (1993, 2002) offer some approaches for doing this. Once the story is established, it requires playing with the number of words, the word sequence, line breaks, pauses, breath-points, and emphasis to get at the essence of what is being recounted, and to create a rhythm and sound that reflect the voice of the speaker. Creating found poetry is a process that moves from the linear thinking that is evident in transcripts to a more embodied form of text that represents feelings and essences expressed in the poetic form. Some found poems almost seem to write themselves, while others remain unfinished over long periods, and require many reiterations before they near completion, if they ever do. There may be some good reasons for this, as I will show in the example that follows.

THE 'SUMATHY' STORY

As I immersed myself in found poetry through poetry reading and workshops, in my classes with students, and in explorations with various forms of data, it became very clear that poignant memories and moments are best suited to this form of representation. I found myself becoming increasingly alert to voices and aspects in my work that I had not previously considered. I wove in theoretical and practical work on alternative representational forms in my research methods courses, and encouraged graduate students to explore these avenues themselves (Butler-Kisber and Borgerson 1998; Davis and Butler-Kisber 1999). The response was very encouraging.

An interesting juncture in these explorations occurred when Mary, a graduate student, gave me a journal entry she had written about the emotions of loss she had experienced after adopting her daughter. Mary had adopted Sumathy from an orphanage in India when she was four years old. Mary realized that she had been mourning the loss of Sumathy's early years, years she had treasured with her two older sons during which time very intimate connections had been created.

Touched that Mary wanted to share these experiences with me, and moved by the poignancy of the story, I asked her permission to work on turning her text into some found poetry. She was pleased, and excited by the prospect. Interestingly, I discovered while doing this that transforming the more linear, written prose of her text into poetic form was much more difficult than using the found words from oral discourse with which I had previously worked. In spite of the fact that I knew Mary quite well, and could imagine how she might tell her story in a conversational context, the nuances of her speech were not present in the prose.

I began the process by retranscribing Mary's prose into a reduced narrative using Labov's (1972) structural approach. This includes an abstract of the substance of the narrative, the orientation of time, place, situation, and participants, the complicating action in terms of the sequence of events, the evaluation showing the significance and meaning of the action, the resolution showing what finally happened, and the coda that returns the narrative to the present. This exercise reduced the prose from six pages to two. Space does not permit me to reproduce all of the retranscription but I have inserted the 'abstract', 'orientation', and 'complicating action', and part of the 'evaluation' to illustrate how this process works and to show how the narrative is then reduced further to get at the essences expressed in the found poetry.

Abstract

It seems over the last two years since adopting Sumathy
I've spent a lot of time trying to make up for time lost with her
during her first four years when she was in India

Orientation

First, there was the course of September 96 where I studied S's
    reaction to being adopted
That was time when my whole life was still absorbed with her
Then I felt I was looking at that whole compensating stage in
    retrospect
That was over after 1½ years
and I wanted to move on
Yes, my monograph topic would be about adoption
but not specifically about S
I thought she had her place in the family
and that the transition to our family had been completed

Complicating action

But then I started to see that although a lot of her/our adjustment had
    been made
I was still coming to terms with a lot of important issues
This realization occurred around the time I was talking to you about
    my proposal
I had mentioned that when S first came
and it was important for me to pick her up and hold her like a baby
    after a bath
and also to have a bath with her
in the same way a mother would with an infant
I didn't know how important all this was to me
I hadn't made any sense of it at all
I got to think that maybe it represented some compensation for the
    time S & I didn't have earlier
I thought about it a lot
because I felt that anything that racked that amount of emotion in me
and still does even as I write
had to mean a lot
and was important to get to the bottom of

Evaluation

. . . whenever as a 4/5 year old I held her bare feet and kissed them
I was always in my mind picturing her as a baby
. . . one night when I was tucking her in
and lying down for a few minutes, afterwards
she kind of nuzzled her head against my chest and went to sleep

> This position was very reminiscent of when I used to nurse the boys
> and I loved that moment
> Just to make it clear – nothing sexual – but very sweet
> And when I noticed that there were tears running down my cheek
> I knew this was what I had been trying to make up for all this time . . .

As I moved into the process of creating the poetry, I found myself struggling to produce a rhythm and flow. In retrospect, I realize that I had attempted to artificially impose a rhythm on the text; to make up for what, at the time, I knew intuitively was missing. In some verses I was much more successful than in others.

Mary was less critical of what became the first iteration of the work. We talked about this, and agreed that it was not because of the power differential between us. It was more that Mary was satisfied she had been able to articulate a story that had remained for some time beneath the surface of her consciousness, and that would now be shared by someone other than herself. This theme has emerged in my other work on found poetry. It suggests that there can be a personal reticence and modesty about telling these kinds of stories, and yet an interest and satisfaction in getting them told. It provides an interesting lens on the discussions that have taken place around the ethical issues of whose story gets told, and by whom (Kirsch 1999). Perhaps there are some stories that are best told by others. It also suggested to me that the wonderful duality that exists in poetic representation is particularly suited for the retelling of these stories. It allows the writer to hone in on the pivotal and poignant aspects of a story, but at the same time to retain a veil of ambiguity that cloaks the story and somehow makes it less raw, subtler. This may be why Ann and Mary so embraced my telling of their stories.

For a long while, I remained dissatisfied with the 'Sumathy' poem. It felt cumbersome and less fluid than I had hoped. I put it aside for some time, and then decided to return to the work, and reshape it by paring it down, and by changing the rhythm, and sequencing. During a period of several months, I enjoyed Mary's responses to my work and the creative play it involved. Sporadically, over five years, I nudged the poem to its present form, having learned how much easier it is to produce found poetry from transcripts of oral discourse. It was a lesson that has helped me subsequently both in my own research and in my qualitative work with students.

Sumathy

> Adoption
> my whole life
> absorbed with her
> pretending to make up

those first years.
Still cuddly
at four or five
I held her bare feet
and kissed them
picturing her as a baby.
At six one night
nuzzled against my chest
she went to sleep
this moment
running down my cheek
reminiscent of how
I loved to nurse the boys
.

I wonder why women
have to
hide this feeling, a gift
clear it's not sexual
just sweet compensation for need.
Guess I missed all that touching
Guess I felt the loss
I can mourn
what I missed now
come to terms with it all.
I know
I'm not alone now
I can't go back and nurse
I know I'll continue to hold her
forever and ever
I hope.

LETTING GO

The next step in the autobiographical turn in my work was a series of poetry workshops that I took with Charlotte Hussey, who was at the time a Ph.D. student and faculty lecturer at McGill. The workshops were centered round a number of exercises that involved free-write sprints, or quick writing, which were meant to help us to 'leave our intellect behind,' and allow more intuitive thoughts to emerge. This was followed by 'nuggeting,' which is extracting key words and phrases from the sprints, followed by longer and slower writing, more nuggeting, and then by a process in which we shaped the results into poems. We often used memories, pictures, and photographs as prompts for the work. I found that through the exercises I gained confidence in using my words rather than found ones, and began to understand more fully how attending carefully to the sounds, rhythms, and sequencing of words helps to produce poetic descriptions. I learned how strongly I needed to identify with visual forms/memories to generate words for a poem. I also discovered how freeing it was to step beyond the boundaries of found words into the realm of my 'own words.' I believe it laid the groundwork for what followed, and helped me to develop poetic work with students by making poetry workshops a part of my courses.

The poem, 'Dusk,' was inspired by a picture in one of the workshops. I developed it by recollecting visions of sunsets that remain etched in my memory. I was compelled to write 'Death Eyes' after watching a woman (whom I knew was quite ill) and her husband during a meal in a restaurant.

Dusk

> Bunchy, voluptuous
> clouds
> beckon
> in fiery hue
> to dream.
> With a crimson sigh
> the sun slips
> evening
> into night.

Death Eyes

> They sat
> silent
> an invisible shroud
> warding off intrusion.
> Knowing pools sunken
> reflecting
> on bloated cheeks
> flickering fear
> agony of the inevitable.
> They gazed
> transfixed by food
> slow ritual
> mundane promise
> frozen
> amid a kaleidoscope
> of life.

During approximately the same time that I was participating in the poetry workshops, I began a project that involved revisiting my dissertation data with a more feminist lens (Butler-Kisber 2002b). I became particularly interested in re-examining the videotapes I had of the young girls in a multi-age grade one and two class in both the large group and small group contexts. In large groups, in particular during circle time where they came together early in the morning to share personal events and stories, the girls were often barely audible, while in other contexts they were playful, feisty, and confident. By carefully analyzing their quiet comments, I was able to show how they built on each other's contributions and engaged in exchanges about relational issues, and how the teacher was both sensitive and responsive to their whispered comments. This talk contrasted sharply with that of the boys during these times, and resonated with the work of Belenky *et al.* (1986) that indicates girls' propensity for relation and connection, and that of Barbieri (1995), which shows how often girls' voices get silenced in schools.

I used found poetry to create a cluster of poems depicting the playful, assertive, and empathetic conversations, as well as the quiet talk of these 'whispering angels.' In the following poem, I show the girls' quiet talk as they contributed collaboratively in circle time to express how much they had missed their teacher who had been absent for a month. When teased out from the transcripts, their remarks stood in stark contrast to the more boisterous, individual stories of weekend events, sports, and play contributed by the boys (Butler-Kisber 2001, p. 31).

Whispering Angels

> I missed you
> When you weren't here.
> Me, too.
> Me, too.
> I started
> dreaming about you.
> I was up all night.
> Every night.
> I was wishing on a star
> that you would come back.
> Me, too.

The girls' voices, preserved on videotapes from a decade previously, enabled me to get at the nuances and rhythm of their speech. During this work, I discovered how the use of poem clusters provides an interesting way to illuminate simultaneously a myriad of essential ideas while allowing room for the reader to make meaning, or particularize, in individual ways

If a goal of ethnography is to retell 'lived experience,' to make another world accessible to the reader, then I submit that the lyric poem, and particularly a series of lyric poems with an implied narrative, comes closer to achieving that goal than do other forms of ethnographic writing . . . Lyric poems concretize emotions, feelings, and moods – the most private kinds of feelings – so as to recreate experience itself in another person. A lyric poem 'shows' another person how it is to feel something. Even if the mind resists, the body responds to poetry. It is felt.

(Richardson 1994, pp. 8–9)

My increasing confidence in using poetic form, the on-going thinking that my 'whispering angels' work evoked about the silence and voice of girls in school, and my interest in continuing an exploration of poem clusters are probably what sparked my idea to revisit my own school days. I hoped to transform some of the sights and sounds of my memories into a cluster of poems. Thus, I ventured into the realm of self-study.

SCHOOL DAYS

Self-study or autobiographical qualitative research has increased exponentially in the last decade as the roots of feminist research, post-modern thought, and arts-based work have taken hold in the educational research community (Bullough and Pinnegar 2001). Self-study is seen as a way of addressing the ethical issues of voice and power by turning a study inward and making the researcher and participant one and the same. It is an important reflective component in any study for examining researcher assumptions. It is a way of putting issues of bias clearly on the research agenda by acknowledging that they exist, exploring what they are, and sharing them with the participants in whatever becomes the public representational form. Self-study is also increasingly being used as a way of becoming more reflective about our educational practices: 'Our autobiographies as learners in childhood, adolescence, and young adulthood frame our approach to teaching at the start of our careers, and they frequently exert an influence that lasts a lifetime' (Brookfield 1995, p. 50).

When I began the work on 'school days,' I was most interested in the analytic and representational aspects of the work. I wanted to see if I could move from videotapes, found poetry and poetry exercises, to introspection, memory, and the use of my own words. The question I posed to frame the work was, 'What was school life like for me as a girl?'

I began the process by identifying pivotal or nodal moments (Bullough and Pinnegar 2001) of my schooling at both the elementary and high school level, while trying to recall the visual and auditory context of each. I have described elsewhere that to avoid the linear thinking that produces more traditional textual forms, I did not 'free write' in the way associated with most memory work (Haug 1992). Rather for each episode, I brainstormed a series of words that seemed most reminiscent of the inner, visual and auditory world I revisited. Then I worked from these words, eliminating some and adding others, to shape the poems using rhythm, line breaks, pauses, repetition, and word play to recreate each memory in an attempt to show some of the 'sights and sounds.'

(Butler-Kisber 2002b, p. 29)

The result was a cluster of six poems about my school days. They are not reproduced in their entirety here, but the theme of 'silence' was very prominent in all of them. At first, I attributed this to the fact that in my 'whispering angel' poems the theme had been about silence as well, and had unconsciously influenced the memories that I had selected. However, upon further reflection, I realized that only the 'Whispering Angel' poem had been about silence; the rest were about playfulness, feistiness, and empathy. Interestingly, though, I had entitled the whole piece 'Whispering Angels,' unconsciously signaling the salience these quiet voices had for me. Fortunately, these young girls had a sensitive and empathetic teacher who noticed what they said even when it was barely audible.

The two poems reproduced here evolved from the most poignant memories for me, one from elementary school and one from high school. Both illustrate a form of silencing through intimidation. The 'Miss Good' story is one I have shared frequently in non-poetic form with pre-service teachers for many years. It serves to juxtapose the context of my schooling, now many decades earlier, with contemporary classrooms, highlighting the changes that have occurred regarding the permissibility of physical punishment, yet opening the conversation about other forms of non-physical intimidation and humiliation that can or might be present. The 'Despicable Bill' story is not one that I had shared with students before I created the poem. Perhaps this is because, in undergraduate courses, I work mainly with elementary teachers and it never surfaced as an example in the storying that I do in classes (Butler-Kisber, in press). But it may represent a darker side of intimidation that goes on in schools along the lines of gender, race, and culture, which inflicts a deeper kind of humiliation, and results in a more profound form of silencing about which I was less able to be vocal.

Miss Good

A grade one teacher
called Miss Good
at her desk
never stood.

A rule of silence reigned supreme
launched each day
by the queen.
A small black notebook
provided means
keeping track
of grand misdeeds.
Question
secret
wonder
dream
Monstrous crimes
indeed.
A twelve-inch weapon
marked the way
doling out
smacks each day
A thunderous call
strike of three
lurking demon
unleashed all.
A ruler-wielding power source
eliciting fear
not remorse
Anna
David
Paul
and Lynn
delinquents
of course.
A searing moment
acute chagrin
not what exists
deep within.
A grade one teacher
called Miss Good
pillar of pedagogy!
never
understood.

Despicable Bill

Where are you despicable Bill?
Still
carving insults on a desk
sexist slurs
women's breasts.
Lurking, slinking
down the hall
raiding lockers
grabbing all.
Sporting leather
boots and chain
sneering threats
bully's game.
Colour yellow
underneath
running scared
of pending heat.
Leaving scars along the way
faceless wounds
etched to stay.
Where are you despicable
Bill
Oblivious
Colourless
Mindless Bill
Still?

When I created the 'school days' cluster of poems, the theme of silencing was not a conscious one. Rather it emerged as an insight after the work was done. The introspection and analysis that resulted from this work enabled me to see a more pervasive pattern that is woven through all the work described earlier. I understand more profoundly why I pursued Ann's story of finding her voice in a study that was focused on the role of adult collaboration, not silencing. Her story was hidden in the transcripts, but my schooling experiences as a girl drove me there. The 'Sumathy' poem is yet another story with a similar theme. A power of the poetic process in self-study is that by examining life experiences, by 'turning logic on its head, reversing images, looking at situations sideways, and making imaginative leaps we realize that things are the way they are for a reason' (Brookfield 1995, p. 87). As a result, unconscious connections and themes emerge, we understand ourselves better, and we become better teachers and researchers.

1 Poetic representation is an arts-based vehicle in qualitative research that allows the heart to lead the mind rather than the reverse, and in so doing elicits new ways of seeing and understanding phenomena. It allows the researcher to hone in on the important aspects of a story, but at the same time retains a veil of ambiguity that cloaks the story and somehow makes it less raw, subtler.

2 Pivotal stories or nodal moments in qualitative research are the ones that lend themselves to poetic representation. There are some stories that participants want to be made public, but they prefer to have them told by the researcher.

3 Found poetry is an approach that distils words from transcripts and transforms them into poetic form to evoke feelings and different kinds of understanding. The process limits the range of poetic possibilities because the researcher is tied to the words that are present in the transcripts. This limitation also provides a certain sense of security, particularly for a novice.

4 Audio and videotaped field texts, which retain the sounds and sights of interactions, can be transformed more easily into poetry than other written texts. The researcher is able to return to the melodic nuances of the interactions. This facilitates the creation of the rhythm and tone in the poetic form.

5 Not every poetic rendition should necessarily become public, but poetic approaches in qualitative research can provide interesting analytic insights which otherwise might not emerge (Butler-Kisber 2002a).

6 Arts-based explorations in qualitative research courses necessitate risk-taking among the participants. The resulting vulnerability produces empathy and collaboration among peers and contributes to the learning context (Butler-Kisber *et al.* 2003).

7 Poetry reading and poetry workshops are good vehicles for moving from found poetry to autobiographical forms of poetic representation.

8 Poetry clusters are an interesting way of producing a kaleidoscope of essential ideas around a narrative theme.

9 Autobiographical poetic representation, where the researcher explores her memories and translates these into poetic form, provides an interesting approach to researcher reflexivity. Helpful themes can emerge which might remain dormant while using other more linear reflective tools such as memos and journals. These otherwise hidden themes produce a deeper understanding of researcher interest and stance.

REFERENCES

Barbieri, M., 1995, *Sounds from the Heart: Learning to Listen to Girls* (Portsmouth, NH: Heinemann).

Belenky, M.F., Cinchy, B.M., Goldberger, N.R. and Tarule, J.M., 1986, *Women's Ways of Knowing* (New York: Basic Books).

Berger, L., 2001, Narrative autoethnography. *Qualitative Inquiry*, 7(4), 501–18.

Bolster, S., 1983, Toward a more effective model of research on teaching. *Harvard Educational Review*, 55(3), 294–308.

Brookfield, S.D., 1995, *Becoming a Critically Reflective Teacher* (San Francisco: Jossey-Bass).

Bullough, R.V. and Pinnegar, S., 2001, Guidelines for quality in autobiographical forms of self-study research. *Educational Researcher*, 30(3), 13–21.

Butler-Kisber, L., 1988, Peer collaboration around educational tasks: a classroom ethnography. Unpublished doctoral dissertation, Harvard University, Cambridge, MA.

Butler-Kisber, L., 2001, Whispering angels: revisiting dissertation data with a new lens. *Journal of Critical Inquiry into Curriculum and Instruction*, 2(3), 34–37.

Butler-Kisber, L., 2002a, Artful portrayals in qualitative research: the road to found poetry and beyond. *Alberta Journal of Educational Research*, XLVIII(3), 229–39.

Butler-Kisber, L., 2002b, School days, school days: a feminist retrospective. *WILLA Journal*, 11, 25–29.

Butler-Kisber, L., in press, Student-oriented teacher inquiry and action research. In Shore, Aulls, Delacourt and Rejskind (Eds) *Inquiry in Education: Where Ideas Come From and Where They Lead* (Mawah, NJ: Erlbaum).

Butler-Kisber, L. and Borgerson, J., 1998, Alternative representation in qualitative inquiry: a student/instructor retrospective. Paper presented at the American Educational Research Association Annual Meeting, Chicago, IL (April). *Resources in Education*, 33, 11, 142 (ED 420 680).

Butler-Kisber, L., Allnutt, S., Furlini, L., Kronish, N., Markus, P., Poldma, T. and Stewart, M., 2003, Insight and voice: artful analysis in qualitative inquiry. *Arts and Learning Research Journal*, 19(1), 127–65.

Conle, C., 1996, Resonance in teacher education inquiry. *American Educational Journal*, 33(2), 297–325.

Davis, D. and Butler-Kisber, L., 1999, Arts-based representation in qualitative research: collage as a contextualizing analytic strategy. Paper presented at the American Educational Research Association Annual Meeting, Montreal, Quebec (April). *Resources in Education*, 34, 11, 135 (ED 431 790), 1–10.

Diamond, C.T.P. a nd Mullen, C.A., 1999, *The Postmodern Educator: Arts-Based Inquiries and Teacher Development* (New York: Peter Lang).

Donmoyer, R., 1993, Generalizability and the single-case study. In Eisner and Peshkin (Eds) *Qualitative Inquiry in Education* (New York: Teachers College Press), pp. 175–200.

Eisner, E.W., 1991, *The Enlightened Eye: Qualitative Inquiry and the Enhancement of Educational Practice* (New York: Macmillan).

Gardner, H., 1999, *Intelligence Reframed: Multiple Intelligences for the 21st Century* (New York: Basic Books)

Haug, F., 1992, *Beyond Female Masochism: Memory Work and Politics* (R. Livingstone translation) (London: Verso).

Kirsch, G., 1999, *Ethical Dilemmas in Feminist Research: The Politics of Location, Interpretation, and Publication* (Albany, NY: State University of New York Press).

Labov, W., 1972, *Language in the Inner City: Studies in Black English Vernacular* (Philadelphia, PA: University of Philadelphia Press).

Lincoln, Y.S. and Denzin, N.K., 2000, The seventh moment: out of the past. In Denzin and Lincoln (Eds) *The Handbook of Qualitative Research* (2nd edn) (Thousand Oaks, CA: Sage), pp. 1047–65.

Mishler, E., 2000, *Storylines: Craftartists' Narratives of Identity* (Cambridge, MA: Harvard University Press).

Onyx, J. and Small, J., 2001, Memory-work: the method. *Qualitative Inquiry*, 7(6), 773–86.

Personal Narratives Group (Ed.) 1989, *Interpreting Women's Lives* (London: Midland Books).

Reissman, C., 1993, *Narrative Inquiry* (Thousand Oaks, CA: Sage).

Reissman, C., 2002, Analysis of personal narratives. In Gubrium and Holstein (Eds) *Handbook of Interview Research* (Thousand Oaks, CA: Sage), pp. 695–710.

Richardson, L., 1992, The consequences of poetic representation: writing the other, rewriting the self. In Ellis and Flaherty (Eds) *Investigating Subjectivity* (Newbury Park, CA: Sage), pp. 125–37.

Richardson, L., 1994, Nine poems: marriage and the family. *Journal of Contemporary Ethnography*, 23(1), 3–12.

Richardson, L., 2000, Introduction – assessing alternative modes of qualitative and ethnographic research: how do we judge? Who judges? *Qualitative Inquiry*, 6(2), 251–52.

Chapter 10

Truth in fiction

Seeing our rural selves

Tony Kelly

PROLOGUE

In this chapter I take the position that the anthropological use of literary texts to examine aspects of the self in connection with others has the potential to shine a light on how we, as teachers, construct ourselves in relation to colleagues, family, and friends. Such texts provide a means of staging, or bringing into view, what is otherwise a taken for granted or commonplace mode of existence. The literary text has what Iser (1993) in his work on literary anthropology refers to as a doppelgänger effect both on the lives of ordinary readers and on the invisible surround we call culture. 'Staging,' according to Iser, 'is not a compensation but a doubling that enables the hidden aspects of a situation to assume a form' (pp. 54, 55). As Iser suggests, staging is a means of making available that which is generally unavailable or sealed off (p. 55).

The staging which occurs during the act of reading is akin to a dream state wherein the dreamer dreams herself outside and above mere corporeal existence and yet retains much of what has been set aside during the dream. Literary fiction makes accessible that which happens to humans during the act of dreaming and 'reveals itself to be pure semblance as regards whatever gestalt human beings make themselves into' (p. 86). 'Semblance itself,' according to Iser, 'is the propellant for a variegated and limitless self-invention of what human beings are like' (p. 86).

SOMEWHERE

I should like now to relate a brief anecdote drawn from my experience as a teacher and a teacher of teachers. The anecdote is suggestive of the desirability of introducing fiction as propellant into the field of self-study methodology. Recently, I participated in the ritual of introductions at the welcoming class in a graduate research course at McGill University in Montreal. My experience in studying at larger universities in Canada and abroad is that students tend to come from all over the world. In fact, in this case the students were not only from Montreal but some were from rural and urban China, from various parts of Southeast Asia, from the Gaspé in rural Quebec, from the Canadian prairies, as well as from the Atlantic coast. A student from Moscow had lived in the Sudan and later in the United States; one from Cairo had migrated to Old Montreal. Indeed we had all come from some very specific place and, although some were wont to indicate they are citizens of the world, once familiarity gained a foothold in the class the students' individual and rich experience of place added much color and context to the various research projects. And yet, during the introductions, I noticed that almost no one had much to say about where they came from. Most simply indicated their name, their interests, and when pressed stated they came from China or some such large geo-political unit. This puzzled me because, as a teacher, I like to know where my students come from, in part, I think, because I want to acknowledge their differences and at the same time learn from their experiences.

All experience is situated. The 'where' in somewhere is important. Certainly when I try to understand how I became the particular teacher I am, I cast my net back to a little river in rural Nova Scotia and I re-imagine my beginnings, my family, my school, and most particularly my village. I used to ring the church bell on Sunday mornings and my hands felt the roughness of the hemp rope attached to the bell. Through the vents in the belfry I could smell the salt air from the nearby river. The bell summoned the church-goers and then I made my way down to sit with my mother in a pew near the back of the church and always on the right-hand side. I point this out because as the minister delivered the Word and the picture of the thorn-crowned Christ gazed down at us we were on the left. Positioned thus, I learned to read as I frantically searched the hymnal for the words to the various songs the choir wafted into the church, out the main doors, and into the village.

When I look back on this it is as if I have entered a richly textured, living museum, a museum of memories organized in a spatial surround. The structure of those spaces in that tiny village provides many of the clues as to who I am now; they set the story as it were. I am convinced that teachers who attend to various life settings will have fuller understandings of their selves. Methodologically, an outward gaze provides access to much of the fabric necessary for the recording of a richly textured self. In my case, in the beginning there was the river. For the teacher, *sui generis*, there was a place. Re-establishing contact with place must therefore be part of the self-study project. The means for doing so are to be found in such textual artefacts as church bells, personal memories, and most especially the literature of place.

And so in this text, which bears witness to my experience, I work to tease out aspects of teacher identity as they are revealed through the interplay of lived texts. With respect to how I imagine myself and my own life story, I aim to explore teacher identity in rural environments. I want to share what particular rural teachers make of the way their environments are represented within rustic literature. To approach these issues I first consider the way in which reading texts contributes to a kind of distraction of the mind, a distraction which achieves focus through the act of writing, and then gives way to a form of drift or release as multiplicities of the self are set free within the culture. The texts I use, to 'inhabit my thoughts and direct my tongue' (Scholes 2001, p. 81), include Alistair MacLeod's (1999) *No Great Mischief* as well as material provided me by two former students/colleagues who live and work in rural Nova Scotia. I am grateful to the latter for giving me permission to quote from their written course material.

OUR TEXTUAL SELVES

Too much reading or reading without pause constitutes a kind of scattering, a distraction, an agitation of the mind. So says Foucault (1997) whose turn to the ancients for countermeasure suggested a form of contemplation, a gathering up of life's threads known as self writing. Such writing works to assimilate in ways which produce identity: 'Through the interplay of selected readings and assimilative writing, one should be able to form an identity through which a whole spiritual genealogy can be read' (p. 214). Such writing is a form of taking care, taking care of oneself in relation to others (Olssen 1999, p. 144).

Teachers who write must therefore be engaged in a process of identity formation. Genealogically such writing offers traces of our ties to each other, of our commonality. The traces are, in Cixous' poetic and metaphoric sense, a means of mapping a return to the Imaginary, a mythological time when mother and child were one, entering life's stream by means of the economy of the gift, an uncontrollable offering, brought into circulation by means of writing (Moi 1995, pp. 115–19). Cixous' sexual textual sense of the act of writing is homologous to that of the late Latin American novelist, Clarise Lispector, whom Cixous intensely admires.

> What shall I tell you about? I shall tell you about the instants. I exceed my limits and only then do I exist and then in a feverish way . . . I'm a concomitant being: I unite in myself past, present, and future time, the time that throbs in the tick-tock of clocks. To interpret and shape myself I need new signs and new articulations in forms which are found both on this side of my human history and on the other.
>
> (Lispector 1989, pp. 14, 15)

What Lispector's novel appears to offer is the impression that the work of the self is immediate both in the temporal sense of a present moving through time and in the spatial sense denoted and demarcated by the notion of 'sides' used to create the self in a particular place.

The clock's rhythm mimics that of the heart beat giving rise to the possibility of language (cf. Barthes 1991, p. 249) and language as Williams (1977) insisted 'is not a pure medium through which the reality of a life or the reality of an event or an experience or the reality of a society can "flow". It is a socially shared and reciprocal activity, already embedded in active relationships, within which every move is an activation of what is already shared and reciprocal or may become so' (p. 166). Williams' pulsating 'or' is suggestive of the richness of the possibilities embedded in an examined life, or of what may become so.

Experience then is the stuff which gives rise to language. The connection between experience and language necessitates a fuller appreciation of the role of literature in moving or situating writing beyond mere communication and placing it in the realm of one of the 'most distinctive, durable, and total forms' (p. 212) of the social. The act of reading literature is a process akin to what might be called a bricolage of the self in society. Men do it. Women do it too. In the context of teachers' lives shared reading can contribute to a realization that identity, the id, is bound to the social in ways which suggest that multiplicities of` the self are the flip side of a coin upon which I am we, not one but as Irigaray (2001, pp. 62–67) provocatively suggests two, perhaps more.

(OUR) SELVES IN CONTEXT

With this notion of the alterity of the self in mind I should like now to consider the response of two women teachers to a particular text offered in a course called 'Literacy, School, and Community'. The course was offered in rural Nova Scotia in the spring of 2001. The instructors, myself included, had set the course to allow teachers to engage the topic through auto-biographical and community investigations. Participants were expected to develop a response to a novel through which it was hoped they would be able to consider their personal and professional identities in the context of a particular place, which we loosely referred to as their community. In addition, participants were asked to produce a photo essay showing evidence of the linkages amongst the key themes of the course.

Most of the participants were women teachers who met on a bi-weekly basis in the staff room of the school. The school was located within a few kilometres of a magnificent harbour, famous I suppose for the ships whose holds had for centuries been laden with the unprocessed resources of this now underdeveloped province struggling to find its place amidst disturbingly familiar global realities. As my colleague and I crossed the province for the weekend sessions we caught glimpses of the tenacity of the inhabitants who continue to make their living in this place. As we drove along, domestic junkyards, and barren clear-cuts pocked the landscape eventually giving way to more groomed and urban spaces.

But the appearance of urbanity was betrayed by the clientele of the local liquor outlet lining up with their cases of twenty-four, the contents of which would disappear within hours in the trailer parks and outer reaches of the town. These things we noticed as we, ourselves, joined the queue to purchase the two cans of imported highland stout we had carefully selected from the specialty section of the store. In paying ancestral homage to our perceived bloodlines we, the now middle-aged university instructors, had perhaps failed to observe this small slight our choice objects presented to our Nova Scotian working-class roots. Our loyalties betrayed, we drove quickly to the school in order to offer brief book talks on the key literary texts we had hoped the students would use to refract their professional experiences of school, literacy, and community.

TEXTUAL SEDUCTIONS

Alistair MacLeod's (1999) magisterial novel, *No Great Mischief*, was one text which attracted several of the women in the course. The novel is the grand tale of the MacDonald clan whose exodus from the Scottish Highlands in the late 1700s marked the beginning of the families' journeys to the highlands of Cape Breton in Nova Scotia. This was followed by two centuries of struggle for survival within the harsh realities of an unforgiving climate, fortuitous circumstance, and diasporic shifts. Over the long centuries, various members of the family move from Cape Breton to other parts of Canada, including mining towns, lumber camps, the cities of Calgary and Toronto, and indeed further afield to the New England states, to South America, and to parts of Africa.

This family and clan story is told by the narrator, Alexander, an accomplished orthodontist whose ambivalence towards his own success is slowly revealed as he tells the haunting tale of his family and especially that of his eldest brother Calum, whose life story underpins that of the successful professional. Calum's tragic life was one of hard labor and generous support for his family members up until the time of his imprisonment for the death of a fellow worker which occurred as the result of the treachery of a distant relative working in the same camp. Upon Calum's release, his younger brother Alexander, the story's narrator, cares for the increasingly isolated and alcoholic Calum. The young Alexander is known as the *gillebeag ruadh* or the 'little red-haired boy'. The reddish hair color is the distinguishing hereditary feature of the larger clan.

The story, as a whole, is mythic in scale. At the same time, it is a conflicted meditation on the relationship between the life of the educated, professional, and privileged member of the middle class and that of the seething mass of humanity who literally drift about the continents doing the work of the harvest, and that of resource extraction. The bone tired dreams of such workers offer no solace to the migrant except perhaps that of reconnecting to family and kin in a place called home.

This (re)connection in MacLeod's work is a kind of return motivated and occasioned by love, family love, and intense loyalty to kin accompanied by strong desire for the lost home. This longing borders on lust for place and it drives those in difficult circumstance to persevere despite the rather dismal odds:

> Grandpa used to say that when he was a young man he would get an erection as soon as his feet hit Cape Breton. That was in the time, he said, when men had buttons on the front of their trousers. We, his middle-aged grandchildren, do not manifest any such signs of hopeful enthusiasm. But we are nonetheless here.
>
> (p. 282)

MacLeod's apparent ambivalence is embodied in the life of the orthodontist and resides in the latter's relative privilege in relation to his male siblings.

The novel as a whole is detumescently structured as wave after wave of family history is revealed, poignant and arresting in each moment, only to return for eventual and final subsistence in the calm drift encapsulated by the book's constant refrain, 'All of us are better when we're loved.' This sexual formula bags sentimentality and exudes seductive charm.

TWO (+ ONE) READERS RESPOND

I begin with the one in part because of the surprise I recently experienced when I opened a text in a Montreal bookstore to find my own conversation recorded by Neilsen (1994) in her book, *A Stone in My Shoe*. At the time, over a decade ago, I was reflecting aloud on the discomfort teachers must pass through if they are to achieve 'professional' growth (p. 40). In the years since then a certain discomfort has clung to my professional life. As a man, performing the male gender role, in the woman's world of elementary schools and teacher education, I am acutely aware that there are marked differences in the way women and men read their worlds. This awareness makes me want to cross borders whilst it makes me extremely cautious about reading the texts I now encounter. These are the texts authored by two women in response to their reading of *No Great Mischief*.

In the novel the title phrase is attributed to Wolfe's correspondence prior to the Battle of the Plains of Abraham wherein Wolfe wrote that it would be no great mischief if the Highlanders were to fall (MacLeod, p. 109). Positioned first in the scaling of the cliffs of Quebec, fall they did. MacLeod's use of the phrase suggests the ruthlessness and cynicism of those aligned against his Highland ancestors and in a metaphoric sense suggests his overall distaste for the arrogance of the powerful. I am conscious that the pen is powerful and I intend no mischief, great or small, when I unpack two themes which appear in the literary responses of Sandra Graham-Muise and Katherine MacPherson.

The quest for truth in fiction describes Graham-Muise's response to *No Great Mischief*. Throughout her writing Graham-Muise is concerned to authenticate the experiences MacLeod shares and she does this by interviewing her own family members who had been to Cape Breton. She in fact traveled to Cape Breton where she gathered images for her photo-essay. What she discovered was a view, shared by many in connection with Cape Breton, that the past is always close to the residents' experience of the place. She blended her observations with memories of the clannishness of the characters in the novel as well as their love of the music. She searched the Cape Breton she visited for evidence of music, drink, and song and she was not disappointed. Graham-Muise's response reads like a detective file. Something has happened here and she sets herself the task of assembling the evidence:

> I searched for a house similar to the one I imagined the older brothers living in after the death of their parents. I chose this house because of its appearance and location. There were different pieces of fishing equipment in the yard which made it even more realistic. On one side of this house you can see the buoy; on the other side just out of picture range were traps. You can imagine Chrissy, the horse, running to meet Calum when he whistled, ready to haul the boat up the incline to receive her award.
>
> (Caption taken from the twelfth photo in the
> Graham-Muise response)

It was important for Graham-Muise to gain a sense that the story MacLeod offered was something more than a story. The difficulty is that the thing which happened is itself a fiction and the camera at best plays tricks. The quest for certainty is in large measure beyond the grasp of the reader.

In relation to the camera, Barthes (2000) suggests: 'No writing can give us this certainty. It is the misfortune . . . of language not to be able to authenticate itself. The *noeme* of language is perhaps this impotence, or to put it positively: language is, by nature, fictional' (pp. 86, 87). With the advent of photography, people's resistance to believing in the past collapsed and 'henceforth the past is as certain as the present, what we set on paper is as certain as what we touch' (p. 88). What Graham-Muise found in Cape Breton were, of course, mere shadows of the vividness of MacLeod's world. As she retreated to her own home far removed from Cape Breton, her camera found images of her own son, Graham, learning to read. She ends having positioned herself in full view of her own story pinning her hopes on the new generation of the family Graham Muise.

Recognition and self-recognition are strong unifying themes woven into Katherine MacPherson's response to *No Great Mischief*. She found herself fascinated with this novel for reasons connected to her own life's story. For a person whose *pater nomen* dates back to the Highland clearances, her family's story runs parallel to that of the six generations of MacDonalds. Born into a family of twentieth-century Scottish Canadians, Katherine became a MacPherson or the 'son of a parson'. Over the centuries, Katherine relates how her family has maintained the tradition of producing a parson in each generation. Her father was a distinguished Baptist minister as is her brother. On the maternal side of her family there were many more Baptist ministers. In her response, however, Katherine is most concerned to offer glimpses of the life of her brother and less concerned to offer insight into the many women in the earlier generations of her family who married pastors.

Katherine focuses on her brother's accomplishments, which are many in diverse parts of the globe, particularly in the realm of social justice. The strong political ethic of caring was learned, Katherine suggests, in the many hours of talk around the family's table where the children were exposed to 'all manner of social, political, and literary criticism'. Like the MacLeods' accomplished orthodontist, the MacPhersons' sibling parson is presented as a restless character at times engaged with farm workers in the United States, working with Japanese in Chicago, studying in prestigious universities, writing theological treatises, and traveling to the Isle of Skye to be told stories of the Battle of Culloden.

As with the MacDonalds, there is in Katherine's family a desire to explore the history underpinning their particular fascinations. This link to the past is not about nostalgia. It is more about uncovering those things which need care and attention. Katherine, herself a traveler, ends her photo-essay with disturbing pictures contrasting the extreme disparities in people's living conditions in the city of San Francisco. She concludes, 'I am my grandfather's and father's child because I believe my job is to teach more than just skills and a set of competencies. It is to prepare a way for children to find expression and justice in a peaceful world.'

I believe Katherine's discussion of her family's story was occasioned by her apparently ludic[1] reading of *No Great Mischief*. She claims her experience was characterized by vivid imagery and language with the 'picturing' being accomplished through the words and pauses between the scenes. She read with both anticipation and retrospection. She felt herself in the thrall of great literature. With little doubt her reading exemplified the fantastic state of being lost in a book.

There is a scene in *No Great Mischief* where Alexander visits his twin sister at her home in Calgary. During the visit the conversation is all about the past and the struggle to understand the family's story. The sister, an actress by profession, assumes the persona of the listener as Alexander commiserates with the past. She waits; silence and pause prompt her brother's reflections. He tells stories told him by his brother Calum.

He tells of a tree once cut near the roots which refused to fall and was held firmly in place by the branches of the entire grove. The tree could not fall whilst the grove stood. The sister hears the story and offers the photo album. In the album there is an outdoor picture of the clan which contains images of their parents. The sister had tried to have a photo technician remove the parents from the large group but the result was disappointing. The only thing to do was to leave them in the larger photo. It was the only thing to do (MacLeod 1999, pp. 239, 240).

As I imagine this scene I fantasize Katherine, son of the parson, listening across oceans and time to her brother's well-written sermons, imagining their good works in church, community, and school. Like the technician in the photo shop I fail to separate the images. I conjoin my informants in what Rose (1998) calls a state of fantasy.

MOVING ON

I began by wanting to think about teacher identity within particularities of place and culture. To do so I suggested that literary anthropology has a certain utility within the self-study project in that it helps us explore the limitless self-invention of what we as human beings are like and it does so by shining a light on those inventions or semblances of ourselves represented in both place and time. The self-study project helps us gain insight and as I move across textual representations of the culture of rural Canada, a kind of trouble or agitation confronts me. Partly the trouble arises from a sense that the state we find ourselves in is a problematic and conflicted one where issues of rurality conjure a sense of loss and yearning. MacLeod's genius resides in how beautifully he conjures not only the loss and yearning, but also in the life-affirming quality of his text; how he allows his readers to capture bits of themselves within the frames and pauses. The countryside, it seems, must always thrash its way into a modern culture. That is history. But history plays itself out in the real life stories of individuals, individuals who dream as I dream, as MacLeod dreams, and who hope as Katherine MacPherson and Sandra Graham-Muise hope. Rose suggests:

> We cannot bypass modern statehood; we are living in its world. Fantasy allows us first to acknowledge that as a more than external matter. But we should not forget fantasy's supreme characteristic is that of running ahead of itself . . . If fantasy can give us the inner measure of statehood, it might also help to prise open the space in the mind where the worst of modern statehood loses its conviction, falters, and starts to let go.
>
> (1998, pp. 14, 15)

We know where we are; it's just that in this now instant we might not want to be here. Self-study then, for this teacher, involves a kind of methodological trawling of the spaces we have inhabited in an attempt to weave credible narratives, narratives which point toward open spaces whether in the classroom, the home, or in the larger community.

NOTE

1   Refer to Nell 1988, p. 75 for more discussion of the fantastic state of the ludic reader.

REFERENCES

Barthes, R., 1991, *The Responsibility of Forms* (Berkeley: University of California Press).
Barthes, R., 2000, *Camera Lucida* (New York: Hill & Wang).
Foucault, M., 1997, Self writing. In P. Rabinow (Ed.) *Ethics: Subjectivity and Truth* (New York: The New Press), pp. 206–22.
Irigaray, L., 2001, *to be two* (New York: Routledge).
Iser, W., 1993, *The Fictive and the Imaginary: Charting Literary Anthropology* (Baltimore: Johns Hopkins University Press).
Lispector, C., 1989, *The Stream of Life* (Minneapolis: University of Minnesota Press).
Macleod, A., 1999, *No Great Mischief* (Toronto: McClelland & Steward Inc.).
Moi, T., 1995, *Sexual, Textual, Politics* (London: Routledge).
Neilsen, L., 1994, *A Stone in My Shoe: Teaching Literacy in Times of Change* (Winnipeg: Peguis Publishers).
Nell, V., 1988, *Lost in a Book* (New Haven: Yale University Press).
Olssen, M., 1999, *Michel Foucault: Materialism and Education* (Westport, CT: Bergin & Garvey).
Rose, J., 1998, *States of Fantasy* (Oxford: Oxford University Press).
Scholes, R., 2001, *The Crafty Reader* (New Haven: Yale University Press).
Williams, R., 1977, *Marxism and Literature* (Oxford: Oxford University Press).

Part 3

Reflection, life history and self-study

Chapter 11

'It was good to find out why'

Teaching drama planning through a self-study lens

Linda L. Lang

PLANNING FOR DRAMA: PUTTING MYSELF UNDER THE MICROSCOPE

Preparing pre-service teachers to practice a pedagogy that they have never experienced is challenging. Because most of the students in my undergraduate drama education courses have little or no school experience in improvisational process drama (O'Neill 1995), I include an extensive experiential component in my introductory drama education course. But I must also address issues related to teaching and the pedagogy of process drama in this one-semester course. I decided to meet the 'not-enough-time' challenge by inviting my students to critique – as teachers – the drama units they had experienced as students in my class. When they are in the critical/teacher role, they are asked to scrutinize and criticize my instructional planning practices.

Teaching process drama involves risks for new and experienced teachers alike. Process drama lessons depend upon student input and ownership of ideas and therefore disrupt more traditional teaching practices where the teacher plans, parcels up, and delivers the content of the lesson. No matter what you, as a teacher, think will happen in a lesson, your students-in-role are empowered to take the drama in unanticipated directions. I needed to find a way to convince my pre-service teachers that ambiguity is built into planning for drama lessons while at the same time maintaining the importance of preparedness. Putting myself as drama teacher and my own planning under the students' 'microscope' for examination seemed to be a worthwhile risk for me to take to achieve my teaching objective. Putting my self under my *own* self-study microscope seemed a natural extension of this decision, an extension that would also model reflective practice (Taylor 1996) as an important aspect of drama teaching.

This chapter recounts the self-study process I entered into with my students. The understandings the students revealed in their roles of participant and assessor are juxtaposed to the meanings and insights I constructed about my own role as drama teacher educator.

A CONTEXT FOR SELF-CRITICAL EXPLORATION

I teach my introductory drama education curriculum course for two seventy-five minute periods per week over the course of a thirteen-week university fall semester. During this time period, twenty-five to thirty-five second-year pre-service teachers participate in a fairly structured progression of activities that are designed to introduce them to the theory and practice of process drama in K-12 classrooms. I usually begin the semester with a unit of instruction that I present as a 'drama sequence'.

A unit or series of drama lessons that develops from and expands upon a single source, theme, topic, or selection of literature may be referred to as:

- a drama structure (O'Neill and Lambert 1982);
- a story drama (Booth 1994);
- a process drama (O'Neill 1995);
- a drama in context/contextual drama (Bolton 1984);
- a role drama (Tarlington and Verriour 1991); or
- simply as 'a drama'.

Bolton (1992) discusses planning a 'sequence of drama experiences' from a specific focus (p. 65). I have shortened this description to 'drama sequence' since the phrase indicates both connections between activities and a progression of activities that build upon each other in a unified and cohesive pattern.

Each of my drama sequences consists of approximately eight to ten drama 'episodes' (O'Neill 1995). Each episode explores one aspect of the theme, source, or topic and uses one or two drama conventions to facilitate that exploration. One example of a drama convention (Neelands and Goode 1999) would be 'still-image' where small groups of students create a still picture with their bodies. Sometimes episodes develop chronologically and create a story or narrative around a theme or idea. In some drama sequences, episodes explore different viewpoints on one event or circumstance and students assume a variety of different roles to examine that event. A drama sequence is usually completed within four or five class periods with the fifth or sixth class period used for reflective discussion. Direct instruction or lectures that deal with methodology, history of drama education, and theoretical underpinnings occur in one-week blocks between drama sequences.

Rather than relying on pre-planned dramas that have been published by authorities in the field of drama education, I plan almost all of the drama sequences I use with my students myself from a variety of sources, themes and materials. I plan in such a way that I combine sources or 'pre-texts' (O'Neill 1995), drama conventions, episodic structures and teaching approaches in a variety of different ways to demonstrate the innumerable teaching possibilities of process work. I also create my own drama sequence plans because this work allows me to exercise my own imagination in a playful way for a practical purpose.

Students participate in three or four instructor-planned drama sequences over the course of the term. The culminating experience of the term involves students working in small groups of three or four to plan a drama sequence using the conventions and patterns they have read about or have experienced as participants.

MAKING PLANNING PRACTICE TRANSPARENT

Most teacher educators insist that pre-service teachers learn to write out lesson plans and unit plans to practice and develop instructional planning skills. My first step in making my own planning transparent to my students is to 'practice what I preach'. I develop a full written plan, complete with learning objectives, lists of materials, motivational set, procedures and closure activities, for each drama sequence that I implement. Even though I usually deviate from this plan in response to my students' ideas and input, it is available for their reflection and critical evaluation.

To give students the drama sequence plan ahead of time, however, would be analogous to reading the last chapter first in a mystery novel! Students must be free to participate in the drama episodes in the 'here and now' as students without concern for pedagogical implications and teacher purposes. In this way, they can experience the impact of the unfolding pattern as it would be experienced in a K-12 classroom. I do have printed copies of my drama sequence plan prepared for distribution during the last session in the drama sequence. Students then have time to read over the plan before the reflection session.

I structure the post-drama reflection session so that students reflect on the drama sequence at two levels. Morgan and Saxton (1987) refer to Geoff Gillam's (1974) distinction between the 'play for the students' and the 'play for the teacher' in relation to the way a drama is experienced in the classroom (p. 164). I try to address both perspectives in our post-drama reflections. First we talk about what the drama was like for them as students. How did they experience the roles they played? Which episodes helped them deepen their understandings and insights about the topic or theme? What did they learn about themselves or about human nature from their participation?

During the second part of the reflection session we examine the drama sequence plan that I used to guide the drama from a teacher perspective. Students are invited to contribute their opinions about what worked and what did not work in our classroom context. I make sure that I am well prepared for this session. Between the final session in the drama sequence and the reflection session with the students I engage in some serious reflective practice of my own.

The weekly drama journal entries I asked my students to record were so interesting and valuable to read that I decided to assign myself the same task. The professional journal that I've kept for the last three years has become an excellent data source for my own self-study and reflective practice. As well as providing information, this journal also details my reactions to what happened in class.

In addition to students' journal entries and my own professional journal, I've explored students' course evaluation responses, student assignments, and my own instructional plans and planning notes in my efforts to identify the implications of teaching planning pedagogy through my own self-critical practice and self-study. I want to note that students voluntarily contributed their written responses/journals *after* they had completed and received a grade for the course. They also signed ethics board approved consent forms before any of this material was analyzed for research purposes. I've achieved some valuable insights about the benefits for my students and for my own practice as a teacher educator through approaching instructional planning through a self-study lens.

'IT WAS GOOD TO FIND OUT WHY': STUDENT RESPONSE TO SELF-CRITICAL PRACTICE

The majority of my students were very positive about my approach to reflection sessions and my self-critical stance. The following excerpts from student journals, evaluations, and assignments reflect some of the reasons that the students provided for appreciating my willingness to critically analyze my own teaching. All students' names have been changed to honour confidentiality.

> There did seem to be something not quite working in the overheard conversation strategy. I couldn't really put my finger on it though so I'm glad it was discussed. You said it needed more structure – people had good ideas about how to do that.
>
> (Sally, 2000)

Sally's comment represents one of the benefits that students identified in their written responses to reflection. Sometimes they knew something wasn't working but they weren't exactly sure what was wrong or how to fix it. Reflective discussion enabled them to identify causes and collectively generate solutions.

A second benefit that students noted was that they felt the written unit plan provided them with a starting point for analysis and reflection:

> It was interesting to receive a copy of the original plan of the drama then compare it to what actually occurred. There weren't many changes but it was good to find out why some plans were left out.
>
> (Loreen, 2002)

Loreen's comment indicates that the use of written planning documents as reference points for reflective discussion and analysis supports the importance of creating written plans, even for the most experienced teachers. Students traditionally communicate that they believe experienced teachers do not need to write out lesson plans when they prepare to teach. They learned that written plans may be both necessary and important for all teachers.

Another interesting benefit for students was the opportunity that the reflection sessions provided for students to achieve a level of praxis (Freire 1970; Taylor 2000). Students in my classes learn about the importance of injecting tension into drama episodes as part of their study of drama education theory (Bolton 1979; Morgan and Saxton 1987; Taylor 2000). However, the meaning of the word 'tension', as it applies to drama, becomes much clearer when it is connected to an actual experience or problem that students confront in the drama:

> At first, we weren't really going anywhere because we seemed to have no conflict or tension so I learned something by you addressing the issue of needing to raise some conflict or tension in the episode.
>
> (Beth, 2000)

Some students commented that this approach to talking about instructional planning was an unfamiliar practice:

> In all of the dramas we had a chance to reflect on the drama. I felt this is where I learned the most. Working on improving things that didn't work was most gratifying to me. Looking at it from a teacher's perspective is new to me.
>
> (Melody, 2002)

The most frequently cited benefits identified by students, however, related to the way they felt and learned about themselves as a result of being invited to contribute their perspectives, opinions and criticisms in class discussion:

> We often take a fair bit of time for reflection because it is what the student experiences that is at the center of educational drama. Everyone's ideas are important and they were taken seriously.
>
> (Kendra, 2002)

> I believe that when we are sharing ideas in the large circle after the drama I learn the most about my classmates and my professor. I really get to understand where they are at and everyone has something different to offer.
>
> (Chelsea, 2002)

> In a university class, professors tend not to be open-minded (not always) – it's a challenge worth taking on, though.
>
> (Marty, 2002)

Some students were also able to understand the differences between the 'play for the students' and the 'play for the teacher' because of reflective discussion:

> Some students did not agree with all the techniques. My experience from this was being able to better understand why certain things were done in the dramas and what you hoped would occur from us doing these things.
>
> (Cheryl, 2002)

Especially exciting to me was the attitude of willingness to take risks that emerged from the students' responses to drama plans that needed reworking:

> I think the stress comes with putting it into action and planning on your feet. Such knowledge can only be gained by practical experience – so my first few dramas may be disasters – if at first you don't succeed, try again!
>
> (Corrie, 2000)

'I NEVER THOUGHT OF THAT!': SELF-STUDY FROM THE INSIDE

The insights I uncovered about my own practice as a teacher educator are framed within the field of drama education but they may indeed be relevant in any context where teacher educators are helping pre-service teachers to explore the messy realities of planning for instruction in schools.

My self-study of my own planning practices helped me to move closer to becoming the kind of reflective practitioner I teach my students *they* should become. I have learned to plan for quality over quantity and forgive myself for not including every drama convention that is listed in the textbook (Neelands and Goode 1999) in my drama sequences. I have learned to try out drama conventions that I am unsure about because I know that if I fail I will be able to turn the failure into a teachable moment for my students. I have also learned to be more sensitive to students' feelings and responses to the drama work we do together, both inside and after the role-playing experience.

I have become aware of tensions within myself that need to be monitored and occasionally addressed. I do have an ego that influences me to believe I'm right about most matters related to drama pedagogy. Just as I ask students to suspend their *disbelief* and enter into drama experiences with commitment (Morgan and Saxton 1987), I have learned that I must suspend my *belief* in my own 'rightness' and listen to students' opinions about my teaching choices openly and without defensiveness. I have learned that it is important to know when to compromise and when to make my compromises explicit and transparent to students.

An unexpected benefit for me, however, is that I have experienced many of the benefits for myself that I hoped to achieve for my students. I am feeling more respected and supported by them. I am a better and more thorough instructional planner because I know my plans will be available to students for their scrutiny. I have refined my abilities to think 'on my feet' or engage in reflection-in-action (Taylor 1996) because of ideas and suggestions from my students that inform the on-the-spot choices that I make.

I have also developed a stronger understanding of the relationships between my philosophy of drama education – my beliefs – and the way I practice that philosophy in my own practice as a teacher educator (Louie *et al.* 2003). This first voyage into the seas of self-study has both affirmed my beliefs about the power of drama education to transform students' understandings and made me a humbler practitioner of my pedagogy and my art.

REFERENCES

Bolton, G., 1979, *Toward a Theory of Drama in Education* (Harlow, UK: Longman Group Ltd).

Bolton, G., 1984, *Drama as Education: An Argument for Placing Drama at the Center of the Curriculum* (Harlow, UK: Longman Group Ltd).

Bolton, G., 1992, *New Perspectives on Classroom Drama* (London: Simon & Schuster Education).

Booth, D., 1994, *Story Drama: Reading, Writing and Roleplaying Across the Curriculum* (Markham, Ontario: Pembroke Publishers).

Freire, P., 1970, *Pedagogy of the Oppressed* (New York: Continuum Publishing).

Louie, B.Y., Dreydahl, D.J., Purdy, J.M. and Stackman, R.W., 2003, Advancing the scholarship of teaching through collaborative self-study. *Journal of Higher Education*, 74(2), 150–71.

Morgan, N. and Saxton, J., 1987, *Teaching Drama: A Mind of Many Wonders* (London: Hutchinson Education).

Neelands, J. and Goode, T., 1999, *Structuring Drama Work: A Handbook of Available Forms in Theatre and Drama* (2nd edn) (Cambridge, UK: Cambridge University Press).

O'Neill, C., 1995, *Drama Worlds: A Framework for Process Drama* (Portsmouth, NH: Heinemann).

O'Neill, C. and Lambert, A., 1982, *Drama Structures: A Practical Handbook for Teachers* (Portsmouth, NH: Heinemann).

Tarlington, C. and Verriour, P., 1991, *Role Drama* (Markham, Ont.: Pembroke Publishers).

Taylor, P., 1996, Doing reflective practitioner research in arts education. In Taylor (Ed.) *Researching Drama and Arts Education: Paradigms and Possibilities* (London: Falmer Press), pp. 25–58.

Taylor, P., 2000, *The Drama Classroom: Action, Reflection, Transformation* (London: RoutledgeFalmer).

Chapter 12

Speak for yourselves

Capturing the complexity of critical reflection

Vicki Kubler LaBoskey[1]

The self-study I report upon in this chapter[2] utilized critical reflection as both the practical activity under investigation and the method for studying that activity. I was doing more than just reflecting on my practice, which as Loughran and Northfield (1998) have noted is not the same as self-study. They argue, 'Reflection is a personal process of thinking, refining, reframing, and developing actions. Self-study takes these processes and makes them public, thus leading to another series of processes that need to reside outside of the individual' (p. 15). Reflection is, therefore, a necessary, but not sufficient, aspect of self-study. I did what they felt was necessary to move from reflection to self-study – made my reflections on my practice a public activity. What happened in this instance was that the study became the reflection.

Since context matters, I need to provide some information about the Mills College Credential Program, called Teachers for Tomorrow's Schools. It is a two-year graduate program that results (in the case of the student teachers in this study) in a multiple subject teaching credential and a master's degree in education. The student teachers complete the credential and half of the master's during the first academic year. In that year credential candidates teach in the mornings, beginning on the first day of school and ending on the last, and take courses at the college in the afternoons. Both their cooperating teachers and college supervisors direct the student teachers in their field-work. The main responsibilities of the supervisors at Mills College are to observe each of their student teachers every other week which includes a post-observation debriefing and write-up; planning, attending, and co-facilitating a two-hour student teaching seminar every week; responding to the inter-active reflective journals of their student teachers every week; and evaluating each of their students at the end of both semesters. At the time that this research was undertaken, I had five supervisors, who were all former students of mine. Four of the supervisors participated in the study with me. In addition to being the director of the program, I am also a supervisor.

The purpose of our study, as co-written by my supervisors and myself in our research proposal, was to determine what college supervisors actually do to enable student teacher growth and learning. In our view, there is no easy answer to this question. The profession requires teachers to give their whole selves to the endeavour: mind, body, spirit, values, past experience, ethics, politics, passion, intellect, hope, vision, organizational skills. College supervisors are called upon to mentor beginning teachers as they explore who they are, what they believe, and how to teach to all of the diverse children in their classrooms in ways that are educative, effective, nurturing, empowering, and inspiring.

Because both the people they mentor and the profession of teaching are complex and demanding, the job of college supervisors is not simple. Supervisors mentor, coach, listen deeply, and share information, as well as their own past experiences. They prod people to become more reflective about themselves and their teaching practice through thoughtful questioning and dialogue, encourage new ways of self-expression, offer emotional support and career counselling, and facilitate and mediate the student teacher/cooperating teacher relationship. They also assess and document student teacher growth and learning.

The purpose of the project, then, was for student teacher supervisors in the elementary credential program at Mills College to work together over the course of one school year to identify and document the key components of successful student teacher mentoring. In so doing, we hoped to develop a new, holistic way of thinking, talking, and writing about our job that accurately reflects its complexity. We needed a way to capture our work in its everydayness, its sophistication. We decided, therefore, to document our regular reflective interactions with our students and with one another. To this end, we would collect the following data, all of which were normal components of program activity: tape recordings of our weekly supervisor planning and student review meetings; copies of the interactive reflective journals of some of our students; and all end-of-semester student teacher reviews of their supervisors.

We also needed a way to critically reflect on this work and to capture that meta-reflection. Thus, we instituted some additional data sources: five supervisor reflective journals that we circulated amongst ourselves over the course of the year and an end-of-the-year questionnaire administered to all student teachers. The combination of these data sources and our collaborative analyses of them constitute our research method: critical reflection. It is so because it includes:

- Multiple perspectives on both process and outcome – that of all of the supervisors and the student teachers;
- An on-going search for evidence of reframed thinking – both our own and our students – as a result of collaborative reflection on our own practice, the practices of our student teachers, and the relationship between the two;

- Instances of changed practice resulting from this transformed thinking;
- The asking and investigating of the political questions associated with equity, social justice, and the use or misuse of power in our director/supervisor, supervisor/student teacher relationships (see Wilkes 1998, p. 206).

Recognizing the complexity of our task, we employed other methods in the practice, analysis, and representation of our reflective interactions and deliberations: dialogue, journaling, and narrative. We also drew upon many other studies when we designed this project.

METHODOLOGICAL SOURCES

The impetus for the research question derived from previous research that some of my colleagues and I had done on the fieldwork component of our program. These studies showed that college supervisors play a central role in helping student teachers connect theory to practice and learn from their placements in the field (LaBoskey and Richert 2002; Richert *et al.* 2000). Even in placements that were not ideal, strong supervision enabled student teachers to learn and grow and, in so doing, become well prepared to teach on their own. Though we had some indications of certain supervisor interventions that were helpful to student learning, we did not have a very complete picture of the nature of the relationship, of what the supervisors were doing that seemed to result in both highly positive reviews by their student teachers and the documented growth of the credential candidates.

Turning to the self-study literature for guidance in how we might best capture this complexity, we found examples of collaborative inquiry that seemed to use critical reflection as both practice and method (e.g. Berry and Loughran 2002; Conle *et al.* 1998; Lomax *et al.* 1998; Schuck and Segal 2002). A primary insight gained from this review was that, in order to turn our reflective practice into self-study, we needed to share and deliberate our fundamental views about the means and ends of our work as teacher educators. As noted by Bass *et al.* (2002), 'Reflexivity, wherein worldviews clash from the input of critical friends and theory, can push reflection past defensiveness into transformative learning' (p. 67). We also needed to capture and make public the nature of that deliberation.

Insights on how to accomplish this goal came from studies utilizing narrative inquiry in general, and dialogue and personal history via journaling in particular. Scholars employing these research methods have argued that these strategies are particularly conducive to capturing the knowledge and practice of teaching and teacher education. One of the fundamental reasons posited is that teacher knowledge can best be characterized as narrative knowing, in Bruner's (1986) typology (see, for example, Clandinin and Connelly 1996, Lyons 2002).

Guilfoyle *et al.* (2002) suggest that dialogue can serve as both methodology and method in self-study research because 'the use of dialogue can be seen as a basis for making meaning, establishing the validity of ideas and promoting action' (p. 97). The dialogue community can construct together new understandings of themselves and their work, which was certainly an aim of our study. They found that 'The dialogue seemed to run in cycles of personal reflection, professional interchanges and public analysis, followed by private analysis' (p. 98), which in turn provided an impetus for transformed thinking and practice: 'We come away renewed because we have reached new epiphanies about the analyses that brought us together and new questions to explore. We leave with new ways to walk our talk and learn' (p. 99). This characterization maps well onto the process of critical reflection, which suggested to us that we needed to both engage in dialogue and utilize it as a method for studying our practice.

We considered interactive journals to be another way to extend and capture our dialogue, our critical reflection. Each of us would make a new entry in one of our journals every week, as well as read and respond to whatever else was there; then we would rotate them. This allowed us to add the benefit of more prolonged and deliberative reflection to the process; we could step back from the rapid-fire interchange of face-to-face interaction to think more deeply about our experiences and our emotional and intellectual reactions to them. In the words of Joanne Cooper (1991), 'Journals allow us to examine our own experiences, to gain a fresh perspective, and by that means begin to transform the experiences themselves' (p. 99) – certainly one of our goals, and a goal of critical reflection in self-study.

We knew that this comprehensive data gathering would capture much; that was the point, after all – to document the whole of our practice, the details. We decided that our analysis of the data would be enhanced if we focused on particular aspects of the work during each review cycle. In the first round, we chose to focus on the interpersonal qualities of our critical reflection.

RESEARCH FOCUS

Our reasons for focusing on the interpersonal aspects of our mentoring process were twofold. First, the literature makes clear the importance of establishing a community based in trust, if meaningful dialogue and critical reflection are to occur (e.g. Berry and Loughran 2002; Conle *et al.* 1998; Guilfoyle *et al.* 2002). Since trusting relationships are fundamental to accomplishing the other goals of collaborative critical reflection, we felt a focus upon that issue – on whether and how we were able to generate caring relationships amongst ourselves and with our student teachers – was a sensible place to start.

A second reason for this focus is that this aspect of our work was consistently noted as a strong point in the reviews of our student teachers. The following comment is representative:

> Luz was fabulous! amazing! wonderful! supportive! generous with her time! nurturing! She consistently related her feedback to readings, which was extremely helpful. I always felt safe with her even when my lesson was partially falling apart. I wish that I could have been supervised every day because her critiques were always supportive and insightful. I felt that I was challenged each time to move my teaching forward. Initially I needed support and encouragement on classroom management, then on assessment and now I have been working on connecting the social/ emotional needs of students with moving the lesson forward. On each of these issues, she has helped me immensely!

We wanted to know more about how we were able to create a safe context for our student teachers, especially since in the heat of the moment we did not always feel confident about our nurturing efforts. We aimed also to be able to say something more to one another and to other teacher educators interested in critical reflection than 'you need to establish trust'. We wanted to understand more clearly what that process might look like, both in the moment and over time.

Fortunately, our first review of the data did give us a sense for what we were doing. It was clear to us that we were engaged in critical reflection and that we were transforming our thinking and our practice, and, in turn, the thinking and practice of our student teachers as a result. Our challenge became: How do we represent both our process and our findings to other teacher educators?

METHODOLOGICAL CHALLENGES

All five of us read the data: twenty-two transcripts of our supervisor meetings over the course of the year; our five dialogue journals; the two sets of supervisor evaluations; and the end-of-the-year questionnaires. We each made notes of instances of our own learning, both as documented in the data – transformations that occurred during the course of the year – and as lessons we were learning from the data analysis process, after the year was over. The former might be characterized as 'reflection-in-action' in Schön's (1983) terms, and the latter as 'reflection-on-action.' We knew that simply making lists of what we found would neither serve our purpose of better understanding our interpersonal process, nor be of much benefit to anyone else. Believing that our knowing was narrative knowing, we then decided to generate personal stories of self learning that would include instances of both what we had learned and how we had learned it. As an example, I include here my narrative.

Pretty please

Jean,[3] who referred to herself as the polite Canadian, had a habit of framing her requests to students as questions – questions that invited alternative responses: 'Will you please bring your papers to the front of the room?' 'Can you quiet down now?' I regularly pointed out to her that this might be confusing to some students, and that in certain circumstances might even invite chaos. Yes, in a student-centered, democratic classroom, we aim to provide children with the chance to voice their opinions, to have input into what they learn and how. But, even with such aims there will still be instances when we really do not want to provide options, when simple compliance is what is necessary. I suggested to her that if she really wanted everyone to come to the front of the room, she should tell them so, not ask, which could still be done respectfully, for example, with polite, yet directive vocabulary: 'Please come to the front of the room now.' Or as an 'I' statement that let them in on the reasons behind the request: 'I need you all to come to the front of the room now so that we can better hear Julio share his story.' Jean had trouble making the shift, in part, because evidence for the need to change was transitory and indefinite and, in part, because it was an aspect of her personal and cultural identity.

Meanwhile in our supervisor meetings and reflective journals, Luz had been sharing her practice of helping her student teachers to focus on student needs and student learning by bringing along to the debriefing sessions all of the student work produced during the lesson. For example, in one of our supervisor meetings in November Luz talked about the importance of using student work to determine whether lessons are providing equal access to all learners:

> That's why I think we need to really use student work . . . I was just thinking about how we need to get our students thinking about how to teach a lesson, how to understand what it is that you're going to teach, making sure that everybody has equal access to whatever it is that we're trying to do. And then, when we get a student's work back, we don't know what to do with it. Or we, sort of, we have a really hard time analyzing what it is that is happening. And I think that one of the things that we need to do is shift it and have a good foundation in defining these lessons, but also have good tools to look at these things that don't make sense and I, as a first year teacher, I think it's one of the biggest things.

Perhaps it should have been obvious to me before, that we ought to base our lesson reflections and assessments on an analysis of what the students actually produced. I had often directed student teacher attention to what I had seen on student papers or heard in group-work discussions, but never in a very systematic way. Luz's arguments convinced me that a more regular examination of full sets of student work could be beneficial in a number of important ways. As a result, I changed my practice. I started asking student teachers to collect all student work, if appropriate, at the end of their lessons and to bring it with them to their debriefings with me.

At a subsequent observation of Jean, we did just that. It was a fifth-grade math lesson on fractions. After some demonstrations and hands-on manipulations, Jean distributed a worksheet she had created that would give the students a chance to practice what they had been learning. One of the questions was constructed in this way: 'Can you now create and solve a similar problem of your own?' When reviewing the papers together afterward, we came to one where the student responded to that question in this way: 'NO, I can't.' This was one of those moments when you could see the proverbial light bulb go on above Jean's head: 'I finally see what you mean about the problem with framing my requests as questions.' This was a pivotal moment in Jean's developmental process, which is apparent in her reference to it in her mid-year review of me, her supervisor, in which she was asked to give an overall assessment and an example of where my feedback had translated into changed practice for her:

> I felt really lucky that Vicki was my supervisor. She was the perfect mix of stern, constructive, and nurturing all rolled into one. Even though I always experienced a tinge of nervousness with the advent of each observation, I also looked forward to them because they were such great learning experiences. Example of a translation of my feedback: First thing Vicki noticed was my voice control and use of words, the fact that I was giving orders/instructions but making them sound like requests. (We Canadians are very polite.) Anyway, I changed that and found that it helped my being explicit and it helped immeasurably in my classroom management. Also applied the same rule to my assignments that I make for the kids. Worked wonders.

Jean acknowledges here that she did change her practice with regard to that particular issue, in both her relational efforts and her assignment structures, and that she found it to be an improvement. In her end-of-the-year response to our questionnaire about supervision, five months later, she was asked to 'describe specific instances in which your supervisor had an effect on your development because of an interaction you had after an observation.' She wrote:

> I felt that I had had a bad lesson and that she witnessed my teaching at a time when things didn't go as I had planned. Vicki taught me to look

beyond that – she got me to look at the work that my students did from my lesson and made me realize that they were learning: moreover, what I had viewed as a poorly controlled classroom was not really the case. I learned how to let go a little more at that point.

Here Jean identifies the same practice – of looking at student work – more broadly. She moves beyond the circumscribed incident and issue, of how to formulate requests, to embrace the general value of looking carefully at student work to assess her effectiveness and student progress.

So, as a result of interactions with my fellow supervisors, deliberations about our mentoring, I decided to change my practice. The resultant change in my practice then had a demonstrable and lasting impact on Jean's understanding and the practice, which in turn transformed my knowledge about my work in important ways – the light bulb went on for me as well. I came to realize that a careful review of a full set of student work was more than just a useful strategy for demonstrating the need to alter particular behaviours such as request formulations. It was an embodiment of much of what we value in our credential program:

- It encouraged and facilitated teacher reflection based on evidence of student learning and student need, which, as Luz pointed out, is very hard to do and so requires frequent practice and careful scaffolding.
- Including all student responses in each analysis provided the opportunity to consider issues of equity – who was being reached and appropriately challenged by the lesson, and who was not and why.
- Careful review of student work could help to suggest how any behavioural challenges the student teacher experienced during a lesson might be related to student outcomes, and thus how their social/emotional/caring goals for their teaching are connected to the development of powerful subject matter knowledge.
- It could reveal where there might be evidence of cultural difference, and thus suggest the need for cultural accommodation.

As Roo, another supervisor, said in one of our meetings: 'The purpose of observations is not judgment, but to provide a common text for discussion – to give us the opportunity to engage in a meaningful conversation about education that will further our thinking.' Student work helps to render that experience text, to make debriefings such opportunities to engage with our student teachers in meaningful conversations about education – meaningful and transformative for both of us, which was a new and very illuminating way to characterize the experience for me.

The reason why this happened was that I was engaged in substantive, supportive dialogue and journaling with knowledgeable and passionate colleagues over time and I examined with them evidence provided by student teacher performance and commentary. It also happened because, in Jean's words, I provided 'the perfect mix of stern, constructive, and nurturing.' In her end-of-the-year questionnaire she talked about how the journal we shared supported her development:

> I think one of the biggest pluses of my journal was just the sheer emotional comfort and support I received. In Vicki's case, I went through all sorts of ups and downs, but was comfortable enough with her that I could be that open and really reveal, complain, ask, etc., of her. It really helped me with my second semester when I became a little more balanced and able to focus on greater issues of classroom development rather than student teacher angst.

Because her emotional needs were met early on in the program, Jean was then able to concentrate on learning what she needed to learn. Attention to the evidence, a focus on student work and student learning in systematic ways, was key to her move toward teaching guided by an inquiry orientation and equitable goals. The two – emotional nurturing and quality teaching – are not mutually exclusive; in fact, just the opposite. What I learned from this self-study is that we, both supervisors and student teachers, need time, support, critically reflective collegial interaction, and encouragement to do both.

CONCLUSION

The purpose of this chapter has been to share and interrogate one of the methods I utilize in my self-study research: critical reflection. Thus, I have not focused upon a discussion of the results of this research, though some should be apparent in the narrative. What I have shown is one way to use critical reflection as both a practice and a method in self-study and how dialogue, journaling, and story writing can aid in that process. I have also provided an exemplar for how the methodological challenge of the representation of critical reflection self-study might be met – through the telling of our stories. The initial success of this strategy is especially encouraging in the current international educational climate which is calling for simplistic formulas on how to engage in effective teacher education. Those of us in the field know that it is much more complex than that; that it is a context-specific, individualized, interpersonal, highly intellectual enterprise, but we have been hard-pressed to offer either convincing evidence of that fact or alternatives for self- and programmatic improvement that could substitute for iterative, disconnected standards and the associated standardized tests. Perhaps the direct representation of critical reflection self-study can help us to transform our own practice, and provide evidence that more holistic, responsive, and humane education is both necessary and do-able.

NOTES

1   I am indebted to my co-researchers in the primary study reported upon in this chapter for their input and general colleagueship: Sarah 'Roo' Cline, Debbie Mitchell, Tali Reicher, and Luz Salazar (see Cline *et al.* 2003).
2   This research was made possible (in part) by a grant from the Spencer Foundation. The statements made and the views expressed are solely the responsibility of the author.
3   All student teacher names are pseudonyms.

REFERENCES

Bass, L., Anderson-Patton, V. and Allender, J., 2002, Self-study as a way of teaching and learning: a research collaborative re-analysis of self-study teaching portfolios. In Loughran and Russell (Eds) *Improving Teacher Education Practices through Self-Study* (London: RoutledgeFalmer), pp. 56–69.

Berry, A. and Loughran, J., 2002, Developing an understanding of learning to teach in teacher education. In Loughran and Russell (Eds) *Improving Teacher Education Practices through Self-Study* (London: RoutledgeFalmer), pp. 13–29.

Bruner, J., 1986, *Actual Minds, Possible Worlds* (Cambridge, MA: Harvard University Press).

Clandinin, J. and Connelly, M., 1996, Teachers' professional knowledge landscapes: teacher stories – stories of teachers – school stories – stories of schools. *Educational Researcher*, 25(3), 24–30.

Cline, S., Laboskey, V.K., Mitchell, D., Reicher, T. and Salazar, L., 2003, The role of relationship in teacher education: self-study as interpersonal nurturing. Paper presented at the annual meeting of the American Educational Research Association, Chicago, IL.

Conle, C., Louden, W. and Mildon, D.A., 1998, Tensions and intentions in group inquiry: a joint self-study. In Hamilton (Ed.) *Reconceptualizing Teaching Practice: Self-Study in Teacher Education* (London: Falmer Press), pp. 178–93.

Cooper, J.E., 1991, Telling our own stories: the reading and writing of journals or diaries. In Witherell and Noddings (Eds) *Stories Lives Tell: Narrative and Dialogue in Education* (New York: Teachers College Press), pp. 96–112.

Guilfoyle, K., Placier, P., Hamilton, M.L. and Pinnegar, S., 2002, Exploring the concept of dialogue in the self-study of teaching practices. In Kosnik, Freese and Samaras (Eds) *Making a Difference in Teacher Education Through Self-study. Proceedings of the Fourth International Conference on Self-Study of Teacher Education Practices, Herstmonceux, East Sussex*, England (Vol. 1) (Toronto, Ontario: OISE, University of Toronto), pp. 96–103.

LaBoskey, V.K. and Richert, A.E., 2002, Identifying good student teacher placements: a programmatic perspective. *Teacher Education Quarterly*, 29(2), 7–34.

Lomax, P., Evans, M. and Parker, Z., 1998, For liberation . . . not less for love: a self-study of teacher educators working with a group of teachers who teach pupils with special educational needs. In Hamilton (Ed.) *Reconceptualizing Teaching Practice: Self-Study in Teacher Education* (London: Falmer Press), pp. 167–77.

Loughran, J. and Northfield, J., 1998, A framework for the development of self-study practice. In Hamilton (Ed.), *Reconceptualizing Teaching Practice: Self-Study in Teacher Education* (London: Falmer Press), pp. 7–18.

Lyons, N., 2002, Why narrative inquiry or exemplars for a scholarship of teaching? In Lyons and LaBoskey (Eds) *Narrative Inquiry in Practice: Advancing the Knowledge of Teaching* (New York: Teachers College Press), pp. 11–27.

Richert, A., Laboskey, V.K. and Kroll, L., 2000, Identifying good student teacher supervision: a programmatic perspective. Paper presented at the annual meeting of the American Educational Research Association, New Orleans, LA.

Schön, D., 1983, *The Reflective Practitioner: How Professionals Think in Action* (New York: Basic Books).

Schuck, S. and Segal, G., 2002, Learning about our teaching from our graduates, learning about our learning with critical friends. In Loughran and Russell (Eds) *Improving Teacher Education Practices through Self-Study* (London: RoutledgeFalmer), pp. 88–101.

Wilkes, G., 1998, Seams of paradoxes in teaching. In Hamilton (Ed.) *Reconceptualizing Teaching Practice: Self-Study in Teacher Education* (London: Falmer Press), pp. 198–207.

Chapter 13

Just where do I think I'm going?

Working with marginalized and disaffected youths and their self-study

Katharine Childs

> Work of sight is done; now do heart-work on the pictures within you.
> (Rainer Maria Rilke)

INTRODUCTION: JUST WHO AM I AND WHERE DO I THINK I'M GOING?

I am an adult educator and an academic mentor who teaches Language Arts to young adults in a full-time high school program in the Province of Quebec. The student population in my center could best be described as marginalized and generally disaffected; in fact, many of my students are young adults from 16–19 years of age who have previously been unsuccessful in school. A growing number of the people I teach have few academic skills; for the majority of them, my school is their last chance at getting a high school diploma – and perhaps qualifying for a job.

All students who want to get their diploma need to pass Senior English. The most difficult part of this course is the ten-page research paper; most students struggle to choose a subject and then find it difficult to produce the required ten pages. My role as a teacher then becomes one of motivation – of pushing and prodding, of suggesting and wheedling these reluctant students to write more and to finish as best they can.

I had just about become resigned to this unsatisfactory situation when one of my most capable students – a bright young woman whom I shall call 'Robin' – who was tired of the usual subjects and anxious to learn more, began to work on an autobiographical self-study. What I learned from working with her made me realize the tremendous power and promise that self-study possesses for significant learning. I also discovered that it was a wonderful tool that could be effectively used with young adult learners.

Since Robin, there have been several other students who have decided to write self-studies, many of them following her lead by using narrative vignettes, coupling them with poetry, photographs, and/or other image texts as a way of articulating their findings and helping others to connect to their experiences. The high quality of the work that these students have produced and the soundness and 'rigor' of their research have convinced me that allowing students the freedom and the responsibility to determine what and how they learn is worth 'bending the rules', of trying something new. Because of this, self-study autobiographical work is now firmly established as one of a number of options for research in my secondary level Language Arts classes.

THOUGHTS ABOUT SELF-STUDY

Self-study is a powerful tool for uncovering and discovering one's underlying values and the manner in which actions and beliefs intertwine. This form of critical reflection has been used almost exclusively by practitioners who study their own practice through the lens of their personal beliefs and values by adopting a form of autobiography or auto-ethnography (Cole and Knowles 1995) with the intention of aligning their practice more closely with their values.

Becoming reflective practitioners involves a process of on-going critical reflection and self-study, involving an in-depth look at our experiences and ourselves. Our interpretations of experience are shaped by our assumptions, by our biases, by our own worldviews. In the same way, those assumptions and beliefs shape our decisions and our responses. Any investigation into one's own practice should, therefore, be an account of uncovered assumptions and of on-going attempts to live up to one's professed beliefs.

The emphasis of self-study is usually placed on the growth and understanding that develops from critical reflection. Because it looks at the way that the personal and professional aspects of an individual impact and interact, I believe that studying oneself can be beneficial to all – practitioners and non-practitioners alike.

WHY I USE SELF-STUDY WITH HIGH SCHOOL STUDENTS

A number of practitioner friends of mine have wondered aloud whether self-study is appropriate for young adult learners and have asked me whether I have any idea of what I'm doing or where I'm going with this. Their main concerns seem to focus on the age and abilities of the young adult student in general, pointing out that many students this age have limited experiences to draw upon and that most of them probably aren't either mature enough or capable of reflecting upon those lived experiences they do have. When they read the work that some of my students like Robin have produced, they inevitably pass the rest off as being products of students who possess tremendous insight and superior abilities, choosing to believe that those students are exceptions and not the rule.

Although their concerns could be well founded, they have not considered an important point: self-study may not be right for everyone – be they practitioners or non-practitioners, experienced or inexperienced, mature or young, brilliant or not. I don't believe that every high school student can or should write a self-study any more than I feel that every practitioner can or should; many of us simply aren't ready to take that particular journey. I do believe, however, that self-study should be a viable option for those who are seriously willing to engage in this type of investigation, and I am more than ready to offer that opportunity to my students.

Self-study requires critical reflection

Probably the single most important aspect of a self-study is its use of critical reflection. Critical reflection itself is not limited to experienced adults, professionals or practitioners – that is, we are probably not born critical reflectors/reflective thinkers. Instead, this is a skill that needs to be taught, practiced, and refined. My own experience leads me to believe that very few people are immediately good at it. Of course, it would seem that the younger we are exposed to this type of processing, and the more we use it throughout our lives, the better we will become at it. If we educators want to see greater depth and scope in terms of reflective thought in the work that our students produce, then it would appear logical that we introduce it as early and whenever we can to the learner population. Self-study is one way in which this can be encouraged.

Self-study aids self-knowledge

In the same way that many of us have a 'felt need' to explore aspects of our personal and professional lives, so, too, there are those young adult students who feel the same way. In these days of constructivism and student-centered learning, self-study makes a tremendous amount of sense for those students who wish to focus on certain aspects of their lives, who wish to understand themselves in alternative individualized ways that might allow them to learn more effectively and well.

Self-study and self-knowledge should not be exclusive

To suggest that young adult learners might not have experiences worthy of investigation – or that they might in some way be incapable of deriving valuable lessons from those experiences or of learning from lessons drawn from experience – strikes me as being a bit short-sighted. High school students have, indeed, lived a number of years on this earth, accumulating valuable life experience that they are attempting to understand and put into perspective in the same way that the rest of us are. The desire to know and learn about ourselves and our place in the world is not restricted to certain age or vocational groups. Offering the possibility of doing self-study work to young adult learners may well be a leap of faith, but to me it is more than that: it's a question of valuing and a matter of trust.

WORKING WITH YOUNG ADULT LEARNERS: WHERE I THINK I'M GOING

I always hope that students will become so involved in what they're doing that they will care deeply about their research and the way that it is presented; usually this is the case, but not always, so it is very helpful to the students if I let them know what I feel a good self-study might contain.

Like any other piece of research, a self-study should be as 'polished' a piece of work as the student can make it, but there is something else that I find to be quite important – credibility. For me, the single most important expectation I have is that the self-study has a 'ring of truth' (Eisner 1991) – that it is eminently believable. A good self-study should demonstrate evidence of authentic growth and of lessons learned, and I believe it does so through the thoughtful gathering and use of artefacts and data as illustrations and verification.

Generally speaking, I see self-studies as searches for personal understandings of sorts, of attempts to come to terms with the whys that make up the who and the what we are as human beings, and the exploration of those perspectival factors in our lives that determine the ways in which we live and work in the world. Undertaking a self-study is a tremendously personal and usually difficult experience – one worthy of great respect. A completed self-study is, for me, a celebration of the individual: in so many ways, it is validation and valuation made visible.

AN EXAMPLE: WORKING ON SELF-STUDY WITH ROBIN

Robin came into my Senior English class in the middle of an academic year, which I found a bit unusual. She mentioned that she was sick of the local high school, but didn't volunteer anything else. In class, she was a very competent student, more than capable of even the most difficult English assignments. She was smart, always neatly dressed, pretty, always finished everything quickly and well – and she had attitude. Yet when it finally came to the research unit, Robin started floundering – quietly, but devastatingly

Her malaise became evident: she was bored and totally unengaged. When I finally asked her, 'What do you care about?', her answer was so simple that it was profound – and unusual in a young adult. She valued herself.

When she said that, it occurred to me that a self-study might be exactly the type of thing that Robin might enjoy. She was fascinated by the idea, and completely captivated by the notion that she could investigate herself as if she were a subject of great interest. I not only assured her that she could, but let her know that that was exactly what I was doing as part of my Master's thesis. We spoke a bit longer about what types of things might constitute data, and what could be considered as 'evidence', and then arranged to meet the next morning so that I could give her a couple of books and articles to read.

The next day – that first morning – established our working pattern: for at least three mornings a week for the next couple of months, I would arrive at a very early hour, unlock my room and unpack my briefcase – and there Robin would be, ready to work with me.

That morning I brought a couple of books on self-study, narrative, and methodology in general. As I turned them over to her, I remember wondering what had ever possessed me to think that a high school student might be interested in reading books like this, but Robin had seemed to be different. She flipped through them as we talked and I saw that she didn't seem to be looking as much for content, for answers, as she was for process, for a framework to help her structure her own information.

We finally decided to begin with the questions that most teacher researchers ask themselves, some of those basic questions that I had first been given to help me focus on my own research:

- What do you want to know?
- Why?
- What do you already know?
- How do you know it?

Some of her immediate responses involved her perception of herself as always having been different and having felt differently from other girls her age. We brainstormed ways she could gather information on herself to prove or disprove her theory. She decided to begin that very day by asking her two closest friends to list what they felt were her most outstanding traits, and to interview her mother and her sister to see what anecdotal evidence she could find to 'trace [her] uniqueness' ('Gibbson' 2001a). We looked forward to our meetings together, which were grounded in learning. I found that I was able to model some of the research behaviour that had been modeled for me by several of my more experienced research partners, but most importantly, we talked: we looked at each other's research and made comments and suggestions, we found paragraphs and chapters in books that seemed to support our evidence and shared them with each other, we speculated on how best to present material. We became research as well as mentoring partners.

Our job in those early stages was to gather as much information, data, evidence as possible. Robin would decide what to do with it. I realized that I had immediately begun this as an adult relationship with Robin, even though she was fairly young. I had approached her quite frankly as a fellow learner and treated her as a fellow researcher. I was doing more than modeling research techniques: this was learning the way I wanted to see it – in myself and in others.

Robin felt that there was at least one other side of her that people didn't see, that the side of herself that she presented to the world didn't reveal:

> In the eye of the public, the [Robin Gibbson] that most people believe they see, is this snobby little girl with an attitude. They think I am better than everyone else, like a rich brat who receives everything she wants with the snap of her fingers. These people, fellow students, see me walking in the halls and automatically do not want to spark up a conversation with me. I guess I don't have a friendly face, and people are afraid.
>
> My friends, who see the public me, think that I don't have a single care in the world. When I am not walking with my head high, I choose to take it easy, nice and calm. The public aspect of me is very sarcastic. I will try to make a joke out of anything, just to relieve any tension within myself.
>
> All of my little 'public' characteristics began in primary school . . . Primary school was the beginning of my public face. The snobby little character that most see, isn't in fact a lie, it is what they see because that is what I want them to see . . . this is the reason why I wear my public mask.
>
> ('Gibbson' 2001b, pp. 1–2)

Her focus became trying to find evidence to support or topple her claim that her public side of being sarcastic, snobby, and determined was a mask to protect her private side, which she saw as being highly creative, self-reliant, and imaginative.

During this time, members of the class were watching. They saw research data and artefacts being collected, selected, and manipulated. Many of them now point to the beginning of Robin's research as the moment when they started thinking about what they wanted to do for their research project.

When Robin was ready, she presented her research to an audience made up of her fellow classmates and a couple of teachers. Her self-study ended with the following:

> My reflections, creations and ideas hold a final purpose. They hold my future. This effectively made me face some of the most difficult aspects

in my life. I now know that I must indulge a little more of myself to the public. I need to let the public discover how beautiful I am on the inside. Studying my inner child reminded me, that I am extremely talented, and that I have the potential to accomplish anything I wish. My private life influences me to become aware of my feelings, and act upon them. My over all [*sic*] view is that I may never completely understand myself, and that is more than enough for me now.

('Gibbson' 2001b, p. 11)

To me, this is very powerful writing, writing that indicates the kind of thinking that I hope to encourage in my students.

Robin's self-study was a watershed for the class and especially for me as a teacher: never again would the research paper be the same, never again would I be able to look at student research in quite the same way as I had previously. From that moment on, the research paper took on a far more personal and pertinent aspect. It became a vehicle of exploration, scholarship, celebration, and personal validation.

CONDITIONS ON SELF-STUDY WORK

I feel that, whenever possible, work submitted as a self-study should comply with 'accepted' research techniques. It should be focused around a thoughtful research question, include a thesis or artist's statement, and have a reference section and references cited wherever possible. Written self-studies should conform to normal mechanical considerations in terms of word usage, spelling, and grammar.

Although I try not to interfere too much with the author's voice or the actual writing of a self-study, I do insist that in-text citations and references be used. This is probably because of a couple of things – not the least being that I feel it 'legitimizes' the entire process. Since one of the requirements for the research paper in the provincially approved program is that a list of sources be included, I feel that this is one way that my students who have chosen to do self-study can appear to be abiding by some of the 'rules'.

Unlike the traditional research paper, a self-study does not necessarily need to rely on a group of outside sources for information. Based on critical reflection and often on memory work, self-studies may use outside sources as memory prompts or confirmation, but rarely for much more than that. Consequently, I do insist that students involved in self-study work read some of the literature published on or about self-study, and that they investigate various readings concerning, for example, the narrative (and/or poetic) form, image texts, memory work, etc. – depending on the methods they may decide to use. It seems only logical to me that students openly acknowledge the deliberate decisions that they make in terms of the ways in which they frame their work – and making a connection to the relevant literature in their work is an appropriate way to do that. I ask that they do this partly from a sense of duty and respect for the work that goes into all research, and partly from a sense of inclusion, a desire to welcome them into the 'fold' as self-study people and fellow researchers.

To begin with, I like students to be aware that there is valuable and pertinent information out there for them to access and use, and that this literature should be consulted and then 'honoured' by being cited. Second, I hope that by asking them to acknowledge these connections and research contributions they will realize that they are not alone, that they are becoming a part of a particular literary and research tradition, and that they are joining a group as fellow researchers. By being rigorous and responsible enough in their research to include the mention of relevant readings they have encountered, I feel that others will be more likely to consider the work that they do as actual contributions to the field of self-study.

THE BASICS

There is a definite mentoring aspect to my work with students. Much of the way that I teach relies strongly on the relationship and the rapport that I build with each individual. The teaching-learning process, therefore, becomes quite dynamic in nature because it builds upon what each learner knows, and how that particular person learns. Of course, because each student is so very different, there seems to be no quick and simple recipe – no one single tried and true method that I can consistently use; instead, I use whatever works with the particular individual.

In spite of these individual (and frequently unpredictable) variations, there are three common threads in the way that I approach self-study with each of the people who have chosen this research option:

1   I set the stage for our work together, using a friendly yet respectful conversational tone, often asking questions to help focus the research.
2   I make time and space for this work with frequent one-on-one conferences.
3   We work together as co-learners and co-researchers, sharing our work and acting as 'critical friends'.

I believe that this acceptance and caring concern for the individual, for each person's distinctive voice, and for the emotional learning journey that each one of us embarks upon is essential for a 'successful' self-study.

1. Setting the stage: first steps

The basic procedure that I use when working with anyone on a self-study follows the general pattern I established with Robin. This involves a number of one-on-one discussions, non-judgmental conversations that explore the student's answers to the following questions:

- What do you want to know?
- Why?
- What do you already know?
- How do you know it?
- What do you care about?
- What evidence can you provide to support those perceptions and to convince others of this?
- How can you best present this information – in what form(s) – so that others can understand and connect on various levels with your experiences and your findings?

This idea of using questions to help with decision-making corresponds to a Quaker practice called the 'Clearness Committee'. The person looking for answers or solutions articulates the problem as clearly as possible to the committee who has gathered to help. The helpers cannot offer answers or solutions; they are confined to asking only questions. Usually before much time has elapsed, it becomes evident that the individual has had the appropriate inner answers all along – and that those questions that have been asked have actually served to uncover and reveal it.

Palmer (1998) talks about this same process of respect by referring to it as paying attention 'to a voice before it is spoken' (p. 46). I interpret this to mean that making space for other people and honouring them means not rushing silences with speeches of our own and not trying to force them into saying things we want to hear – in essence, being open enough to hear (and accept) another's truth. This is tremendously important in all aspects of teaching and research, but acceptance of this nature is essential when dealing with young adults whose voices do not always seem to be heard or considered valid in our school systems.

2. Making time and space

Finding time and space to work individually with a student is one of the many challenges we face in our day-to-day teaching life, yet the emotional aspects inherent in working with self-study indicate that students need to be continually supported as they stretch, risk, and explore. Being sensitive to the individual personal needs of young adult learners as they negotiate the often tricky and muddy waters of self-study is vitally important to the way that they may view their 'success' as people and as researchers.

Because of its very personal nature and the fact that it is not a traditional form of research, I believe that it is vitally important to establish a support system for each student undertaking this work – a support that will be sustained throughout the entire research process (from conception through 'publication'). The best way to do this is to be able to conference daily with each and every individual who is working on a self-study; unfortunately, the reality of my teaching life makes this close day-to-day contact difficult. Making space for a self-study research consultation in the midst of all the demands that a busy classroom and other students place upon me is a bit tricky, yet I try to make a point to do it as often as possible because I feel that it is important to confirm and nourish each student as an emerging researcher and to validate the work that that person is doing.

Because I am convinced that this type of support is important, I have had to learn how to be more flexible and creative in the use of my time, grabbing moments whenever and wherever students and I can fit a chunk of time in – before school, after school, during mealtimes, in the evenings, and even on the weekends, if necessary. I take my role as 'critical friend' as seriously as my own critical friends have taken theirs: students have my home phone number and my e-mail address and I assure them that I will do my best to get back to them as quickly as I can should they feel they need me during non-school hours.

Many times we use a tape recorder or a video camera in our sessions together just so that we can have a record or a memory prompt of our work. This has proven to be a wonderful tool: it can work as a placeholder, providing us with a place or a conversation to start up another session, or as a device to prompt student writing and/or promote further reflection.

3. Working together

Researchers come in all shapes and sizes – and ages. Working with a student as a co-learner and co-researcher can be a wonderful space to inhabit. I strive to be continually open to new ideas and different representations, without censure or preconceived notions of what research is, or what others say it should be.

I do, however, have a bit of a bias about learning that extends into much of what I do and the way that I view research: I believe that personal experience is a source of valuable knowledge, a knowledge that reflects the diversity of real life and resonates with its complexities. Using this as a resource gives us an opportunity to examine our actions and to consciously construct and reconstruct a personal identity that responds to a newly transformed worldview. Mitchell and Weber (1999) refer to this same process as the 'pedagogy of reinvention' (p. 8).

This is research that requires a continuously questioning and open mind. Trying to maintain that openness to new ideas is one of the ways which leads to our perpetual becoming and growth as aware and 'wide-awake' (Greene 1978) individuals.

As I work with students, I try to make the process a bit more comprehensible and comfortable for them by modeling appropriate research techniques in terms of the type of questions we ask and the way we examine data.

In self-study, the manner in which we look at problematic experiences involves several steps: first, we scrutinize and clarify those complex situations in terms of the data and our personal interpretations of them; next, we examine our own assumptions based on those interpretations; and then, we frame and reframe those experiences in a variety of ways and perspectives in order to better understand and learn about ourselves. Finally, we try to decide on how to represent and communicate this new knowledge in ways that are both personally satisfying and aesthetically pleasing.

Because I seem to be continually at work on various aspects of my own self-study, this modeling process usually takes on very real dimensions. Often after discussions about data, I will bring in some of my own to analyze or work on. In a like manner, when we are working on the writing aspect, I am apt to consult students about the wording of certain passages in my own work that I find problematic – over and above the work we do together on their writing. Frequently, we team up to work on the various images or pictures we have chosen, carefully sorting, placing and rearranging them, going back and forth from one person's work to the other's until we are both satisfied with the results.

I have found that when students are placed in the role of being 'critical friends' and are seriously regarded as fellow researchers, they begin to understand first-hand how challenging and rewarding self-study can be – all the while learning that research is something that can, indeed, be undertaken and shared with another.

CONCLUSION: OUR STUDENTS/OURSELVES

Teaching – good teaching – demands a respect for life and learning. Self-study may well be one of the greatest tools we teachers have that embodies that belief, that can foster the kind of healthy respect and recognition of the individual that is essential to lifelong learning. Engaging in self-study teaches us that we teachers and teacher educators must first learn to take our beliefs and ourselves seriously – to learn to listen and pay attention to our own voices so that we can then take those we teach just as seriously. This is a chain reaction that is part of the profession we have chosen.

What I have learned from others is that it is important that we make connections between what and how we learn and what and how we teach. We know that when we teach – no matter what the subject matter may be – we actually teach what we value and love; therefore, in order to foster stronger and more thoughtful teachers and students, we educators need to value authentic and on-going self-reflection in ourselves and in others. I believe that we need to teach it when and how we can, and build it into the very foundations of our academic systems.

What I have discovered in my work with young adult learners is that self-study is a powerful tool for all those who choose to use it. If it can be used effectively by young adult learners who are relatively inexperienced in the research process and generally not accustomed to academic work, then it is, indeed, a wonderful vehicle for authentic self-development and enhancing new understandings about teaching and learning. My own work with students indicates that self-study is capable of engaging even the most disaffected individuals. When students realize that they are experts in this subject (themselves), their interest in learning and their use of critical reflection expands: their writing then becomes stronger and filled with their own distinctive voices. This, in turn, propels them onward – towards pride in oneself and in one's work.

REFERENCES

Cole, A.L. and Knowles, J.G., 1995, Methods and issues in a life history approach to self-study. In Russell and Korthagen (Eds) *Teachers Who Teach Teachers: Reflections on Teacher Education* (London: Falmer Press), pp. 130–51.

Eisner, E.W., 1991, *The Enlightened Eye: Qualitative Inquiry and the Enhancement of Aesthetic Experience* (New York: Macmillan).

'Gibbson', R., 2001a, Self-study research diary: November, 2000–May, 2001. Unpublished raw data.

'Gibbson', R., 2001b, The three within. Unpublished manuscript.

Greene, M., 1978, *Landscapes of Learning* (New York: Teachers College Press).

Mitchell, C. and Weber, S., 1999, *Reinventing Ourselves as Teachers: Beyond Nostalgia* (London: Falmer Press).

Palmer, P., 1998, *The Courage to Teach: Exploring the Inner Landscapes of a Teacher's Life* (San Francisco: Jossey-Bass).

Chapter 14

Pathlamp

A self-study guide for teacher research

Carol A. Mullen and William A. Kealy

THE PATHLAMPS PROJECT: LIGHTING THE WAY FOR NOVICE RESEARCHERS

This case study is for teacher researchers who are interested in applying theory to practice in partnership settings. We define *teacher researcher* inclusively to mean those university students researching in school settings, pre-service university students preparing for school careers and as teacher educators, and teacher educators committed to reflective inquiry and teaching practice.

Here, teacher researchers are invited to take a stroll along an unlit walkway. Imagine being alone and having to find your destination without a map or directions. Picture yourself walking along a path that leads to a house in suburban woodland. It is a moonless night. Groping in the dark, you feel for the edge of the path with your foot. Tentatively proceeding, your arm scrapes against something rough. Then you bump your head on a tree bough (ouch!). Working your way to the journey's end, you fumble about to flip a light switch. A door illuminates. Looking back, the pathway now seems all too obvious. You survey the meandering trail, noting the accidentally trodden flowerbed and the points at which your physical injuries occurred. You wonder what safeguards might assist future travelers.

Struggling in the dark while learning how to conduct school-based action research – alone and without a guide – is a familiar scenario. While one can argue that this 'growth opportunity' is essentially a trial-by-fire, we believe this is an antithetical consequence of learning to do research. By contrast, mentoring accounts that offer a 'behind the scenes' view can be of enormous benefit to new researchers.

But even a well-lit walkway may pose dangers for the teacher researcher-traveler trying to spot the ruts and crevices along the way. When a researcher stumbles from an unexpected setback, what are some ways for getting quickly back on track? Experienced teacher researchers reflect after overcoming an obstacle, perhaps asking themselves: What could have been done differently? What ethical issues and concerns arose that could have been revealed more readily? What twists and turns or unplanned forces were encountered? Also, how might problems that arose during the process have been approached differently or even reframed as opportunities for deeper connection and material for writing?

Reflecting on experience, what do teacher researchers learn from their action research projects that may be helpful in guiding others? Metaphorically put, what *pathlamps* or mentoring strategies might teacher researchers put in place during their research journeys to serve as guiding steps for doing teacher research? Pathlamps that signify pivotal or breakthrough approaches might even be 'best practices' in action research. Figure 14.1, 'Pathlamp for planting,' is our visual guide that encourages anyone who has taken the teacher researcher journey to share their deeper learning with the academic community.

In this spirit and based on our own introspection, we discuss some ideas here that can be used for developing a school-based research guide. We underscore productive, empowering, and ethical action for teacher researchers using autobiographical techniques. These take the form of personal footpaths created with two purposes in mind: to aid effective mentoring and provide material that can be adapted or critiqued. Such self-study or auto-ethnographic approaches to memory emphasize reflection and invention, and help 'make the past usable [and] illuminate and transform the present' (Mitchell and Weber 1999, p. 5).

Figure 14.1 Pathlamp for planting.

Researchers can realize their own teaching capacity or mentoring responsibility by 'planting pathlamps' (or footlamps) for others. This can involve a process of *self-study*, which Mitchell and Weber (1999) say is 'not only about ourselves . . . it serves other teachers and students, and can provide both the impetus and the blueprint for change' (p. 217). To successfully assist others, as we see it, there are at least two approaches: (1) light the walkway – that is, offer external forms of support to the teacher researcher, and (2) provide a map – give the traveler access to professional knowledge or internal support.

We think of it this way: If you had just completed a challenging hike from here to there, how might you guide others taking a similar path? One way would be to install a spotlight and then sweep away debris to make the path more visible or install a railing to steady walkers' steps. Another strategy involves sharing one's story of the journey with prospective travelers that illuminates the pathway taken to reveal clues. We all benefit from inheriting stories about the 'ruts' and 'crevices' – barriers, mistakes, ambiguities, and surprises – encountered by others. However, even with assistance the research journey to be taken must be forged to the traveler.

Teacher researchers have various kinds of assistance at their disposal. Examples include the organizational structure in the schools, administrative personnel and faculty, and cultural rituals. It is reassuring to remember that teachers and administrators can, because of their training in making complicated ideas accessible, help frame and implement a research project in a way that makes it less daunting. Also turn to the information available on-site, such as official reports, documents, and program curricula. This category of 'external support' also refers to trappings of the research practice itself: Surveys, inventories, and technologies (e.g. electronic servers, tape recorder). In this chapter, we present successful pathways for carrying out school research.

A SELF-STUDY GUIDE FOR TEACHER RESEARCH

This self-study guide is for teacher researchers who are partnership-oriented and hence value collaborating across university and school domains. It is specifically for those seeking ideas and techniques for taking this journey. We highlight the importance of learning from others' footpaths combined with self-study practice – strategies for empowering one's capacity to be an inquirer. While algorithms and checklists have their place, they can sometimes devolve into 'cookbook' approaches that undermine reflective thought, suspend critical judgment, and abdicate intellectual responsibility. The footpaths we propose do not dictate or predict the shape of the story told and ways of living and telling it. On the contrary, we view the process of learning from others' experiences as broadly creative opportunities for shaping our own research journeys and decision-making, not as templates to be imitated.

It is natural for novice researchers to long for maps that will support the success of their projects. Those searching for footholds can learn from the chalk marks, grips, and knots of others whose discoveries hint at complex decision-making, breakthroughs, compromises, and even hardships. Experienced researchers can also offer guidance by demystifying how their work was actually undertaken and how it unfolded. In this way, novices benefit not as blind followers but as informed agents who can in turn extend the circle of knowing available to others.

Beyond technique, in this text we raise issues about the underlying theoretical and cultural frameworks that shape action research studies. Through such dialogue, research 'maps' can be created that convey to new teacher researchers and the entire school/university community alike more empowering ways of doing research. We have grounded this text in the lessons learned and the knowledge generated from our own relevant research and that of others. Hence, the pathlamps we discuss are not randomly planted but rather optimally placed on the research pathway so that newcomers can traverse this foreign territory with sure-footedness.

Teachers, administrators, and other school personnel are traditionally cast as gatekeepers, data producers, and participants in research. Such stances feed the persistence of norms in educational research that fail to provide footholds for emancipatory or non-conformist, status-defying relationship building (Mullen 1999). We expose some of the ethical issues embedded in research and possible solutions based on our revisioning process.

Pathlamps to plant

 Offer practical guidance and professional knowledge to novice school researchers.

 Assist by establishing external and internal forms of support.

 Provide maps that give beginning researchers a sense of direction for their projects.

FINDING THE FOOTPATH: HOW TO GET STARTED

Even as a beginning researcher, you have influence. Consider how tourists obtain critical information from insiders to find their way, using this knowledge to adapt, improvise, and culturally adjust to the unfamiliar surroundings. Similarly, 'researcher insiders' give recent arrivals assistance and advice about the domain of inquiry that makes all the difference.

As a newcomer, turn to school/university professionals to become your supporters, critical friends, and maybe even research partners. In addition to inviting people to participate in your research, you can join others in their projects, building a network through reciprocity. As you mesh the needs of others with your own, it is also important that the needs of the group take into consideration the goals and interests of each member.

You will soon realize that you have less control over your study than anticipated. Exerting the will to have things 'just so' will be compromised by the contextual realities and obstacles you will no doubt encounter; always remember that you are dependent on the goodwill and investment of the insiders. Further, absolute control, even if it were possible, might be un-desirable. In the 'give and take' of everyday life, serendipitous events often provide new insight and richer, more meaningful experiences. For instance, a PE coach, who at first may have been overlooked by you, could embody deep historical knowledge of the local context.

Given this dimension of the unseen in your setting, you will want to participate in what appear to be tangential school events and rituals. Accept invitations to do so. You can establish a footing on the inside in a range of ways to help foster your research goals. For example, introduce yourself and your project to key stakeholders and top leaders; invite colleagues to join your project and related opportunities that arise; and distribute a research statement addressing how your project fits with the mission of the institution. Think about how to contribute to the survival and success of future research at the school site – part of the legacy we owe others.

Also reflect on the private or public dimensions of your project and how best to handle these. Darling-Hammond and co-authors (1994) caution that many innovative projects need to escape notice until they have become strong enough to take root. But new research studies can also be fostered within the mainstay of school environments, and with the visible support of leadership. To what extent might public visibility facilitate or hinder your project? For example, you might avoid announcing your project to the top leadership at your university or school if your primary contact advises otherwise. Likewise, it makes sense to seek counsel from leaders. Some might recommend, for example, that a public announcement be made for soliciting volunteers.

As mentioned, the tactic of low visibility for ensuring the success of an innovative project is not always the best route. The Partnership Support Group (PSG) that Carol Mullen formed at a school/university collaborative in Florida in the late 1990s seemed ripe for peripheral operation (Mullen and Lick 1999). Given the serious lapse in a shared vision between the school and university at the time, in addition to the facilitator's newness to the culture, the researcher could have opted for a low profile until support was secured. But key decision-making events occurred early on that brought public visibility and high interest to the project. Consequently, top leaders, mid-career practitioners, and beginning teachers all merged as synergistic players who contributed to this study of collaborative mentorship. The sixteen participants included membership of respected leaders; in this case, the public dimension of the work proved crucial.

Pathlamps for creating a footpath

Based on the PSG project and other school/university projects resulting from our leadership and participation (e.g. Mullen and Lick 1999), we offer some pathlights. Together, these may assist novice researchers in gaining a foothold within their own places of study.

IRB approval. Have your project endorsed by the university's Institutional Review Board (IRB) and also by the school's research committee. Read about the IRB process on the Internet to learn how this federal policy informs both national and regional policies (Mullen 1999). Expect to undergo two official approval processes through the university and school channels. The IRB process governing schools may require compliance with a separate set of policies; any products of the study, such as final reports and publications, are filed at the school site. The school leader's annual productivity briefs may reference your documents – media publicity could also follow, so use jargon-free language in all communications that include synopses and outcomes of the research. Relevant requests of a school's leadership must be respected.

Talk with key administrators at the school to obtain a practical foothold. Also consider the issue of 'fit' – to what extent are your research goals 'do-able' given the school's mission, values, and resources? Address this matter of congruence in your IRB protocol and, more importantly, in your orientation to the school. Meet with insiders to clarify the study objectives and identify areas of support. Document conversations and follow up with a summary. Such processes are essential for facilitating entry and building trust.

Formalize your invitation to a targeted audience. Ask your point of contact – the school's research coordinator or someone else – if you can announce your project (goals and invitation). One context for this purpose is a staff meeting. Your insider might want to inform the staff of who you are, what you plan to do, and what you need to be successful. It is good practice for a research plan to be circulated to leaders and potential participants.

If you will be addressing the staff, see yourself as a symbiotic agent, not as an outsider bent on satisfying your research needs. Address the school's goals or vision. Share a relevant story, incorporate facts about the school, or mention points of pride. Discuss any research conducted by the staff and how your own project complements or extends it. Invite your audience (e.g. teachers) to join you in exploring a topic of interest. If this is a dissertation, it is all the more critical to be 'other-oriented.' Focus on how the school can benefit, perhaps through accommodations of the faculty's workload, support of professional development, or modeling of particular skills. Share the purpose of the project, the timeline, and the specific steps to be taken.

For the PSG effort, Carol Mullen's sharing at the first school staff meeting of the year highlighted these points: the value of community building between the school and university; mentoring within a heterogeneous group of professionals and on a shared action research study; previous projects on mentoring, self-study, and action research; and writing a book for publication, with the contributors as authors (Mullen and Lick 1999).

In various contexts you can solicit input. Avoid being too tentative and wide open or too narrow and overly specialized. Invite your audiences to shape the project collaboratively. A primary goal here is to be flexible enough with your own project goals to generate interest and build momentum. The staff will try to 'get a handle' on the commitment required for your project relative to the time required and the payoff for personal investment. Address these issues without being prompted. Obtain names and contact information. Follow up with an official invitation and a clear plan that addresses any feedback received. Rethink your study through the lenses of your informants.

Encourage stakeholders and leaders to join. If appropriate, instead of involving primary stakeholders on the sidelines only, offer them a role to play in your project. Exhibit confidence in your capabilities as well as your study, and a constant willingness to learn from the insiders. Your success at the site relies to some degree on influential members (e.g. popular teachers) whose collective goals (e.g. generating a data-based school profile) or personal goals (e.g. learning to write for a public audience) ideally converge with your intentions.

Two important questions for shaping your project are: What role could top leaders and influential stakeholders have in my project? And what criteria do I have for involvement in my project? Criteria could include strong mentoring and leadership qualities, a value for applied research in schools, community-based involvement and knowledge, risk-taking and responsiveness to program innovation, diversity and affirmative action advocacy, strong problem-solving skills in groups, and more. Those leaders and stakeholders who would sincerely like to become involved but are unable to attend meetings can be accommodated as 'extended collaborators.' Some may even be willing to participate via conference calls or telecasting.

Strive to exhibit a strong problem-solving capacity during the lifespan of your site-based project. The scenario that follows is from a 1998 meeting of the PSG of the Florida collaborative. This audio-recording segment demonstrates how the participants mutually found solutions to problems.

Participant speaker (university administrator): My problem is that I don't have enough data to prove that the mentoring program we established in the College of Education for untenured faculty of color was as effective as it appeared to those of us who directed and experienced it. It became obvious that the untenured faculty could become successful in terms of tenure and promotion, but we failed to determine whether their success was a direct correlation of time spent with designated mentors.

Responder 1 (university professor): Concepts of data and validity have changed in the social sciences. Narrative qualitative methods give importance to storytelling, experiences, and memories. Even 'significance' can be thought of in nonstatistical terms as a quality relationship that has had an impact on one's professional development and career. In other words, you can reconstruct the event to highlight its value.

Responder 2 (school administrator): Yes, all of that but you [to the participant speaker] can also collect data even now to develop a retrospective picture and assessment of the program. You could interview some of the protégés and even mentors in your university program to learn what this experience has meant in their lives.

Hold meetings at the school. By holding project meetings at the site, the value of the local context is communicated and an appreciation fostered. The importance of this symbolic gesture and ritual cannot be overstated. It signals a range of political and practical messages, namely that researchers understand the schedules of school personnel to be less flexible than their own, and that school researchers are equal to university researchers. The PSG always met in the school's media center, a building that was literally located on the walkway adjoining the school and university – a symbolic, unifying image of collaboration.

Consider having an 'open door' policy during your project meetings. Why? (1) to invite those who are curious to join the endeavor, (2) to replace those members who may withdraw, (3) to dissipate any suspicions or jealousies by nonmembers, and (4) to create momentum for community building that respects the fluidity and spirit of membership in a volunteer project.

Pathlamps to plant

 Obtain IRB approval for your research project and accommodate the school's mission.

 Exert influence as a researcher but also understand that forces will shape the conditions of your work.

 Decide how private or public you want your project to be.

 Encourage a gatekeeper to introduce you and your project to the target population.

FROM TENTATIVE STEPS TO CONFIDENT STRIDES: USING RESEARCH MAPS

We next offer three research maps: *traditional-historical*, *traditional-progressive*, and *progressive-radical*. Each one provides a basic theoretical orientation to school-based research. The first and second portraits underscore that the socialization of university researchers sets the tone for 'participation' in school culture that is limiting. We believe that researchers need to search for ways to conduct inquiry that light the walkways between universities and schools.

The research maps we present reflect an ideological grounding of teacher research, broadly speaking, in a traditional model, a more current model, and an emerging possibility. We see ourselves as ideologically grounded in what we portray as a 'progressive' worldview. However, the first two models have been a core part of our academic socialization where progressive thinking and action can amount to 'wishful thinking' (Mitchell and Weber 1999). As dissertation directors, we have found that institutional models are antiquated, in part because these do not encourage student researchers to negotiate the role and needs of schools.

Before turning to the maps, we wish to emphasize that the sources cited within each are *not* intended to categorize them but merely to illustrate some key ideas.

Pathlamp: Traditional-historical map. This research model can have the unintended effect of working *on* rather than *with* others to achieve mutual goals. Underscored are issues of abstract generalization, data gathering, and analysis, rather than local theory and human interests. The issue of negotiation with 'subjects' is relevant only in the context of the researcher's goals, which, it is presumed, are to be selflessly accommodated by one's participants. Also, the idea for this type of work is to reduce complexity and control for human interference.

In contrast, local theory (the thrust of research maps no. 2 and no. 3) wrestles with how to change school cultures for the better (Rorty 1995). Local theory brings to the fore human-powered stories of those who 'have been marginalized . . . or forgotten in the telling of official narratives' (Peters and Lankshear 1996, p. 3). Local theory compels activist agendas that promote 'vigilance against the predictable attempts by the rich and the strong' (Rorty 1995, p. 204). Stories matter and they can inflame activism.

The traditional model tacitly endorses exploitation of what Rorty refers to as 'the poor and the weak.' This allows for a self-serving, authoritative perspective on knowledge, ownership, and even reality. It also resists the use of critical, feminist discourses relative to authority, power, gender, and race. The traditional-historical model perpetuates a view of reality that depends on the separation of classes for socioeconomic privilege and educational opportunity. Critically speaking, from this worldview democracy has been infected with a cancer – for many who are disenfranchised have been programmed as such by being structurally disadvantaged.

The traditional-historical model presents life from a distant cultural perspective. As Heilbrunn (1996) asserts: 'The scientific quest for a generic model of leadership can take one only so far . . . the field repeatedly loses sight of one of the principal reasons for its subject's essentially unpredictable nature – the environment in which leaders function' (p. 8). General theory creates distance from 'ordinary' people by, for example, using numbers to represent hardship. Statistical abstractions substitute for human lives. However unintentional, the effect can be dehumanizing.

Pathlamp: Traditional-progressive map. Traditional-progressive map users elect to 'know' differently as investigators, even if only vicariously. Consider how Kozol (1991) writes about kids who are 'handicapped by scarcity' – such as the boy who, when asked where he lived, responded, 'Times Square Hotel,' a homeless shelter in Manhattan. When we describe such powerful events, we can connect deeply with our readers, possibly stimulating action. A salient marker for research map no. 2 is the educator's responsibility to improve the quality of others' lives. Fullan (1997) reminds us that '[l]eadership with a small "l" has to do with how we all can exert greater control in the complexities of everyday experiences' (p. 225). Change must be made 'with' our clients, not 'for,' 'to,' or 'on' them.

Variations on the current traditional-progressive model connote shifts in the educational field. Notably, the popularity of using narrative to understand school culture and critique research culture is evident in studies of practitioner knowledge and researcher activism. An example of the traditional-progressive model is participatory action research (PAR). This North American framework was derived from the grassroots movement in Brazil that activist Paulo Freire (1996) perpetuated. The PAR model upholds principles of collective negotiation and confrontational dialogue among research parties. A new research ethic supports reaching out to participants who are disenfranchised relative to the context at hand, not to the lives of Brazilian peasants. Action researchers' use of the PAR model focuses on moving beyond the creation of shared knowledge to changing organizations; for example, co-authorship and shared reward as possibilities for educational change have not seeped into political self-consciousness.

Yet another example of the traditional-progressive model is the post-modern feminist framework. Among other re-culturing agendas, this expands the role of self, voice, and method in research and teaching (Mitchell and Weber 1999). New educational discourses include *collaborative co-mentoring* where researchers and participants together deconstruct power while honoring cultural diversity (Mullen and Lick 1999).

Another current initiative spearheads study of the expressive side of organizations through emotion and symbol (Bolman and Deal 1997). Notably, Hargreaves (1998) and Fullan (1997) identify the 'emotional politics' of schools. Emotions are political – they can be catalysts for change. However, human emotions are often subsumed through mechanisms of repression. Resurrecting a countering gaze, arts-based educational research offers a hybrid of emotional politics and personal expression (e.g., Barone and Eisner 1997).

The traditional-progressive model values change agency. Lieberman and Grolnick (1997) critique the researcher's exclusive expert status and engage participants in constructing cultural knowledge. This ethical orientation has yet to become an ingrained part of teacher research. It signals a transformative phase in teacher research – shifting from *thinking about* studying egalitarian practice to actually *doing* this. Such re-culturing efforts depend on self-study practice, partly because it is challenging to translate vision into practice and partly because 'it is tempting to think that we can easily change what we do' (Mitchell and Weber 1999, p. 229).

Pathlamp: Progressive-radical map. For university researchers, authorship is a vital source of power, status, and reputation. Yet, we are not generally encouraged to consider innovations in authorship in our institutional collaborations. Nor have school practitioners been socialized to expect credit for their research contributions or to see activism as a form of dissemination. Mainstream research pathways presume a narrow view of authority, privilege, status, and reward. An alternative path would force researchers to set, implement, and assess research goals collaboratively as authentic change agents.

Ethics is at the center of the progressive-radical model, shaping everything from the researcher's perspective to research outcomes. This model deliberately aims to enrich the lives of participants. Those embodying this worldview reflect on the shortcomings of their academic socialization and on the need to compensate as 'self-giving' professionals. In contrast, it is easy to assume that teachers lack the ability to conduct research and represent their own learning. Has this bias been inadvertently used as a rationale for negating the contributions of practitioners?

Central to progressive forms of action research is the reflective risk-taker, a hallmark of the researcher's changing identity. Lincoln (1997) asserts that the act of transforming participants into co-researchers shifts the treatment of relationships as part of a deeper gestalt that involves 'breaking out of our scholarly "native languages" and learning new ones to match our new commitments' (p. 42). Mitchell and Weber (1999) link this process of identity/language renewal to that of self-study, which 'involves a "whole self" [that] speaks directly to the heart of our identity . . . with the "we" containing some "me", "us" and "you"' (p. 231).

Pathlamps to plant

 Create your own research map that builds on the three frameworks (i.e. *traditional-historical*, *traditional-progressive*, and *progressive-radical*).

 Study the tension between general and local theory in your study and use the learning that emerges to clarify your own thinking, purposes, and future actions.

 Document the words you naturally use, and then deconstruct them to see what insight may be gained into your own native scholarly languages.

FLIPPING THE LIGHT SWITCH: STRATEGIES FOR ILLUMINATING THE WALKWAY

We now turn to specific approaches that can assist in the development of school-based projects and participant groups. For this purpose, strategies that enabled the PSG collaborative project are discussed.

Introductory survey. This tool was used for developing a portrait of the PSG. In the PSG, Carol Mullen used the survey results to create a matrix that compared members' perceived strengths and weaknesses to the project goals. Gaps in knowledge and skill (e.g. awareness of the mentoring research; facility with electronic attachments) were identified and addressed.

Regular communications. Electronic communications, follow-up, and news flashes kept everyone posted, motivated, and team- and goal-oriented. These may be indispensable these days.

Readings. Researchers can assemble relevant readings into packets for or with participants. In the PSG, members read and discussed the relevant literature on mentoring and support groups, as well as action research and teacher development.

Nuts and bolts tasks. The development of salient 'items' (e.g. key terms, titles, and table of contents) for a work in progress, such as a book, keeps negotiations ongoing. In the PSG, members examined the contents page for the book and, by doing so, gained clarity of purpose.

Audiotaped meetings. For each meeting, the PSG reviewed the transcription from the previous session. As members conducted their studies and wrote the chapters, they used the transcripts as a vital source of information and as a memory trigger.

Local records. Exploring a local culture and its history puts the current study in context. The PSG teachers felt empowered when they shared material that had been generated by their school, such as productivity reports. This process legitimates the local context in scholarly work.

Learning logs. Members can document research ideas, questions, responses to the literature, and material for writing. Rituals within the meeting itself can be built around sharing from learning logs. The PSG found this strategy helpful for exchanging ideas about each other's works.

Storytelling exchanges. Storytelling can be used as a conversational structure for promoting learning and analysis as well as feelings of safety and belonging. The PSG told stories as a way of personalizing formal research, and the literature on mentoring and collaboration.

Disseminating phase. Editing material being prepared for release is important. In the PSG, the facilitator edited all book chapters, with input from a member. Participant involvement in managing the dissemination phase contributes to group solidarity.

Pathlamps to plant

 Use strategies for developing your network to inform the directions of the study.

 Develop roles (e.g. communicator) to ensure participant ownership in the project.

 Establish a research dissemination plan (including timeline) and an editorial team.

PLANTING PATHLAMPS FOR THE FUTURE

The centrality of the pathlamp is our symbol of authentic guidance for assisting new researchers in their partnership journeys. On another level, this symbol is one of hope, sending the message that traditional maps can be transformed. We look forward to a world where people have made mentoring an integrated part of learning and connecting. New lenses and practices in 'carrying the lamp' are needed. Mentoring tends to stand apart from the greater totality of our profession: 'Mentoring practice may fall short of its ideals . . . because we fail to regard mentoring as integral to our approach to teaching and professionalism' (Hargreaves and Fullan 2000, p. 50).

Teacher researchers may choose to use our self-study guide for planting their own pathlamps – guiding steps. Or, they may opt to create their own research maps. Either way, we hope that our readers will plant a pathlamp today.

AUTHORS' NOTE

Graphic designer William A. Kealy created the artwork, 'Pathlamp for planting.'

We thank the book's co-editors for the 'pathlamp' they provided us.

REFERENCES

Barone, T.E. and Eisner, E., 1997, Arts-based educational research. In Jaeger (Ed.) *Complementary Methods for Research in Education* (Washington, DC: American Educational Research Association), pp. 73–103.

Bolman, L.G. and Deal, T.E., 1997, *Reframing Organizations: Artistry, Choice, and Leadership* (2nd edn) (San Francisco: Jossey-Bass).

Darling-Hammond, L. (Ed.), 1994, *Professional Development Schools: Schools for Developing a Profession* (New York: Teachers College Press).

Freire, P., 1996, *Pedagogy of Hope: Reliving Pedagogy of the Oppressed* (New York: Continuum).

Fullan, M., 1997, Emotion and hope: constructive concepts for complex times. In Hargreaves (Ed.) *Rethinking Educational Change with Heart and Mind* (Alexandria, VA: Association for Supervision and Curriculum Development), pp. 216–33.

Hargreaves, A., 1998, The emotional politics of teaching and teacher development: with implications for educational leadership. *International Journal of Leadership in Education*, 1(4), 315–36.

Hargreaves, A. and Fullan, M., 2000, Mentoring in the new millennium. *Theory Into Practice*, 39(1), 50–56.

Heilbrunn, J., 1996, Can leadership be studied? In Temes (Ed.) *Teaching Leadership: Essays in Theory and Practice* (New York: Peter Lang), pp. 1–11.

Kozol, J., 1991, *Savage Inequalities: Children in America's Schools* (New York: HarperCollins).

Lieberman, A. and Grolnick, M., 1997, Networks, reform, and the professional development of teachers. In Hargreaves (Ed.) *Rethinking Educational Change with Heart and Mind* (Alexandria, VA: Association for Supervision and Curriculum Development), pp. 192–215.

Lincoln, Y.S., 1997, Self, subject, audience, text: living at the edge, writing in the margins. In Tierney and Lincoln (Eds) *Representation and the Text: Re-Framing the Narrative Voice* (Albany: State University of New York Press), pp. 37–55.

Mitchell, C. and Weber, S., 1999, *Reinventing Ourselves as Teachers: Beyond Nostalgia* (London: Falmer Press).

Mullen, C.A., 1999, Anonymity revisited: a case study in mentoring teachers-as-authors. *Teacher Development*, 3(1), 129–45.

Mullen, C.A. and Lick, D.W. (Eds), 1999, *New Directions for Mentoring: Creating a Culture of Synergy* (London: Falmer Press).

Peters, M. and Lankshear, C., 1996, Postmodern counternarratives. In Giroux, Lankshear, McLaren and Peters (Eds) *Counternarratives: Cultural Studies and Critical Pedagogies in Postmodern Spaces* (New York: Routledge), pp. 1–39.

Rorty, R., 1999, *Rorty and Pragmatism* (Nashville, TN: Vanderbilt University Press).

Chapter 15

Teaching about teaching

The role of self-study

Amanda Berry and John Loughran

INTRODUCTION

This chapter explores self-study of teacher education practices through an examination of some of the teaching and research that we (Berry and Loughran) have conducted together. We describe this work by responding to the questions that the editors of this book have asked authors to specifically address. Although we do not answer these questions in a simple linear fashion, they are at the heart of the ideas that underpin this chapter. Hence, for each of these questions we offer explanations in line with the following: 'How do we go about engaging in studying our own teaching?' To this question, we respond by illustrating the impetus for, and approach to, self-study that has helped us to become better informed about our practice. 'What studies have informed our work?' To this question, we offer exemplars of similar work drawn from the emerging literature in self-study. 'What aspects of our teaching did we study?' In responding to this question we highlight our commitment to, and the centrality of, pre-service teacher education, for it is through our desire to help student-teachers better see the complexity of teaching and learning, and therefore learning about teaching, that we have been drawn to self-study. Finally, 'What challenges did we encounter?' Not surprisingly, challenges abound in work of this kind, both theoretical and practical. Some of these will be discussed.

QUESTIONING THE STATUS QUO

We would assert that teaching in pre-service teacher preparation is undervalued within the academy. Teaching in teacher preparation is viewed as relatively unimportant work, particularly in institutions whose reputations rest on research and publishing (Dinkelman 2001). Teacher educators' work has received little research attention because knowledge of teaching about teaching has not generally been regarded as a form of specialized expertise within academia. This may well be linked to the view that teaching itself is an under-theorized field. Further to this, those outside the profession often perceive teacher education as little more than the delivery of pedagogical 'tips, tricks and techniques'. The prevailing assumption is that teacher educators require little specialized expertise and that prior school teaching experience is usually sufficient (although not necessarily essential) for teaching prospective teachers how to teach.

For teacher educators themselves, learning to teach teachers is often experienced as a private struggle. The culture of isolation (Brookfield 1995) that commonly exists within teaching institutions reinforces the message that sharing questions or concerns about teaching is not something that teacher educators do (or should do). This, we believe, alienates many teacher educators who prefer to work collaboratively and are professionally motivated by examining their teaching in ways that foster questioning, critique and development of knowledge beyond their individual selves. Interestingly, then, the term self-study seems somewhat paradoxical as, for some, there is unease with the term as a descriptor of their interest and actions (Barnes 1998; Loughran and Northfield 1998; Munby 1996). This is especially so when considering the fact that the involvement of others and the checking of data and interpretations are crucial in addressing the very concerns that may be the impetus for a self-study in the first place.

There have been a small number of studies that have investigated the professional development of teacher educators (e.g. Kremer-Hayon and Zuzovsky 1995; Dinkelman 2001). These studies illustrate that new teacher educators inevitably seem to draw upon their own experiences of teacher preparation as a source of pedagogical knowledge as they are rarely offered any genuine support in their transition to teacher education. Sadly though, drawing on their own previous experiences of teacher preparation often leads them to a traditional technical–rational paradigm of professional knowledge development that involves 'the transmission to its students of the generalized and systematic knowledge that is the basis of professional performance' (Schön 1983, p. 37). Therefore, it becomes too easy for teacher educators to fall into the trap of presenting expert knowledge about teaching to their students, who are then expected to successfully reproduce this knowledge in their classrooms.

This has led in recent times to a growing number of teacher educators expressing their dissatisfaction with traditional teacher education practices and has prompted some to investigate alternative approaches to teaching about teaching. Self-study research, with its emphasis on teacher educators' collaborative learning about their practice, has emerged as a response to such challenges. It is through experiencing this common 'storyline' (above) that we too have been encouraged to adopt a self-study approach to researching our teaching about teaching and our students' learning about teaching.

DEVELOPING A SELF-STUDY

Inquiry may begin from a study of self where 'self' is the teacher educator (e.g. Dinkelman 2001), or investigating an aspect of student teachers' experiences where 'self' is the student(s) (e.g. Freese's (2002) analysis of a student teacher's apparent resistance to reflecting on his own teaching or Hoban's (1997) investigation of his students' understanding about the relationship between his teaching and their learning). Alternatively, collaborative conversations with the 'selves' who are colleagues may also serve as the starting point for a study of teaching about teaching (e.g., Bass *et al.* 2002).

Being able to access the work of others has therefore been important in encouraging us to initiate similar forays into self-study. More than this, though, being able to access others' learning through self-study has been helpful in shaping not only what a particular self-study might involve or 'look like', but also how self-study reports might be organized and constructed to best portray the inherent complexity of the work. Therefore, it is fair to suggest that the work of others has offered us support, methods and insights for exploring the dilemmas of practice so often the catalyst for action.

Berry (2004) highlights these dilemmas through the notion of tensions. She describes these tensions as growing out of teacher educators' attempts to match *their* goals for their students' learning with the needs and concerns that *student-teachers* express for their own learning. This desire to better match teaching goals and learning needs is ever present in the ambiguities in teacher educators' work, yet they are 'more manageable than solveable' (Lampert 1985). From an extensive review of the self-study literature, Berry offers the following as notable tensions that exist in the work of those teacher educators who are drawn to self-study. These tensions are framed as competing goals and needs whereby a teacher educator may recognize (and feel) a sense of dissonance or discomfort between:

- informing and creating opportunities to reflect and self-direct;
- acknowledging student teachers' needs and concerns and challenging them to grow;
- making explicit the complexities and messiness of teaching and helping student teachers to feel confident to proceed;
- exposing one's vulnerability as a teacher educator and maintaining student teachers' confidence in the teacher educator as a leader;
- working towards a particular ideal and jeopardizing this ideal by the approach chosen to attain it;
- a constructive learning experience and an uncomfortable learning experience;
- planning for learning and responding to learning opportunities as they arise in practice;
- helping students to recognize the 'authority of their experience' and

helping them to see that there is more to teaching than simply experience; and,

- the research demands of the employing institution and the interpersonal demands of teaching.

TENSIONS: SHAPING FACTORS IN TEACHING ABOUT TEACHING

This list of tensions is very real to those who have 'felt' them in their practice. In this section, we explore a limited number of these tensions in order to highlight how they might shape a self-study, and therefore bring to the surface our responses to some of the editors' questions in order to open up understandings of self-study.

The first tension we consider is, in fact, two tensions that are closely related. They are drawn together because they both hinge on the contrasting notions of confidence and uncertainty. That is between:

- making explicit the complexities and messiness of teaching and helping student teachers to feel confident to proceed; and,
- exposing one's vulnerability as a teacher educator and maintaining student teachers' confidence in the teacher educator as a leader.

In a third-year education subject (EDF 3002) that we team-teach (the basis for many of our collaborative self-studies; Berry and Loughran 2000, 2002; Loughran *et al.* 2002), we have continually been confronted by these tensions. Because they have also affected our students' learning about teaching, ignoring them is not a viable option. For example, we highlight the problems of practice that confront us as we teach so that our students can see what we are questioning in our pedagogical experiences. However, in so doing, we are also concerned that our behaviour is not viewed as 'peculiar', but rather as a window into the reasoning that informs our teaching. Inevitably, then, the tension created by our choice to illustrate the 'messiness' of teaching also creates a need to know whether this approach helps our students to apprehend (what we think are) important aspects of teaching.

As one component of a recent self-study, we explicitly sought such data by following up, through questionnaires and interviews, students whom we had worked with in the previous year. We anticipated that the separation in time from their involvement in the subject might offer us honest insights into the experiences from their perspective. And, as in any research project, we were also concerned about our influence on the data through data collection itself. Therefore, we chose to distance ourselves from the data collection process by having all interviews and questionnaires conducted by a colleague. This was an important issue for us because teaching is about relationships (see Loughran 1997), hence, despite our (and our students') best intentions, the relationship building that occurs through teaching and learning experiences can make it difficult for many students to be critical of their teachers' practice.

The following data are informative as they illustrate that the purpose of the subject appears to be recognized and appreciated by many of the participants. In making the messiness of teaching explicit, finding out that the purpose for so doing carries through in meaningful ways to the students matters very much to us; if the purpose is not achieved, the practice needs to be even more vigorously questioned. This may in fact be exacerbated if the purpose is not seen as valid by the students – an example of an impetus for further self-study!

> The subject made me challenge the assumptions I held about the way in which I taught. Particularly valuable was the way in which others [tutors and peers] also challenged my assumptions. The pass or fail grade encouraged me to take risks.

> I learnt that real learning about teaching occurs from experience and that reflection is needed to look back and develop from the experience.

> I liked being able to try out ideas while 'they didn't count' [pass grade only assessment] and reflect on how it worked.

Further to this, the data also suggest that there is value in continuing with the approach to risk-taking in teaching about teaching that we employ and encourage, and that highlighting our own personal vulnerability is instructive.

> I felt that the way we were taught (experience leads to deeper understanding) helped me decide that this is the way I want to teach.

> The way our tutors created a safe risk-taking environment really promoted our learning. What we did was not the main importance, but what we learnt about what we had done was.

A danger in reviewing this type of data is that it can easily mask other issues that are not so easily raised or, in some cases, may purposely not be offered (as per relationships noted earlier). The intention, though, is to find ways of apprehending different students' perspectives on the same experiences in ways that may not be so noticeable when using 'front of the room' observations during teaching, or through our own interpretations on situations when reflecting on sessions or discussing sessions after class. Therefore, the following data are also important.

> I felt it [EDF 3002] was too 'airy-fairy'. It needed a more concrete focus and objectives that we as students needed to see.

I missed having a mark instead of PGO [Pass Grade Only] – I realize there were valid reasons!!

Although there was only one 'lacking direction/objectives' type (*airy-fairy*) response from the forty-one students, it is a reminder of the need to continually make our intentions clear and for the teaching to consistently reflect the purpose for 'unpacking' and questioning practice – our own and our students'. In EDF 3002, it would be easy to become involved in making the messiness of teaching so much of the focus that it could inhibit a sense of progress or direction for those involved. Hence, actively seeking disconfirming data matters lest we become too concerned with exploring the 'meta-narrative' and diminish the value of the overall purpose. As can happen in any teaching and learning situation, the taken-for-granted aspects of our own practice can easily lead to a 'routinized' approach; the very thing we are trying to challenge. And, herein lies the tension in practice. By attempting to 'make explicit the complexities and messiness of teaching' we are reminded that this is not necessarily universally helpful. By changing the assessment procedures to encourage risk-taking and honest experimentation in teaching, for some the move away from 'grades as a reward for effort' detracts from the perceived value of making an effort. Hence, what we want to achieve may be countered by the way we attempt to achieve it.

We believe that it is through 'unpacking' pedagogical experiences that understanding the complexity of teaching can come to the fore. Therefore, we must be flexible and responsive to the unplanned; being ready to grasp the teachable moment (van Manen 1991). Nevertheless, in attempting to structure the program to create such situations there is a danger of the antithesis. We need to be constantly reminded that we are asking our students to have 'trust' in us and what we are trying to do (show that there is no one 'right' way of doing teaching). This is despite the fact that, for many, their university experiences generally reward them for finding the 'right' response in most situations – especially when it is being assessed! Therefore, the tension that we are consistently attempting to manage is something that we can neither take for granted nor dismiss. Thus, seeking students' perspectives on our shared experiences makes for an exquisite tension, with important pedagogic consequences. Hearing those matters:

> I don't think I thought at the time that the approach taken in the subject would help in developing my teaching ideas/philosophy, but in retrospect it did equip me with different ways of looking at teaching. The subject created a safe environment for trying/experimenting with teaching for the first time.

We have also come to see the difficulties associated with researching our own practice. This is not so much to do with recognizing the complexities inherent in our work (which is constantly apparent) but in finding ways of representing that complexity to others. Because so little of the world of teaching about teaching has been publicly articulated by others, it is not always easy to know how to proceed. Consider again the brief overview of data above. For the reader, no doubt there are questions, issues and concerns that are raised by having access to such small amounts of data. However, what matters is that such data are actively sought in order to see our practice through our students' eyes; despite it being problematic. In terms of the purpose of this chapter, then, we revisit the editors' questions to ensure that our reasoning is clear.

'How do we go about engaging in studying our own teaching?' We constantly look for different ways of developing alternative views of given teaching and learning situations. In the example above, we have paid attention to perspectives beyond the teacher, yet in our team teaching both the teacher and the colleague are also important perspectives that should not be discounted. By spending time discussing our intentions for our teaching, debriefing these experiences after classes (often audiotaped), maintaining journals and on-going electronic communications, and observing and interacting within the teaching environment through team teaching, we have an array of possibilities for comparing our intentions and actions. The way we engage in studying our teaching offers enhanced professional satisfaction and academic development.

'What studies have informed our work?' The efforts of Dinkelman (2001), Hoban (1997), Nicol (1997), Senese (2002), Russell (1997), Russell and Bullock (1999), Tidwell (2002) and many others have been helpful in highlighting the need to pursue students' perspectives on our practice. Further to this, such literature has also been important in confirming the value of researching practice and has offered new possibilities for approaching analysis and portrayal in ways that might make our learning and our ideas accessible in appropriate ways for others. Familiarity with other studies also engenders the necessary confidence for persevering with self-study as addressing questions, issues and problems that resonate with others creates a sense of validity and purpose that extends beyond oneself.

'What aspects of our teaching did we study?' Through an examination of EDF 3002 we were studying both our teaching about teaching and our students' learning about teaching. However, we were also studying ways in which teaching and learning could be embedded in experience in ways that would make the learning for participants intensely personal. In so doing, we were hoping that such learning would be more meaningful, professionally satisfying and applicable to practice, and be one tangible way of attacking the theory–practice gap that 'haunts' many teacher preparation programs.

'What challenges did we encounter?' It is easy to say that we sought the students' perspective, but inherent in gaining this perspective is a recognition that the power relationship between teacher and pupil simultaneously creates other tensions, doubts and questions about the veracity of the claims to be made. However, such a response is no reason to ignore these perspectives. Rather, it is an encouragement to be realistic about the differences in inter-pretations and to be reminded of the value of seeing and hearing these differences as much as possible. Such a response is one way of challenging our own taken-for-granted assumptions about practice and is an ever-present and real challenge that should be viewed as an enticing encounter.

We now briefly consider a second tension in the hope that it offers another way of seeing how the editors' questions can be answered through our understanding of, and approach to, self-study. This tension is one that has not received a great deal of attention in the literature. It is the tension between *a constructive learning experience and an uncomfortable learning experience.* We argue that good teaching about teaching should lay bare one's practice to the scrutiny of others through honest discussion about the impact of teaching on the development of others' learning. Inquiry conducted into practice in this way may well be confronted by the usual 'rules of politeness' that generally guide the ways that students and teacher educators speak about each other's practice. Clearly, then, working in ways that might genuinely open up practice for honest 'critique' requires a sensitive appreciation of others' feelings in ways congruent with Noddings' (2001) description of caring.

In EDF 3002, we purposefully work to set up opportunities for our students to experience and to articulate the uncertainties of practice as they encounter them through their microteaching situations (Berry and Loughran 2000, 2002). We want to find ways to help our students see into their practice and, sometimes, this is achieved by confronting them with problems or different possibilities as they are teaching. Such actions are not taken lightly but, equally, they are not avoided because they will be uncomfortable. Guilfoyle notes, 'Our students perhaps are seldom faced with "real" learning so they do not know how to deal with the disequilibrium . . . most were good students and did not have to struggle. Why should they have to struggle now?' (Guilfoyle *et al.* 1997, p. 194). Hence, there are sensible reasons why many students happily avoid disturbing or uncomfortable teaching and learning situations.

We now consider how this tension has played out in our practice and therefore become another aspect of inquiry in our teaching about teaching and our students' learning about teaching. This approach of 'confrontational pedagogy' is intended to help students see that their learning about teaching requires much more than accumulating experiences of teaching, but is brought into sharp focus through confronting one's own practice during teaching (in a safe and trusting learning environment). The following account is of a real 'unplanned' situation where the tension between constructive and uncomfortable learning was ever present. In this situation, being responsive to the pedagogic possibilities was perhaps the catalyst for the form of uncomfortable interaction that followed.

Mandi: . . . Two students were up front teaching. When they had finished and were beginning to debrief with the group, you [John] said to them, 'Do you remember what you did when Adam came in late?' They said that they didn't do anything. So, you said, 'Why not?'

'Well it's not a real classroom so I don't need to worry about that stuff' was their response, yet you hit them with, 'What would you do in a real classroom?' When one of them started, 'Well I'd say . . .' you interjected and told Adam to go out and told Sally to say what she would have said to him if he arrived late. Adam looked a bit sheepish when he went out. (He has now been identified as a latecomer!) He had been quite happy just to slip in unnoticed and Sally and the other members of her group had been happy to let him do so . . .

When Sally starts to say, 'You're late,' she stops and just looks embarrassed. 'I guess I'd just say something like that.' . . . Yet, you persist with her by asking her whether she would say anything else. 'Yeah, well probably,' she offers.

Then you said, 'Adam go out again and Sally try to say all the things that you would want to say to him', and Adam exits . . . now everyone is looking at Sally. (Glad I'm not up there; I can feel them thinking.) This scene is then played out twice more as you encourage (persistently!) Sally and her group members to say all of what they think they would say and at the same time questioning them, 'Why would you want to say that?'

I watch this public 'working through' of Sally's thinking along with the others. She is pinned, wriggling, and clearly uncomfortable. You continue questioning. Eventually Sally says what she thinks and she begins to ask questions about dealing with this or other situations. This is the breakthrough; here is where the learning through experience begins to really bite.

For me this has been more powerful than what the group presented in its teaching episode. I wonder if it has been for them? This is where it is not possible to plan, and yet these are the most powerful learning experiences.

(Berry and Loughran 2002, pp. 19–20)

This situation was no doubt uncomfortable for all involved. However, as an aspect of self-study, inquiring into the impact of such a situation is crucial. It cannot be assumed that, just because a teacher educator believes in a particular teaching approach, the desired outcomes will naturally flow forth. Hence, in our case, we were both concerned that the purpose of confronting Sally in this way was achieved and that discomfort rather than hurt was the affective factor impacting on (our) learning.

Following up on the situation involves attempting to gather data from multiple sources and multiple perspectives. Students' journals, the debriefing sessions that follow the peer teaching, our own reflections on practice, and the planned and unplanned responses of those involved are all important ways of gaining insight into the situation. Yet the most powerful form of data is that from the individuals directly involved in the discomforting/ confrontational situation. Interestingly, we have found that some students choose to place themselves in these demanding situations so that they can 'feel' what it is like to 'not know how to act'. More so, those involved often want to discuss the situation at length afterwards. We have found students' journal writing, their seeking us out, and/or staying behind to discuss the situation further, to be a useful insight into their learning through the situation.

> As it turned out, we were confronted with a barrage of comments, questions and opinions that really put us on the spot up there in front of the class . . . certain questioning and opinions did unnerve me . . . however, I think that we are all the better for it now that we have done something like this before we enter a school . . . instead of 'thinking on our feet' we aimed to try and get through the lesson and stick to our plan but it came at the expense of students' learning in what ended up a rather disjointed and somewhat confused lesson.
>
> (Student's reflection following an 'uncomfortable'
> learning experience)

Such uncomfortable experiences are not blithely introduced in our teaching and, just as we are concerned for the students, so too we are ever cautious to ensure that we have not 'gone too far' with our intervention. Hence, another aspect of self-study in this case is the need for us to debrief 'confrontational pedagogical experiences' in order to gain the perspective of a valued colleague; possible because of our team teaching. Trust in one another that the debriefing will be open and honest is another crucial aspect of our learning about teaching in the uncertain land of confrontational pedagogy. Being uncomfortable is not something that is reserved for the students alone!

CONCLUSION

Teacher educators' efforts to address problems of practice rarely result in tidy answers when such problems are viewed through the lens of self-study. Knowledge that is developed through teacher educators' investigations of their teaching about teaching is situated in a complex terrain, sometimes difficult to describe, and with an ever-changing destination. Grimmett recognized this when he noted, 'I was to learn that, although there are solutions to some problems, every solution creates further problems in a classroom of diverse learning needs and expectations' (Grimmett 1997, p. 131). His words could well be regarded as reflecting the process of self-study itself – recursive spirals that lead to continuing investigations of practice.

For many teacher educators, underlying issues associated with change and development in teaching about teaching may well go unnoticed and this is one reason why self-study of teacher education practices is important. Self-study, then, is an approach for those who choose to critically examine their own beliefs about teacher education through challenging their existing practice in meaningful ways. However, as we trust this chapter illustrates, there is no one way of conducting self-study, but the purpose and learning intents are certainly crystal-clear.

REFERENCES

Barnes, D., 1998, Looking forward: the concluding remarks at the Castle Conference. In Hamilton (Ed.) *Reconceptualizing Teaching Practice: Self-study in Teacher Education* (London: Falmer Press), pp. ix–xiv.

Bass, L., Anderson-Patton, V. and Allender, J., 2002, Self-study as a way of teaching and learning: a research collaborative re-analysis of self-study teaching portfolios. In Loughran and Russell (Eds) *Improving Teacher Education Practices through Self-study* (London: RoutledgeFalmer), pp. 56–69.

Berry, A. 2004, Self-study in teaching about teaching. In Loughran, Hamilton, LaBoskey and Russell (Eds) *International Handbook of Self-study of Teaching and Teacher Education* (Dordrecht: Kluwer Press), pp. 1294–332.

Berry, A. and Loughran, J.J., 2000, Developing an understanding of learning to teach in teacher education. In Loughran and Russell (Eds) *Exploring Myths and Legends of Teacher Education. Proceedings of the Third International Conference on Self-Study of Teacher Education Practices* (Volumes 1 and 2), Herstmonceux Castle, East Sussex, UK (Kingston, Ontario: Queen's University), pp. 25–29.

Berry, A. and Loughran, J.J., 2002, Developing an understanding of learning to teach in teacher education. In Loughran and Russell (Eds) *Improving Teacher Education Practices through Self-study* (London: RoutledgeFalmer), pp. 13–29.

Brookfield, S.D., 1995, *Becoming a Critically Reflective Teacher* (San Francisco: Jossey-Bass).

Dinkelman, T., 2001, Self-study in teacher education: a means and ends tool for promoting reflective teaching. Paper presented at the Annual Meeting of the American Educational Research Association. April, Montreal, Quebec, Canada. ED444936.

Freese, A., 2002, Reframing one's teaching: discovering our teaching selves through reflection and inquiry. Paper presented at the Annual Meeting of the American Educational Research Association. April, New Orleans.

Grimmett, P.P., 1997, Transforming a didactic professor into a learner-focussed teacher educator. In Carson and Sumara (Eds) *Action Research as a Living Practice* (New York: Peter Lang), pp. 121–36.

Guilfoyle, K., Hamilton, M.L. and Pinnegar, S., 1997, Obligations to unseen children. In Loughran and Russell (Eds) *Teaching about Teaching: Purpose, Passion and Pedagogy in Teacher Education* (London: Falmer Press), pp. 183–209.

Hoban, G., 1997, Learning about learning in the context of a science methods course. In Loughran and Russell (Eds) *Teaching about Teaching: Purpose, Passion and Pedagogy in Teacher Education* (London: Falmer Press), pp. 133–49.

Kremer-Hayon, L. and Zuzovsky, R., 1995, Themes, processes and trends in the professional development of teacher educators. In Russell and Korthagen (Eds) *Teachers Who Teach Teachers* (London: Falmer Press), pp. 155–71.

Lambert, M., 1985, How do teachers manage to teach? Perspectives on problems in practice. *Harvard Educational Review*, 55, 178–94.

Loughran, J.J., 1997, Principles of practice. In Loughran and Russell (Eds) *Teaching about Teaching: Purpose, Passion and Pedagogy in Teacher Education* (London: Falmer Press), pp. 57–69.

Loughran, J.J. and Northfield, J.R., 1998, A framework for the development of self-study practice. In Hamilton (Ed.) *Reconceptualizing Teaching Practice: Self-Study in Teacher Education* (London: Falmer Press), pp. 7–18.

Loughran, J.J., Berry, A. and Tudball, L., 2002, Teaching about teaching: Learning to help student-teachers learn about their practice. In Kosnik, Freese and Samaras (Eds) *Making a Difference in Teacher Education through Self-study. Herstmonceux IV: The Fourth International Conference on Self-study of Teacher Education Practices* (Volumes 1 and 2) Herstmonceux Castle, East Sussex, UK (Toronto, Ontario: OISE, University of Toronto), Vol. 2, pp. 67–71.

Munby, H., 1996, Being taught by my teaching: self-study in the realm of educational computing. In Richards and Russell (Eds) *Empowering Our Future in Teacher Education. The Proceedings of the First International Conference of the Self-Study of Teacher Education Practices*, Herstmonceux Castle, East Sussex, UK. (Kingston, Ontario: Queen's University), pp. 62–66.

Nicol, C., 1997, Learning to teach prospective teachers to teach mathematics: the struggles of a beginning teacher educator. In Loughran and Russell (Eds) *Teaching about Teaching: Purpose, Passion and Pedagogy in Teacher Education* (London: Falmer Press), pp. 95–116.

Noddings, N., 2001, The caring teacher. In Richardson (Ed.) *Handbook of Research on Teaching* (4th edn) (Washington: American Education Research Association), pp. 99–105.

Russell, T., 1997, How I teach IS the message. In Loughran and Russell (Eds) *Teaching about Teaching: Purpose, Passion and Pedagogy in Teacher Education* (London: Falmer Press), pp. 32–47.

Russell, T. and Bullock, S., 1999, Discovering our professional knowledge as teachers: critical dialogues about learning from experience. In Loughran (Ed.) *Researching Teaching: Methodologies and Practices for Understanding Pedagogy* (London: Falmer Press), pp. 132–52.

Schön, D., 1983, *The Reflective Practitioner: How Professionals Think in Action* (New York: Basic Books).

Senese, J.C., 2002, Opposites attract. What I learnt about being a classroom teacher by being a teacher educator. In Loughran and Russell (Eds) *Improving Teacher Education Practices through Self-study* (London: RoutledgeFalmer), pp. 43–55.

Tidwell, D., 2002, A balancing act: self-study in valuing the individual student. In Loughran and Russell (Eds) *Improving Teacher Education Practices through Self-study* (London: RoutledgeFalmer), pp. 30–42.

Van Manen, M., 1991, Reflectivity and the pedagogical moment: the normativity of pedagogical thinking and acting. *Journal of Curriculum Studies*, **23**(6), 507–36.

Part 4

(Re)positioning the self in and through self-study

The sand diaries

Visions, vulnerability and self-study

Anastasia Kamanos Gamelin

Journal entry, 14 September 2002, Jeddah, Saudi Arabia:

I am awakened by the leaves of the acacia trees that brush against my window. The trees are home to the hundreds of dizzy birds that chirp noisily as they fly from tree to tree, home to home. The lush bouquets of bougainvillaea are fat with fuchsia color. They resist the prodding of the gentle breezes. Wild geraniums of white and clinging vines of green climb the sides of my windows and shield me from the first rays of light. The full sun has yet to dance across the distant horizon – a horizon peaked with mosques and moons. I stretch, wait and listen for the far-away echo of the call to prayer. I arise to a land of mystery and myrrh.

(Kamanos Gamelin, *The Sand Diaries*, 2002, unpublished)

INTRODUCTION

I am a woman, writer, academic, and feminist. I am of both Greek and Turkish ancestry; have dual Greek and Canadian citizenship; speak, live and laugh in both English and French. I came to Saudi Arabia thinking that my work had brought me here, to a place where paradox and contradiction have come to nest. I now know that the self-study begun in my doctoral dissertation (2001) has led, and I have followed.

In this chapter, I will discuss self-study from my perspective as academic, artist and educator, and will explore the contradictions and paradoxes inherent in the self-study process. My purpose here is both personal and political as this chapter serves to recant the epistemic value of self-study, to mark stations along my personal and public journey as a female academic, artist and educator and to illustrate points of digression and intersection between lived experiences, cultural knowledge and academic ways of knowing. How I have come to be a writer, a teacher and an academic is bound through autobiographical narratives to 'making the past usable' which, as Mitchell and Weber (1999) explain, is a remembering in service of future action' (p. 11). Future action, in this case, means looking ahead to the use of self-study with my students, while 'remembering' is a look back through understandings elaborated in narratives.

This process is necessary as self-study defies traditional explanations of methodology. Indeed, it is a process that must be experienced. It requires acute consciousness of process, a heightened awareness and an ability to live at the intersection of past, present and purpose. Understanding self-study involves 'becoming' your work. To borrow Geertz's (1995) words, to do self-study is to put yourself 'in the way' of your work. Therefore, as self-study is an experiential practice, my aim here is to evoke in the reader an understanding of how multiple layers of past and present, experiment and experience, revelation and risk, purpose and position enmesh in this knowledge-making process.

THE JOURNEY

I teach in the Education faculty of Saudi Arabia's first private institution of higher education for women. I attribute my arrival here to the transformative energy of self-study. My work in Saudi Arabia seems to be a designated stop on my journey forward.

In fact, taking leave and returning, packing and unpacking, mimics my own family's history of migration and return, of unsettledness and uprooting, of the longing for memory and the attraction of new beginnings. The voyage was never simply for the trip. Here in Saudi Arabia and in my writing, I am once again challenged to redefine my identity, to review my roles. I must add Western, white and non-Muslim to my self-defining characteristics. The imprint of each of these identities is as different as each finger of my hand . . . yet, all are part of a working whole. I try to engage, interact and integrate the surrounding culture. I learn to walk gracefully within the folds of my flowing black 'abaya' and to expertly wrap the silky, dark 'tarha' around my head. I speak scratchy chunks of Arabic and my students teach me the pillars of Islam. I drink Cava, smoke shishah, and eat dates. For months, I have a burning desire to write something, but cannot write anything. I have a title. I buy a new fountain pen. I am stunned, incapacitated by a sense of responsibility, fear and vulnerability.

Clifford Geertz reminds me that, 'You don't exactly penetrate another culture, as the masculinist image would have it. You put yourself in its way and it bodies forth and enmeshes you' (1995). Therefore, I try to release myself to the culture, the surroundings, the classroom and the page. In doing so, the revelations exacted of self-study challenge me once again. I fear self-study – my body, soul and senses react to the memory of its grip, to feeling very vulnerable, naked to the reader's eyes. I remember how the use of self-study in my doctoral dissertation was considered a risk. I had no idea of how it would be received or if the academic community would accept it. I only knew that it filled a gaping hole evident in so many academic texts.

The travel through self-study taught me that vulnerability is the 'place', the stance from which I write and teach. As anthropologist Ruth Behar explains, 'when you write vulnerably, others respond vulnerably . . . To write vulnerably is like a Pandora's Box. Who can say what will come flying out?' (1996, p. 77) Ah . . . the box again.

If feminism by definition is concerned with social change, self-study as methodology is concerned with personal change. Both, however, enable, support and engage students in a common understanding that the personal is political, that ways of knowing and being are the result of communal effort and support. And so, if self-study travels, if as a methodology it crosses borders, moves mountains, traverses historical, social and cultural boundaries that speak to the essence of identity, dignity, selfhood and knowledge, then it is here, in Saudi Arabia, where I put this to use, both to uplift and be uplifted . . .

WHO DID I THINK I WAS?

The dancing bears

I do not remember exactly how old I was the first time I went to the circus. It was in the old Montreal Forum and the smell of elephant dung and wet straw stuck to the cement like sweat to skin. My school had distributed passes to needy families and I was excited to ride the bus uptown with a sense of purpose and destination. 'No, no', my mother told the driver as she pushed me ahead, holding up her five fingers. I wanted to holler that I was really older, that on Saturdays I babysat Mrs Johnson's baby boy and that I could skip double-Dutch with my eyes closed. Another dime saved.

From our seats in the rafters high above the three rings, I waited in anxious anticipation of the spectacle I had been told to expect. Chequered clowns, pink cotton candy, spinning red-painted ladies and breathtaking, high-wire acts. But all I saw were broken horses, droopy elephants and nervous monkeys. The big brown bears that rolled in were muzzled and chained and wore sequined hats and curled feathers. I was sad for all the animals that were whipped and teased. I secretly wished for the lion tamer to be swallowed up by the beasts. I was envious of the children in the front rows who got to ride in the magic train. Rather than caramel popcorn and Eskimo Pies, our row munched on the hard-boiled eggs and salami on rye bread that our mothers had packed. I brooded and fought against my anger and disappointment all the way home. The next day, a disbelieving teacher proclaimed my perceptions as wild, untruthful and a sign of my acute selfishness, ingratitude and unwillingness to adapt.

Years later, as a graduate student in university, I felt the same sense of contained desolation. I had returned to academia because, as a teacher, I somehow believed that the disappointment and resentment I felt in the classroom had, once again, much to do with my skewed perception of the world. Theresa Amabile (1990), an academic who studies creativity, remembers how her first grade teacher chastised her for being too creative. She questions why she still draws like a first grader and claims, 'I study creativity because I'm still trying to figure out something that happened in grade one' (p. 61).

Rather than integrate my creative perceptions and personal history into my academic work, I believed I had to exorcise them and spent the first few years of graduate school training to be much less than I actually was. I learned to maintain a separation between the university and my private life as a writer and a mother of three. The 'primal scene' that Grumet (1988) talks about was far removed from the university classrooms I attended. Perhaps years of living on social, cultural and economic margins had defeated me. I was tired of figuring things out. I believed it safer to be told how to 'do and be'. I tried to disregard my troubled educational history, my cultural background as a Greek immigrant and my social and economic history as a resident of a housing project in downtown Montreal. I wanted to surrender, to give myself up and to learn the steps to success and conformity. Bring in the dancing bears, I thought.

SELF-STUDY: VISION AND VULNERABILITY

My students in Saudi Arabia are young women from the socially, culturally and economically privileged class. Though quite young, some are married and mothers. Like many other women, they live between two worlds and two languages; between the modern and the traditional, between voice and silence. And, like other women, they too are vulnerable. Engaging in the work of self-study requires that they literally and metaphorically lift the veil separating their inner and outer worlds and make themselves known. Revelation in this case is a difficult balancing act, as the culture requires that separation between the private and public world be preserved. The walls that divide private and public are as thick as they are high, as metaphorical as they are concrete. My students are in a constant struggle to establish the boundaries and determine the limits of self-revelations in their narratives and other work.

HOW DO I THINK I AM?

Teacher's role

As Tillie Olsen has shown, some women spend their lifetimes answering to the echo of 'Who do you think you are?' and remain voiceless, unable to articulate a response developed from their own perspectives. Instead, they hear the uninvited voices of a parent, a teacher, or a husband. Years after Tillie Olsen first introduced her groundbreaking ideas in her book *Silences* (1978), many women continue to grapple with the damage incurred by what she called the 'unnatural silences' that disrupt the creative and intellectual process. These silences, as Hedges and Fishkin (1994) explain, are those that result from 'circumstances of being born into the wrong class, race, or sex, being denied education, becoming dumbed by economic struggle, muffled by censorship, or distracted or impeded by the demands of nurturing' (p. 31).

A teacher's role is not to replicate suffocating conditions that stunt self-awareness and self-knowledge, but to set up conditions that will inspire, that will literally give breath to students' visions of themselves as 'knowers'. Self-study allows us to move from the rigidity of the 'Who do you think you are?' voice to the flexibility inherent in the 'How do you think you are?' question that I ask my students. This question invites a holistic perspective, enables movement, problem-solving, critical thinking, and self-determination. However, moving from 'here to there', from answers provided by the outer world to the sparkling insights of inner worlds, is tenuous. There is resistance, anger, confusion, and chaos. As one student said, 'I don't like this class because now I have to rethink what I thought I knew. I have to rethink who I am.'

Mapping

In every moment of our daily interactions, I aim to help students gain a heightened awareness of the forces that shape who we are in the process of 'becoming'. My students and I map our inner and outer worlds in common-place books, reflective journals, memoirs, response journals, photography, and art and installation pieces. The very act of 'mapping' is transformational. Moreover, every act of knowing and learning transforms classrooms, teachers, students, communities, and worlds and transcends artificial geographical boundaries. Self-study does not determine who we become. Nevertheless, it can be an instrument that helps us to understand and embrace the transformational process by allowing us to get inside it.

My students' insights and knowledge have enriched my teaching. I am witness to their transformational process. I have mapped my own transformational process of self-study in journals, letters, messages, and unpublished manuscripts. This is a continuation of the work undertaken in my doctoral dissertation. Over time, I have learnt that my search for meaning is oftentimes unsettling and causes discomfort for me, and others. That discomfort invites vulnerability. However, I have learnt that vulnerability can be strength rather than weakness, and that there is valuable knowledge that comes from being an outsider, from dual identities and conflicting roles. I can trace the movement and shift in identity when the outer 'who do you think you are?' roar becomes the inner 'how do I think I am?' whisper.

I came to Saudi Arabia to work with women because I recognized both the vulnerable and powerful position of women in a kingdom on the cusp of important social, cultural and educational change. I also needed to reconnect with the transformative synergy of self-study and wanted to 'make the past usable'. This past included a major transformation that was in great part the result of the self-study work elaborated in my doctoral dissertation. This work served to ground my knowing, experience and authority. It helped me frame what it was I knew for sure.

OF THIS MUCH I AM SURE

The journey to my dissertation was an especially precarious and difficult one. As an immigrant, mother, writer and academic I had lived with a sense of social disorientation and cultural dislocation. I had to overcome self-doubt, silence, lack of history, distrust of the future. I also had to overcome the sense of beginning from nothing, of starting from nowhere. To do this, I had to grope my way through gender, cultural and social biases. This meant kicking addictions, examining open wounds and facing impostors. As a private writer, entering the public domain meant leaving the security of my 'writer's closet' and daring to publicly proclaim and confront myself as a writer/artist. This requires conviction of spirit and courage of purpose, as it renders oneself vulnerable to charges of misrepresentation. Are you a real writer? Are you truly an artist? What can you know? For a time, self-doubt settles in. Then, slowly, knowledge thickens. Past all the uncertainty, beyond the hurtful doubts, far from the stabbing criticism, I realize that of this much I am sure.

The uncommon path of my own academic journey challenges widely held assumptions of who academic women are. A significant development of this journey has been my daring to venture into the public domain while struggling to form stylistic techniques that incorporate the public and private, the artist's and the academic's voice (Kamanos Gamelin 1996, 2000).

As a female artist in academia, I make explicit how sensing my self as a 'living contradiction' (Whitehead 1993) is a condition that begs creative resolutions. In my work I describe how I have engaged in the academic landscape from my perspective of artist and reveal how within the tension and inherent struggle of conformity and self-expression, process and product, artist and academic, comes the need to express my knowing in a way that I, as a woman and writer, make meaning of the world.

My challenge in my writing was to find a form that accommodated the messiness of the creative life. In order to flourish in my work I need to maintain a connectedness between my personal and public worlds, a dialectic relationship between artistic and intellectual ways of knowing, between the mundane and the sacred, between emotion and reason. Indeed, authenticity, integrity and creativity are the alpha and omega of artistic as well as knowledge-making activity. As an artist, I therefore need to resolve the problem I live as an academic. That is, to speak in my authentic voice and to answer the creative and intellectual yearning in a way and in a place where my beliefs and practices align. I must reclaim my writer's voice. Only then can my perceptions of the world be rendered in so potently truthful a way that they resonate with meaning and purpose for me, and my readers and my students. My narratives, therefore, are key to my work as a writer and academic.

And of this much I am sure: my relationship with the written word has helped me survive a dauntingly bleak and hurtful childhood and adolescence. Writing allowed me to capture the twinkle and preserve the stardust of the encounter between the natural world and the child. I built soft cocoons of snowflakes and leaves. Bright red huts and sparkling castles. Icicle drawbridges and leafy lakes. Though the years beyond childhood have stretched, the future, it seems, has shrunk. But not in silence.

My cultural, social and educational experiences had taught me that to nurture oneself was narcissistic, self-centered and indicative of a personality stuck in a sort of post-adolescent limbo. I know better now to reject this. My writing, I understand, was a tool for the building of meaning in a world that offered no interpretations for a life like my own. Yet, the writing was never good enough, the experiences too crude. I kept the writing in such a deep, dark place that retrieving it was painful. It was like dragging something up from the depths of the ocean floor with all the vegetation, sea urchins and moss still hugging it for nourishment.

So, my work is a salvage operation of sorts. It means putting what has been buried into a historical context. It means understanding the circumstances behind the sinking of women's treasures and examining what has been uncovered in some contextual light. At times, the feelings of fear and insecurity return, and the conflict between artist and academic resurfaces. Do I really know what I know? Who do you think you are? An inner voice whispers; of this much I am sure: whether painter or poet, writer or weaver, becoming an artist is a continuous process. It is lived daily. It is akin to feeling, loving, and breathing. And once we experience the process unobstructed, we cannot return to a former state of being. The transformation is never complete, the process always on-going, the freedom bottomless. Therefore, my work must rely on a method and theory that gives breath, and that inspires the artist.

My love of the ocean is in-bred. I love the ebb and flow because it reminds me of how things are different, yet the same; of how one travels far, only to return, of how a wave can cradle or swallow you in its undertow. The ocean is a metaphor for the paradoxes and contradictions inherent in knowing and being and becoming.

I live in a country of vast differences; the landscape reflects this. My Mediterranean blood never quite adapted to the glacial winters that make my veins shrivel. Like the waves that wash debris up to the shores, there are certain things that I carried with me into academia. Some were harmful; sticks and stones, others were treasures; shells and bones. Each was a reminder of a long journey. There is also a certain knowledge stored in my body that is triggered off by sensory awakening. These bones rattle with the knowledge of my own journeys past. My supervisor's British accent, for example, is a reminder of humiliation at school; paper napkins, of lunch box notes to the children. 'Hey Jude' still makes me cry. *The Cat in the Hat* still makes me laugh. Bob Dylan makes me happy, Billie Holiday makes me sad. The music, and books and the solitary creative company I keep illustrate my life story.

And of this much I am sure: creative work is as valid and rigorous a form of feminist knowledge-making as other more traditionally defined research in academia. The social, cultural and economic environment and context of my life pervade my work and leak into the crevices of the theoretical meanings I make of the world. I know the world in a certain way because of how I approach and interact with it. I interpret it from my own palette of colors.

Artist and academic are like fingers of the same hand. Though at first glimpse the notion of artist and academic may seem contradictory, it is the possibilities that feminism has imagined for women that make the revelation of academic as artist possible. The paradox inherent in the concept of 'artist as academic' is a useful guide for understanding women's creative lives. In inspiring, literally giving breath to female academics, feminist research has revealed how the absence of the female artist's voice from the knowledge-making process has deprived women of the possibility of reconciling the form and content, process and product of their creative lives.

Not all women think, talk and write alike. Our visions are multiple, our creative forms varied. Our history, knowing and experiences collide, contrast and jostle for recognition. And along with the scientists, historians and traditional female scholars, we need to begin to recognize and acknowledge these alternative ways of women's knowing, being, doing. This cannot be accomplished by replicating what is already in the mainstream, academic picture, but by imagining the importance of what has been left out. In retrieving vestiges of women's knowing, their novels, letters, diaries, quilts and pottery, we understand how women have transformed their lives into artful creations when no other instruments to express their knowing were available. The knowledge that is recognizable to other women, but not many men, has therefore been discounted and recounted as something else. Regardless of what I was told, academic writing was not like learning a new language for me. Rather, it was like learning to be a new person. I felt obliged to sing off key, to paint blindfolded and to write with my hands tied behind my back. The difficulty lies in never being you. Though each day in academia was a challenge to my integrity, of this much I am sure: in becoming an academic I do not want to fulfill the mission that my primary education set me on the path towards. That is, to become someone I am not and to conform to a way of saying and doing that dissimulates my perspective, and my social, economic and cultural background.

I therefore see self-study and creativity as a way of transgressing the traditional boundaries of expression in academia, and view feminism as the political tool that makes this possible. This is the point at which feminism fulfills its political and personal potential for women. Self-study is how the political arm of feminism reveals itself in the personal and daily. It is the manifestation of feminist principles in academia. Though much of what I have experienced as negative in academia might be dismissed as my own misunderstanding of the academic process, of this much I am sure: my perceptions of the world have been borne from the grains of my experience. These seeds were not sown with purpose, row on row. Rather, they flew crazily with the wind, dropping here, growing there. I stand back and look at my experiences as a farmer would look at her fields. There are no straight lines in mine. There are curves, loops, and zigzags. What others see as chaos, I see as the particular design of my life. What others see as mundane, I see as the narrative of daily living. I know that there is harvest and abundance. So that I may maintain a sense of integrity in my work and a sense of authority in my voice, I must take this way of being and seeing into account when I write. Of *this* much I am sure.

CONCLUSION

Climbing the slippery slope of self-study and transformation oftentimes means looking backwards in order to move ahead. This kind of work is what poet Dionne Brand (1994) calls the 'travel back' and is a process that requires a revisiting of sites/sights so that we will be free to ask the questions that we have been forced to repress, questions that may point us toward new paths. Self-study is a way to learn personally and collectively from our experiences. If one of our goals in academia is empowerment and emancipation for women, then transformation is almost inevitable and the process needs to be documented as evidence of women's alternative possibilities and potential.

As methodological tools, self-study and narrative inquiry are ways of revolutionizing and transforming societies, institutions and worlds. As Clandinin *et al.* (1993, p. 18) explain, transformation rests upon an awareness of how our personal, institutional and cultural stories influence and shape our 'lived stories' and experiences. These experiences and knowing form the 'circles within circles' that Ely *et al.* (1991) talk about and the stories within stories that Metzger (1992) talks of. 'Writing', claims Said, 'then becomes a place to live in harmony, in beauty, in understanding' (1996, p. 266). Beyond informing, for many women self-study is a confirmation of what we already know; it is both self-affirming and self-confirming, and returns meaning to the educational process.

REFERENCES

Amabile, T., 1990, *Creativity in Context* (Boulder, CO: Westview Press).

Behar, R., 1996, *The Vulnerable Observer: Anthropology That Breaks Your Heart* (Boston: Beacon Press).

Brand, D., 1994, *Bread Out of Stone* (Toronto: Coach House Press).

Clandinin, D.J., Davis, A., Hogan, P. and Kennard, B., 1993, *Learning to Teach, Teaching to Learn* (New York: Teachers College Press).

Ely, M., Anzul, M., Friedman, T., Garner, D. and McCormack Steinmetz, A., 1991, *Doing Qualitative Research: Circles within Circles* (Bristol, PA: Falmer Press).

Geertz, C., 1995, *The Interpretation of Culture* (New York: Routledge).

Grumet, M., 1988, *Bitter Milk: Women and Teaching* (Amherst: University of Massachusetts Press).

Hedges, E. and Fishkin, S. (Eds), 1994, *Listening to Silences: New Essays in Feminist Criticism* (New York: Oxford University Press).

Kamanos Gamelin, A., 1996, Migrant storybirds: life, language, text. *Feminist Voices*, 9(8), 9–11.

Kamanos Gamelin, A., 2000, The Canadian quilt: image of us in small squares. *Atlantis: A Women's Studies Journal*, 24(2), 147–53.

Kamanos Gamelin, A., 2001, Home and away: the female artist in academia. Unpublished doctoral thesis, McGill University, Montreal.

Metzger, D., 1992, *Writing for Your Life* (San Francisco: Harper Publishing).

Mitchell C. and Weber, S., 1999, *Reinventing Ourselves as Teachers: Beyond Nostalgia* (London: Falmer Press).

Olsen, T., 1979, *Silences* (New York: Delta Press).

Said, E.W., 1996, *Representations of the Intellectual* (New York: Vintage Press).

Sternberger, J. (Ed.), 1991, *The Writer on Her Work. Vol. 1* (New York: W.W Norton).

Whitehead, J., 1993, *The Growth of Educational Knowledge: Creating Your Own Living Educational Theories* (Dartmouth, UK: Hyde Publications).

Chapter 17

A queer path across the straight furrows of my field

A series of reflections

Mary Phillips Manke

Two ways (of many) I identify myself:

- self-study researcher
- queer.

Butler (1990) points out that to name any single aspect of one's identity (say, queerness) is to open the question, what else, and what else, and what else? Similarly, Bornstein (1998) suggests that multiple gender options point the way to multiple paths for one's life. I am not *only* queer, only self-study researcher, only white, only mother, only teacher, only administrator, only . . . My lived life embodies all these aspects and more.

It is exactly the act of looking at self that allows one to identify as queer. A question may be presented, such as 'What is your sexual preference/orientation?' An answer may be elicited by a list of choices (gay, lesbian, bi, trans, straight) that lets me respond without actually looking into myself. No looking within is required to complete this questionnaire. Responses to it can be analyzed by sociologists, who can then say, 'Lesbians 55–65 prefer . . .' or 'Forty-eight percent of white females think that . . .'

But, to choose the could-be-pejorative, has-to-be-explained-over-and-over, always political, designation 'queer' does require that I ask 'who are you?' of myself as if I were some other . . . And this is just what I do in self-study research. I ask, 'Who are you?' as if I were some other. And the designation 'self-study researcher' is also possibly pejorative, also needing explanation, also political.

Queerness and self-study are deeply linked co-expressions of my self. Aspects of queerness intrude into my sense, my preferred definition, and my practice of self-study. Here, I use some of the literature of queerness to offer insights that are opening up my own ideas about self-study.

FIRST REFLECTION: MARGINALIZATION/ 'OTHERING'

Let me begin with the marginalization of self-study in the academic world, strongly reinforced by the new emphasis on so-called 'scientific research' in education. Qualitative research has been research on the defensive since it first claimed to be a research method paralleling quantitative research. Self-study is marginalized even in the qualitative research world. When Ken Zeichner (1999) was vice-president of AERA's Division K, he delivered an address praising the importance of self-study, an event that led to more self-study and more concerns. Some fear that self-study will be transformed into study that ignores the self and looks only at the self's work. Others fear that study too focused on the self is self-indulgence.

Another term for this state of marginalization and defensiveness is 'being othered.' It expresses how a group endowed with power claims to be the center, the real/natural thing, 'us,' and describes the less powerful group as 'the other.' Self-study is 'othered' by the educational research establishment.

In the same way, queers are 'othered' by the straight, heterosexist, male-dominated power structure of our culture. For example, my state's legislature is considering a bill to exclude queers from using sick leave already earned at work to care for an ill partner or mourn a partner who has died – privileges automatically granted to heterosexuals. This bill tells queers that we are not actually human, with human needs to show caring and to mourn. We are some 'other.'

Returning from this excursion into the politics of the worlds of research and policy to a focus on my self, I note that I *choose* both the S-STEP SIG as a center of my professional life, and being queer as a center of my life. I acknowledge a *preference* for being 'othered.' The question of preference as opposed to some inevitable, genetic predisposition is of course important in discussions of varied sexualities. Does one 'choose a lifestyle' or obey some inescapable force that requires one to be gay or lesbian? I have no certain answers to this question, but I assert that, for me, being queer is a choice. Queer names not just my sexuality, but also the direction from which I approach the world. It means strange (as opposed to at home), off-center, slantwise, widdershins, jaywalking, out of sync. It is a political option.

I choose queer and find it suits me better than more conventional choices. Like lesbian, like straight. Before I chose to identify as queer, I had a tendency to want to break things, a mischievous streak, that I had to control. This slightly destructive inner tendency is gone, I think, since I acknowledged my queerness. Yet both in coming out as queer and in identifying myself as a self-study researcher, I dithered on the edges for a long time. Not easy choices, then.

Just as I choose queerness, I choose self-study as a primary mode of research, not in spite of being othered by these choices, but because each offers the opportunity to find myself identified as the Other. In this role of self-as-Other, I can look at the world in a non-obvious way, ask questions not ordinarily asked, walk unusual paths, draw on unexpected resources. I can take risks. I can feel free.

SECOND REFLECTION: PERFORMANCE/GENDER PERFORMANCE

In a recent book review, the author pointed out acerbically that gender studies are not actually about gender, but about homosexuality. One was not to be deceived into thinking that gender studies were studies of manliness and womanliness. Of course, in a sense this is not true at all, since those doing gender studies are often very interested in how the performance of male-ness and female-ness is defined. Butler (1990) writes about gender 'performativity.' She says that gender has to be performed (not put on and worn, like clothing, but acted out). People make choices in the performance of their gender roles, and, in that sense, are free to choose. Yet the culture makes them choose to act one way or another, whether in expected or unexpected ways. Gender *must* be performed, and is constituted in the performance.

As a queer person, I deal with this notion of performativity daily. Queerness, which has been described as 'a critique of identity' (Jagose 1996, p. 131), makes me acutely aware that I am performing my gender role(s) differently according to my company and mood. What do I wear? How do I walk? How do I moderate my choices of language between what I understand to fit others' expectations of my gender role and what I actually want to say? If I say I value being Out, what shall I be Out as, and what will be the impact of being Out in this environment, and what is my judgment right now about the value of being Out versus the value of fitting In? These are choices, constructed in a social, political, and emotional context that shifts constantly as it is constantly constructed. To identify as queer is to be aware of these choices, and of one's life as performance. How surprising is it, then, that the element of performance in self-study research is one that appeals to me?

Cole and McIntyre (1998) first brought performance to the SIG, tap dancing the history of Cole's life as a teacher educator. Music, words, and dance expressed Cole's inner changes in her self and her role as a teacher educator. Other performances in the SIG have included theatre pieces by Weber and Mitchell (2000, 2002) exploring the role of family in the construction of their selves; an enactment of a visit to an art museum by Hamilton (2002); and a reading from Perselli's dissertation that takes place in a display of the imaginary works of an imaginary woman artist (2002).

Performance is a strand of excitement, mystification, and enjoyment that weaves through the self-study experience. It uses symbolic material, blurring the academic prose tradition. It is a link for me to the daily awareness of gender performativity that characterizes my life as a queer person. The self-awareness of stage performance is linked to the self-awareness essential to being queer. The choices essential to performance are linked to the endless string of choices in a queer life.

THIRD REFLECTION: PERFORMING ROLES

De la Huerta (1999) suggests that queers have an historic role of acting out certain iconic types in society. While avoiding stereotypes, I still venture to identify some roles I see myself playing (at). This idea goes beyond the dailiness of the gender-performativity awareness referred to above. It calls on iconic social roles that are not directly linked to the *gender*, but instead to the *otherness* of the performer. Three roles that de la Huerta defines link to my sense of my queer self and to the nature and status of self-study.

First is the role of queers as 'catalytic transformers with a taste for revolution.' In chemistry, a catalyst transforms by being present in a reaction. Though it is not really part of the reaction, not joined with the chemicals really being transformed, the catalyst is essential to the reaction. Perhaps the catalyst performs as 'other' in the chemical reaction. Queerness implies an inclination toward change, toward radicalism, an antipathy to conservatism and stability. It continually calls into question the idea that certain beliefs, practices, bodies are 'natural' or real.' To say, 'I am queer,' is to emancipate oneself from one's own – and others' – expectations of how one should act, dress, be or believe. Queer is not a direction, but an option. I tell you I am queer, but you have no idea in what direction I will go. Queerness is tied to a psychology of constructivism that holds that all social roles, acts, performances, statements are constructed and constantly being constructed by the participants in any social environment. The 'Under Construction' sign is always up, because there is no end to the building project that is queerness.

Self-study research is not necessarily radical. It takes place within educational institutions that aim to conserve the culture. Yet within this fairly narrow context it is continually asking questions about change and seeking self-emancipation. It asks how varied research practices can create something different, something new, in the teachers or classrooms or children of the future.

For example, Bruce Smith (2000) looks at the effects of lying or exaggerating in the stories he tells his teacher education students. A group of self-study researchers from Northern Iowa (Heston *et al.* 2000) ask what happens when together they read literature with a spiritual component, not to abstract from it concepts to teach or strategies to share, but to change their selves and teacher selves. Griffiths and Windle (2002) try new administrative structures and redefine what is needed to make change (A painted picnic table? A box of batteries?) in the culture of their institution. The true, strong core of self-study research is emancipatory, even revolutionary, in focus. It is exemplified in the strand of self-study research that seeks social justice, as when Hamilton (2000), Vavrus (Vavrus and Archibald 1998), or Bass (2002) ask how the culture of an institution can be transformed to embody equality.

De la Huerta's second iconic role for queers is as outsiders, mirroring society. (Remember that a mirror reflects the reverse of what is 'really there.') Looking at myself in a mirror, it is easy to forget that left is right and right is left. Imagine I had a disability that ended the match between my two sides. Then I would know what a mirror does! De la Huerta thinks of society looking into its queer mirrors (are they like funhouse mirrors, distorting the objects they reflect?) and seeing its own diversity. In a way, straightness is defined by its limited thinking. It makes a false claim that it is uniform, consistent, regular, natural, real. Defining as 'other' what it perceives as different from itself, it must overlook the differences it allows to remain within the pale.

Self-study researchers step outside the bounds of proper research, with its pre-arranged mechanisms for defining and guaranteeing truth. In their self-centered research, they reflect the diversity that a post-modern epistemology finds in traditional research. Where traditional researchers seek to exclude the self or compensate for its presence (Peshkin 2000), self-study researchers gladly include their own practices and perceptions. Thus when traditional researchers look in the mirror provided by the 'othered' self-study community, they can see that their work too is produced by the self, is affected by the self, and disowns the self at its own risk.

De la Huerta (1999) identifies a third and last iconic role for queers as what he describes as 'consciousness scouts,' going first and taking risks. They can uncover 'new paths, new answers' (p. 10). Where are these scouts going? Out in search of a Northwest Passage or an open-water route across the pole? Or are they scouting in the unknown terrain of the consciousness, the self? Bornstein (1998), in her popularization of gender theory, *My Gender Workbook*, repeatedly asks the reader to answer gender questions about her/his own self. This can feel like an endless journey through back issues of *Cosmopolitan*, but a serious effort to answer her questions can uncover entirely unknown territory within. Similarly, queer people explore new paths within the category of gender. For me, it is my self-identification as queer that encourages me to pursue new paths of understanding in every part of my life, especially in my self-study research.

Self-studiers are often on these new paths. What happens when I encourage students to critique my work as their teacher (Lighthall 2000; Manke 1995)? What happens when I allow for the possibility that problems I have with students as a teacher educator stem from me, not from them (Dinkelmann 2003)? What happens if I view my experiences as a teacher from the point of view of an artist (Perselli 2002)? What happens if I use in teaching my age peers the very same practices that work so well with children (Austin 2001)?

What happens if . . . Not to say that every self-study is on a new and risky path, but as a queer self-study researcher, I value those that are. Moreover, over the years in which I have come more and more to acknowledge my queerness, my desire to try those paths has increased.

Writing these words on the brink of the second Gulf War, with its many parallels to the Trojan War, I identify another iconic role for queers, that of Cassandra. She was a daughter of the Trojan king, Priam, famous for the gift of prophecy and the curse of not being heard. Christa Wolf (1984) observes that Cassandra sets herself apart from her people. By claiming (or revealing) that she can see what they cannot, she leaves them forever, and in the end is carried off to die in a distant land.

All this is a bit dramatic (as epics are) when placed next to my modern queer life, in which gods do not intervene, let alone my life as a self-study researcher. Yet, I find a thread of connection in that notion of separation. When I write about 'othering,' I think of the establishment, the powers that be, othering the queer and the self-studier. When I write about Cassandra's separation from her people, I think about myself choosing to be separated from my peers by claiming to see and understand what they do not, whether the play of queer sexuality/performativity or the unnoticed play of the self in classrooms and offices of teacher educators.

FOURTH REFLECTION: BEWILDERMENT

To identify myself as queer is to accept that I am confusing for the straight world. The queer other is bewildering. How often, when I say that I am queer, does someone say, with sincere confusion, 'Why do you say that? Isn't that a, you know, like a negative? I would be afraid to say that about someone.' Sedgwick has said (Hodges 1994, cited in Jagose 1996, p. 97) that calling yourself queer 'dramatizes the difference between what you call yourself and what other people call you. There is a sense in which queer can only be said in the first person.' Evidently, queer might mean something beyond a set of subcategories like lesbian, gay, bisexual, transgendered . . . Queer is a mystery . . . Queer is bewildering. And I do not just apply the words mystified and bewildered to the outsiders to queerness who ask those questions. They apply to me as well. I am bewildered, made wild (as opposed to tame), placed in the wilderness (as opposed to ploughed fields and subdivisions), by identifying myself as queer. I am claiming a category that is not defined, that could mean many things, that calls for multiple identities and multiple possibilities for my life. Jagose (1996) confirms my sense that queer is indeterminate, having as its essence the breaking down of 'categories, opposites and equations' (p. 97).

I titled this chapter 'A queer path across the straight furrows of my field' with a double meaning for the final word, because I follow a queer path across my life field, but also a queer path across my teacher education field. I am not only a queer researcher, but also a self-study researcher, and it is certainly true of self-study of teacher education practices that it is a queer path indeed within the study of teacher education. It is mysterious. Entering it is like walking in a wilderness, away from street signs and sidewalks, away from clear and consistent definitions. That, it must be obvious, is what attracts me to self-study.

Let us take an educational walk in the wilderness. Across the meadow, half-hidden by a thicket, we see a group of teacher educators reflecting on their process of becoming part of the field (Arizona Group 1996, 2000, 2002). In a flowered clearing, a teacher educator takes stories his students wrote for his classes and shapes them to express what he has learned about his teacher education practices through the length of his career (Allender 2001). In a valley, another teacher educator works to define the place of reflection in his students' work, and asks how to improve its quality (Russell 2002). Next to the water, a poet uses her art to define the methodology of self-study (Manke 2002; Manke and Allender 2002). Deep in the woods, another teacher educator explores the possibilities of representation of her experience (Perselli 2002). In a sunny spot, two teacher educators consider how their personal pasts illuminate their researcher selves (Weber and Mitchell 2000, 2002).

Now, a quiz. Take a piece of paper and a pencil, and using the information in the above paragraph, write a definition of self-study of teacher education practices. Bewildered? Mystified? Lost in the wilderness? Good. You've got the right answer . . .

FIFTH REFLECTION: ALEATORY THINKING

Sedgwick (1990) writes that within queerness, identity can feel 'aleatory,' 'discretionary' (p. 25). Aleatory means controlled by the roll of the dice, by luck, and Sedgwick, pairing it with 'discretionary,' is clearly thinking of a random, choice-filled identity. The word also brings to my mind a sentence from Latin II, Julius Caesar's words after crossing the River Rubicon, '*Alea jacta est.*' The die is cast. Queerness is like that, an irreversible, uncontrollable event, a path chosen or given, and not to be reversed. After the die is cast, Caesar is committed to his journey to Rome and his plans for the future; on the other hand, all roads lead to Rome, and there are many paths after the irreversible event of recognizing/defining (making definite) my queerness. To stand up in public and say 'I am queer' changes my life permanently. Suddenly I am too big to fit in the closet I once lived in. Even a silent statement, 'I am queer,' heard by no other, begins the change. Claiming queerness multiplies the dimensionality of my life, expands the possibilities of my living, opens me to winds of change from which I once found shelter. Choices, too, but no going back to before the die was thrown, the Rubicon crossed, the words spoken.

For me and at least some others, as self-study practitioners, the act of engaging in study of the self as a study of teacher education practices has a similar flavor. Once I have asked 'What is it about me as a person, my self-ness, my chosen or seemingly not chosen actions, that shapes my practice of teacher education?' there is no going back to thinking of oneself as a technical automaton riding above the straight furrows of the field. Once I had written honestly and reflectively about the role of relationships in my teaching of established teachers, I could never again enter a classroom inno-cent of the knowledge I had uncovered about my practices. Once I had named the fears and weaknesses that shaped my response to those teachers, I could never pretend that the fears and weaknesses found in a classroom where I taught did not include my own.

It is risky to provide examples of others' work that may have changed them in similar ways, so I add here a warning as I do so that I am only guessing about the self-effects of the work I describe. When Antoinette Oberg (in Oberg and Finger 1997) studied, with her Alexander Method teacher, the ways that the posture of her body affected her relationships with the students she advised, could she let go of that awareness? When Rena Upitis and Tom Russell (1998) studied how their use of e-mail created/destroyed/altered possibilities for relationship in their college of teacher education, could they go back to typing and sending e-mails without reflective thought? When Marilyn Johnston (1997) confronted the effects on all the participants of her efforts to remove herself from the center of a professional development collaboration, could she make decisions about where to place herself in the way she had originally made that one?

Choices, possibilities, roads newly opened, but no option to not have chosen, not have moved, not have thrown the dice. Bornstein (1998) asks, 'Would my future [as queer] be a series of becomings, never really arriving?' (p. 107). Queer is an unsettled state, queer is a crooked path, queer is 'I don't know' and 'I am finding out.' Queer is in some deep sense homeless, pushed out of the nest, never quite certain that the feathers needed for flying have fledged. I cherish these aspects of queerness. I hunger for new ideas, new books, new plans, new ways to create, new people. But, with queerness, I'd better like it, because there's no going back to before. And, with self-study, there's no going back to not paying attention. *Alea jacta est.*

SIXTH REFLECTION: DESTRUCTIVENESS/ DECONSTRUCTION

I referred earlier to my perception that before I came out as queer, I saw in myself a minor destructive tendency. After I came out, this tendency seemed to disappear. I want to acknowledge the likelihood that this change took place exactly because within queer there is an element of destructiveness, mischief, the desire to break things and not be sorry afterwards. Queer does not cry over spilt milk, but dances in the puddle and spreads it across the kitchen floor. In a way, it is the same with self-study.

You can't go back after you have opened yourself to the inner understandings that self-study brings, or that choosing to be queer brings. The place where you used to live is broken, uninhabitable, destroyed. As a queer self-study researcher I want to claim that destruction has its place. It is a close relative of deconstruction, that staple of post-modern thought. You have to take a thing apart to see how it works or what is inside it. If you cannot put it back together, you have gained understanding of how to build something you could not have built before.

In my own self-study of my work over two years with a group of teachers performing action research, I raised the question of how I could improve our communication around the content and structure of our classes. Diligently I searched the literature for ideas about improving communication and, almost as diligently, I applied those ideas in class. Each week, I journaled about the quality of our communication and their response to our work together. What emerged was a record of what I came to understand about the teachers, their lives in classrooms and outside them, their needs and wishes for change in their working environments, their beliefs about schools and children and curricula. All this knowledge added up to a connection between and among us that permanently changed my understanding of teaching. What I had thought and believed during the preceding five years of working with similar groups of teachers was deconstructed and rearranged. Cognitive and emotional structures painstakingly built up were destroyed, hammered away by carefully attended to events and my interpretations.

I have never published that self-study. It is too personal, too revealing for me, and too intimate, too critical of the teachers in the class. Under the cloak of anonymity or not, it would not be ethical to publish. Yet of all the research I have done, I learned the most from it.

In the academic world, the purpose of doing research (self-study or not) tends to become the opportunity to publish or present. Not only external rewards, but also the internal reward of self-satisfaction can only be accessed through putting research out for others to see. However, self-study research has the potential to reach deeper, to teach more. It can go so far into the self that sharing it is difficult. I think this difficulty comes from the way self-study can destroy what is taken for granted, and break down the walls that protect us from the pain of self-understanding.

Self-study researchers do not have to go so far, and often they do not. On the other hand, if they do, they may publish or present only so much of the journey as makes them feel safe. Nevertheless, many of them are aware that they are learning on the edge of the destruction, or deconstruction, of their beliefs, values, and ideas about teaching and teacher education. Accepting and valuing this aspect of self-study is one of its greatest challenges.

Last Reflection

Who are you? you? you?
ask yourself
ask myself
as if I were some Other
I am under construction, so
   slow down
   watch out for the workmen
a work in progress
   being created/creating
   being performed/performing
I don't know
I am finding out
I am seeking a Northwest Passage
a clear water route across the Pole
a walk in the wilderness
   on the wild side
I am looking for a direction
   a path
   across my field
   across the straight furrows of my field
I am not a plough
   I am not a harrow
I am a wanderer
   a sideways jumper
   a connection finder
   a catalyst
   an Outsider
   a stranger
because I choose
because I prefer
because I perform my life

REFERENCES

Allender, J., 2001, *Teacher Self: The Practice of Humanistic Education* (New York: Rowman & Littlefield).

Arizona Group (Guilfoyle, K., Hamilton, M.L., Pinnegar, S. and Placier, P.), 2000, Myths and legends of teacher education reform in the 1990's: a collaborative self-study of four programs. In Loughran and Russell (Eds) *Exploring Myths and Legends of Teacher Education: Proceedings of the Third International Conference on Self-study of Teacher Education Practices, Herstmonceux Castle, East Sussex, England* (Kingston, Ontario: Queens University), pp. 20–24.

Arizona Group (Guilfoyle, K., Hamilton, M.L., Pinnegar, S. and Placier, P.), 2002, Exploring the concept of dialogue in the self-study of teacher education practices. In Kosnik, Freese and Samaras (Eds) *Making a Difference in Teacher Education through Self-study: Proceedings of the Fourth International Conference on Self-study of Teacher Education Practices, Herstmonceux Castle, East Sussex, England* (Toronto, Ontario: OISE, University of Toronto), pp. 96–103.

Austin, T., 2001, Treasures in the snow: what do I know and how do I know it through my educational inquiry into my practice of community? Retrieved 22 February 2003 from http://www.bath.ac.uk/~edsajw/austin.shtml

Bass, L., 2002, Self-study and issues of privilege and race. In Kosnik, Freese and Samaras (Eds) *Making a Difference in Teacher Education through Self-study: Proceedings of the Fourth International Conference on Self-study of Teacher Education Practices, Herstmonceux Castle, East Sussex, England* (Toronto, Ontario: OISE, University of Toronto), pp. 20–25.

Bornstein, K., 1998, *My Gender Workbook* (London and New York: Routledge).

Butler, J., 1990, *Gender Trouble: Feminism and the Subversion of Identity* (London and New York: Routledge).

Cole, A. and McIntyre, M., 1998, Reflections on 'Dance me to an understanding of teaching'. In Cole and Finley (Eds) *Conversations in Community: Proceedings on the Second International Conference of Self-study of Teacher Education Practices, Herstmonceux Castle, East Sussex, England* (Kingston, Ontario: Queens University), pp. 213–17.

De la Huerta, C., 1999, *Coming Out Spiritually: The Next Step* (New York: Jeremy P. Tarcher/Putnam).

Dinkelmann, T., 2003, Self-study in teacher education: a means and ends tool for promoting reflective teaching. *Journal of Teacher Education*, 54(1), pp. 6–18.

Griffiths, M. and Windle, J., 2002, Helping teacher educators learn to research: bread and roses – and a phoenix. In Kosnik, Freese and Samaras (Eds) *Making a Difference in Teacher Education through Self-study: Proceedings of the Fourth International Conference on Self-study of Teacher Education Practices, Herstmonceux Castle, East Sussex, England* (Toronto, Ontario: OISE, University of Toronto), pp. 87–91.

Hamilton, M.L., 2000, Change, social justice, and reliability: reflections of a secret (change) agent. In Loughran and Russell (Eds) *Exploring Myths and Legends of Teacher Education: Proceedings of the Third International Conference on Self-study of Teacher Education Practices, Herstmonceux Castle, East Sussex, England* (Kingston, Ontario: Queens University), pp. 109–12.

Hamilton, M.L., 2002, Using pictures at an exhibition to explore my teaching practices. In Kosnik, Freese and Samaras (Eds) *Making a Difference in Teacher Education through Self-study: Proceedings of the Fourth International Conference on Self-study of Teacher Education Practices, Herstmonceux Castle, East Sussex, England* (Toronto, Ontario: OISE, University of Toronto), pp. 109–14.

Heston, M., East, B. and Farstad, J., 2000, A waltz with Chaunce – a polka with Parker using text as a tool for self-study. Paper presented at the meetings of the American Educational Research Association. April, New Orleans.

Jagose, A., 1996, *Queer Theory: An Introduction* (New York: New York University Press).

Johnston, M. with the Educators for Collaborative Change, 1997, *Contradictions in Collaboration: New Thinking on School/University Partnership* (New York: Teachers College Press).

Lighthall, F., 2000, Reflecting with my students on my daily teaching: three case studies of a post-class laboratory. Paper presented at the meetings of the American Educational Research Association. April, New Orleans.

Manke, M., 1995, When a professor does action research in her classroom: a constructivist understanding of power relations. Paper presented at the Annual Meeting of the American Educational Studies Association. November, Cleveland, Ohio.

Manke, M., 2002, The hill one happens to be sitting on: community and validity in self-study research. Invited presentation to the Special Interest Group on Self-Study of Teacher Education, American Educational Research Association, April, New Orleans.

Manke, M. and Allender, J., 2002, Reflecting and refracting self-study artifacts: jazz poetry. In Kosnik, Freese and Samaras (Eds) *Making a Difference in Teacher Education through Self-study: Proceedings of the Fourth International Conference on Self-study of Teacher Education Practices, Herstmonceux Castle, East Sussex, England* (Toronto, Ontario: OISE, University of Toronto), pp. 15–19.

Oberg, A.A. and Finger, S., 1997, Action, reaction, and presence of mind. Presentation at the Seventeenth Curriculum Theory and Classroom Practice Conference. October, Fairfax, IN.

Perselli, V., 2002, The importance of being an artist. In Kosnik, Freese and Samaras (Eds) *Making a Difference in Teacher Education through Self-study: Proceedings of the Fourth International Conference on Self-study of Teacher Education Practices, Herstmonceux Castle, East Sussex, England* (Toronto, Ontario: OISE, University of Toronto), pp. 81–83.

Peshkin, A., 2000, The nature of interpretation in qualitative research. *Educational Researcher*, **29**(9), 5–10.

Russell, T., 2002, Can self-study improve teacher education? In Loughran and Russell (Eds) *Improving Teacher Education Practices through Self-study* (London: RoutledgeFalmer), pp. 3–9.

Sedgwick, E., 1990, *Epistemology of the Closet* (Berkeley, CA: University of California Press).

Smith, B., 2000, Finding and creating my self as a teacher educator and researcher: a ten year self-study. Paper presented at the Annual Meeting of the American Educational Research Association. April, New Orleans.

Upitis, R. and Russell, T., 1998, Building a teacher education community: combining electronic mail with face-to-face interactions. In Hamilton with Pinnegar, Russell, Loughran and LaBoskey (Eds) *Reconceptualizing Teaching Practice: Self-Study in Teacher Education* (London: Falmer Press), pp. 77–109.

Vavrus, M. and Archibald, O., 1998, Teacher education practices supporting social justice: approaching an individual self-study inquiry into institutional self-study. In Cole and Finley (Eds) *Conversations in Community: Proceedings of the Second*

International Conference on Self-study of Teacher Education Practices, Herstmonceux Castle, East Sussex, England (Kingston, Ontario: Queens University), pp. 162–66.

Weber, S. and Mitchell, C., 2000, Prom dresses are us? Excerpts from collective memory work. In Loughran and Russell (Eds) *Exploring Myths and Legends of Teacher Education: Proceedings of the Third International Conference on Self-study of Teacher Education Practices, Herstmonceux Castle, East Sussex, England* (Kingston, Ontario: Queens University), pp. 248–51.

Weber, S. and Mitchell, C., 2002, Academic literary performance, embodiment, and self-study: when the shoe doesn't fit: death of a salesman. In Kosnik, Freese and Samaras (Eds) *Making a Difference in Teacher Education through Self-study: Proceedings of the Fourth International Conference on Self-study of Teacher Education Practices, Herstmonceux Castle, East Sussex, England* (Toronto, Ontario: OISE, University of Toronto), pp. 121–24.

Wolf, C., 1984, *Cassandra: A Novel and Four Essays* (New York: Farrar, Straus & Giroux).

Zeichner, K., 1999, The new scholarship in teacher education. *Educational Researcher*, **28**(9), 4–15.

Chapter Eighteen

Self-study through narrative interpretation

Probing lived experiences of educational privilege

Kathleen Pithouse

In this chapter, I use the research method of narrative inquiry[1] to understand and explain the personal significance of a critical experience that I had as an English teacher in an independent girls' school in South Africa.[2] This teaching experience that I found so intellectually and emotionally intriguing occurred within the context of a grade seven Teen Stories writing project through which the learners in my class made a collection of short stories about teenage experiences for our school library. As part of the project, the learners were asked to record their thoughts and feelings about the writing process in daily journal entries.

To interpret this experience through a narrative lens, I consider it as a part of my unfolding life story. I search inward and outward, backward and forward through my on-going personal experience to uncover, penetrate and lay open the personal tension that moves me to engage in this inquiry, much as an unresolved conflict or problem propels the plot of a short story (Conle 2000, pp. 195–98).

Conle explains how a narrative inquirer's life story provides a context for making meaning of personal experience:

> [We] are burdened with a past for which we are accountable – even though it is not all of our own making – and with a future that is both unpredictable as well as foreshadowed by preconceived images of it . . . Constraints of the past and foreshadowed futures at each point of the writing [of a narrative inquiry] suggest particular horizons within which it can proceed.
>
> (Conle 2000, p. 192)

My effort to comprehend how my Teen Stories teaching experience follows on from previous personal experiences has evoked a collage of memories from my own schooldays. In trying to recognize the powerful energy that pushes me to do something important with this specific teaching experience, I have re-encountered my uneasy, unresolved relationship with the educational privilege that characterized my school experience as a white, middle-class, high-achiever in apartheid South Africa. In addition to revisiting my discomfort at having been advantaged by the fundamentally unjust apartheid education system, I have also become more conscious of my misgivings about the actual *educative value* (Dewey 1963, pp. 25–38) of my privileged school experience.

The apartheid policy of 'separate education' that was in place for the duration of my schooling (1979–1990) meant that South African school-children were set apart according to the National Party government's system of racial grouping. Furthermore, learners who were categorized by the education authorities as being physically or intellectually 'deficient' were excluded from mainstream schools.

In practice, the policy of separate education in South Africa ensured that a rigid hierarchy of educational privilege circumscribed all children's school lives. While 'white' schools received a disproportionately greater amount of government funding and had superior facilities and resources, 'black', 'coloured' and 'Indian' schools were actively disadvantaged in countless respects. The alternative provision made for learners with special educational needs also varied according to race. The majority of special schools were poorly resourced and many children with special educational needs had no access to schooling.

During my early primary school years at a white government school, my separation from other South African children because of restrictive categories of race and intellectual or physical ability did not have much personal meaning for me. My social life took place in the confines of a white middle-class suburb. Moreover, I was in the 'A' class at school and did not ever learn together with or forge friendships with the children who were relegated to the 'B', 'C' or 'mixed ability' classes. Although I had some awareness of the system of separate schooling, I did not really know any children of other races or different abilities and so did not *feel* our separation.

On some level, I must have known about the unequal distribution of resources between schools because I caught glimpses of rural black schools on long road journeys. What I did not see were the urban black, coloured and Indian schools. I do not think that I realized then that these schools did not have the libraries, playing fields and swimming pools that were standard features of white schools.

In my later primary school years, I did become more informed about and critical of the discriminatory practices of the apartheid education system. Because modern South African history was not part of the prescribed school syllabus, my knowledge came from unofficial sources such as my older brother. Another source of 'extra-curricula' ideas was my grade six teacher who often made space in our school day for informal Zulu lessons and discussions about current political issues.

As I approached my teens, I also became more conscious of the practice of intellectual differentiation within my primary school, which offered the A class children additional, purportedly superior learning opportunities and the 'best' teachers. I came to realize that my classmates and I were more likely to be chosen for coveted positions of responsibility and less likely to be suspected of misbehaviour. Our less advantaged peers appeared to regard us with some suspicion and resentment and we did not mix socially with them. I remember feeling intimidated and fascinated by the children in the mixed ability classes who seemed to have a reckless glamour that the A class 'nerds' lacked.

Despite the privileged treatment that I received as a high-achiever, I remember my senior primary school years as an intellectually uninteresting, often stifling, time. Learning to read and write in junior primary school had been exciting and empowering. After that, however, stimulating learning experiences were infrequent. My academic success was rarely the outcome of joyful learning. I think that it stemmed mainly from a personal sense of responsibility and a desire for adult approval. I gained the most intellectual and aesthetic satisfaction from reading books of my choice (I usually kept one open in my desk and read it surreptitiously at intervals during lessons), and from writing my own stories after school.

I do not remember tackling classroom creative writing tasks with the same enthusiasm as my independent story writing. At school, composition lessons usually involved being required to write on a set topic for a limited period. This was standard practice in South African schools where creative writing was regarded as a talent that could not be taught and genuinely creative thinking was not often facilitated or encouraged (Haarhoff 1998, p. 4, 11). I know that for many of my classmates, composition exercises or tests were stressful and demoralizing ordeals.

At the end of grade seven, I was expected to progress to the local white government high school. However, I wanted to follow my best friend to an independent girls' school in my area. My father had died when I was in grade six, and my mother could not afford private school fees on a nurse's salary, but I was able to attend the school of my choice through an academic scholarship. At that time in South Africa (1986), independent white schools could admit a limited number of children from other race groups. I remember feeling a kind of relief (and, I have to admit, a sense of moral superiority) about being able to make a choice to go to a so-called 'multi-racial' school.

Although my awareness of racially slanted educational privilege in South Africa increased during my high school years, my understanding of its impact on other people's lives was still constrained by my mostly white environment. With the exception of two Indian girls, all the learners in my grade at secondary school were white. One of the Indian girls had attended primary school in England and her tales of school life with no uniforms and other unheard of freedoms enthralled me. I do not know where the other girl's primary schooling took place. I presume she must have attended an Indian school, but I do not remember any discussion about it and I did not gain any insight into her earlier school experiences.

By going to a private high school I moved into an even more 'intellectually exclusive' atmosphere. Like many white independent schools in South Africa, my secondary school required all applicants to write an entrance exam and only accepted learners who appeared to have above average academic potential. As a 'scholarship girl', I remember feeling weighed down by a constant environmental pressure to achieve outstanding academic results. Although the learning opportunities offered to me in high school were not generally much more inspiring than my senior primary experiences, I was motivated to work hard by an unspoken fear of not being good enough. In what I have come to recognize as a way of including my thoughts and feelings in largely disaffective curriculum experiences, I developed a practice of writing for my own pleasure and emotional release outside of school, and then adapting these personal stories and poems to fit the set topics in class.

After high school, I went on to study at university. As an undergraduate, I encountered students who had attended a range of schools under the apartheid system. By studying with people from other race groups, I started to understand more about the discrepancies between our schooling.

I discovered more about the educational deprivation of the majority of South African children through my experiences as a volunteer tutor for secondary school learners. These learners from black township schools came to the university campus for extra lessons on Saturday mornings. I enjoyed the contact with the learners, but felt frustrated by the limited intervention that I could make. It was at this time in my life that I really began to comprehend the immorality and destructive power of the apartheid system of race-based educational privilege.

It was not until I started my career as a teacher in 1995 that I began to interact closely with learners who were identified as having special educational needs. Through this contact, I started to gain some insight into how it feels for a child in a mainstream school to be set apart by continual academic and/or social and emotional difficulty. I also began to grasp the extent to which the South African school system had failed children with different learning abilities.

In the eight years that I have been teaching, I have become increasingly aware of an internal dissonance with the *mis-educative* (Dewey 1963, p. 25) system of privilege that enveloped my school experiences in a shroud of separateness and constraint. I have recognized my school experiences in the writings of scholars such as Connell (1993, p. 15) who argues that '[an] education that privileges one child over another is giving the privileged child a corrupted education, even as it gives him or her a social or economic advantage.'

My personal need to understand how the experience of apartheid-era educational privilege impacted on my learning and on my self-concept has led me to question the discourses of privilege that were widely taken for granted during my time at school. By achieving my own agency within my story of mis-educative privilege, I hope to become 'better equipped to turn [my] own discourses and practices against those which constrain [me]' (Gough 2001, p. 110).

In the knowledge of this underlying personal and professional tension, I have engaged in a process of revisiting my Teen Stories experience in an attempt to find out and to make clear what it was about this particular teaching experience that was so emotionally and intellectually valuable to me. I now recognize that the Teen Stories project enabled me to experience, for the first time in my life, the growth of *a community of authors*. Through reflection on my experience, reference to others' stories of teaching writing and broader reading across the education field, I have come to understand that this community of authors developed in my classroom through the interaction of *contribution, sharing and response*, and *ownership*.

From the outset of the Teen Stories writing project, my learners were made aware that I wanted to know their thoughts and feelings about this curriculum experience so that I could use their on-going *contributions* to develop the project as we went along, rather than simply follow a preordained course of learning. Because I asked my learners to vote on whether or not to take part in the project, they understood that they were being given some power over the direction of the actual curriculum. Their journal entries revealed that this opportunity to choose made them feel like valued participants in classroom curriculum decision-making:

> Getting the invitation was exciting. (Leigh)[3]

> I think it was a clever idea to hand out invitations. It was nice that we got to vote just in case some people didn't want to do the project. (Callie)

> I liked the invitation because it made me feel important. (Colleen)

I believe that this initial emphasis on genuine learner input situated the Teen Stories project in a more open, dialogic classroom space than either I or my learners had previously experienced.

As the project progressed, my learners continued to trust that I would value and act on their insights into our classroom curriculum practice (Zaragoza and Vaughn 1995, p. 47). The provision of lesson time for regular journal entries made it possible for each learner to convey both positive and negative opinions about the evolution of the project to me:

> It's nice to work in groups on a story because you can hear all the different ideas and you can really use your imaginations. (Jane)

We progressed well today and are finally starting to get somewhere. (Bridget)

Can't wait to finish our story. It's going to be very exciting! (Lisha)

I could write all day. I think my story is good! (Callie)

My story is confusing me. Can you please give me some advice? (Samantha)

We are taking a long time because we are not agreeing. (Sandy)

Today was OK, but our group was very rowdy and I felt as if I was the only one contributing to the story. (Abigail)

My desire to remain receptive to my learners' thinking throughout the project meant that I had to make myself more vulnerable in the classroom than I had before:

> In this project I feel that I am relinquishing some of my control of the classroom. It's quite scary, but also quite liberating. Instead of my carefully choosing groups so as to avoid conflict, I'm letting them choose their own groups – letting underlying conflict surface and then my role as mediator and counsellor has to come to the fore. Also, with the pre-writing, I have to let them make mistakes and try not to overwhelm them with my opinions. It's a delicate balancing act – like reeling in a fishing-line very slowly – being careful not to lose the fish. I still need to be the manager of the classroom, but maybe not the director. By arranging the groups myself, I may avoid conflict, but perhaps it's not acknowledging conflict that already exists. This will keep me on my toes anyway! I need to remember to explore. I'm feeling my way. But, it's a harder way of teaching. It demands consciousness.[4]

It was often quite difficult for me to remain flexible and open to new contributions from the learners and to the necessarily unpredictable course of the story writing process (Goleman 1996, p. 273). As the project progressed, it became evident to me that the key resources that I could use to chart my way through this dynamic learning journey were my learners and my self (Ainscow 1999, p. 4).

The second factor that I believe supported the growth of our community of authors was a 'writing workshop' atmosphere that allowed for increased freedom of movement in my classroom and fostered genuine *sharing and response* among the participants in the Teen Stories project (Zaragoza and Vaughn 1995, p. 45). Through sharing their stories with one another and me at various stages in the writing process, my learners gained valuable experience of discussing and reflecting on their writing, as well as useful advice about their writing (Zaragoza and Vaughn 1995, p. 45). In many cases, by reading their stories aloud and trying to explain their work to others, the learners became more critical readers of their own writing (Phenix 1990, p. 31). Moreover, when sharing their precious stories with others, my learners began to realize that they were making themselves vulnerable and that their response to other writers who took the same risk should be as encouraging and helpful as possible.

As a teacher-participant in the project, I took on the important role of paying close attention and responding to the unique creative writing process of each learner (Ainscow 1999, p. 6; Roosevelt 1998, p. 81; Zaragoza and Vaughn 1995, p. 46). I was able to discuss every learner's work in regular meetings in class and I also managed to give written advice in the writing process books after each lesson. In this way, I attempted to integrate my on-going evaluation of each learner's writing into the course of the actual learning experience (Phenix 1990, p. 98). By keeping notes on the development of each learner's writing process, I was able to build my knowledge of every individual's achievements to inform my end-of-term assessment (Phenix 1990, p. 98; Zaragoza 1998, p. 93). At all times, I tried to show my respect for my learners by responding to their writing in constructive and supportive ways. I also endeavoured to make the learners aware that they were free to accept or reject my writing advice (Zaragoza 1998, p. 82).

In retrospect, I realize that my participation in the classroom creative writing process would have been enhanced if I had also been writing and sharing stories within the community of writers (Gregory 1990, p. 1). Although I could draw on my memories of my adolescent creative writing experiences, and I was working on my academic writing at the time of the project, I believe that I would have been better placed to advise and support my learners if I had actively participated in this communal Teen Stories writing endeavour.

Sharing and response in the classroom were enhanced by the learners' journal entries. The journals, which had started off as academic journals, became a safe space in which some learners chose to examine and share their personal thoughts and feelings (Gregory 1990, p. 35). Learners were able to mull over and discuss happenings that were of vital importance to them, but that would not usually come up in an English lesson (Goleman 1996, p. 267):

> Life sucked today. Problems are cropping up in all forms! Friends, test results and all sorts! (Carmen)

> Today wasn't the best because someone was quite ugly to me. I know this is not to do with English, but I am quite sad. (Samantha)

> Confidential! Today in English I felt all alone. My friend decided to write a story without me. (Lana)

These more personal journal entries enabled me to gain a fuller understanding of and establish deeper relationships with individual learners (Ainscow 1999, p. 3). Through reading and responding to these entries I became more conscious of the emotional responsibilities that teaching entails and of the extent to which emotional and social issues affect learning (Connell 1993, p. 63).[5]

The third important element of the Teen Stories project that facilitated the development of our classroom community of authors was a feeling of learner *ownership*. Ownership occurs in the writing process when learners are at liberty to pursue their own concerns, to have some power over their learning and, accordingly, to feel more responsible for it. Although my learners were somewhat limited in their choice of topic by having to situate their work within the broad framework of a teenage story, many of their journal entries expressed their pleasure at being given a chance to write their 'own' stories:

> I think that there will be a lot of creativity involved. This project gives us a chance to write our own stories and put them into a book. I'm also quite glad that we can choose who we want to be with and have as many stories as we want. (Maria)

> I liked writing my story because you could write anything you wanted to. (Christine)

The learners seemed to feel that their interests, preoccupations and desires were being acknowledged as important because they were able to choose particular story topics that were significant to them (Connell 1993, p. 187; Goleman 1996, p. 263; Zaragoza and Vaughn 1995, p. 43). I believe that so many of my learners were really inspired by and absorbed in crafting their stories because they had a sense that they were free to be true to their own concerns when writing. Zaragoza confirms the value of empowering learners to pursue their own interests when writing:

> When children are given the time and opportunity to choose and develop personal topics, they begin to feel control over the writing process . . . Writing becomes connected to their personal work, activities and social interactions . . . Their control over decisions produces the desire and motivation to learn and be active participants in the writing process.
> (Zaragoza 1998, p. 78)

Because the Teen Stories project involved the writing of fiction, my learners had the freedom to imagine new stories as well as to draw on their own or others' teenage experiences (Gregory 1990, p. 192). While some stories were based wholly on real events, most were created from diverse snippets of experience and imagination that were fused and transformed through the writing process. The extent to which my learners communicated in their journals on the creative possibilities of this writing project made me more aware that genuinely creative learning experiences were not an integral part of their school lives (Haarhoff 1998, p. 46). The Teen Stories project seemed to offer the learners fertile openings for the private and shared making of meaning. One learner explained that the project enabled her to make use of ideas that had been 'overflowing in [her] head'. I believe that the project allowed me space and time to acknowledge and cultivate my learners' largely unexplored desire to use written language to actively create their own fictions, rather than merely to decode or transcribe adult narratives (Ritchie and Wilson 2000, p. 43; Zaragoza and Vaughn 1995, p. 46).

The Teen Stories project required me to step back from the chalkboard and to bear witness to the dynamic encounter of the learner-writers 'and the world of culture, imagination, morality, hope, and doubt' (Roosevelt 1998, p. 82). My work in this context of the creation of fiction was to make meaning with my learners by being a serious, appreciative and reflective reader of their stories (Roosevelt 1998, pp. 81–82).

Another significant characteristic of the project was that it gave my learners the opportunity to work through, understand and 'own' the processes involved in writing a short story. According to Phenix (1990, p. 35), this explicit knowledge of how to go about a task, step by step, is essential to learners' success in writing. I believe that because my learners were guided through the writing process that all authors experience in some form (Phenix 1990, p. 1; Zaragoza 1998, p. 77), and were allowed to concentrate on each aspect of writing at a time in the process when it was most meaningful, they felt more in control of their own creative writing work. Consequently, almost every learner was enabled to author a story that she was proud of (Phenix 1990, pp. 35–36; Zaragoza 1998, p. 78).

The demanding, often frustrating journey through the writing process helped my learners to appreciate that good writing involves hard work and commitment and that to produce a final draft of a story is an admirable achievement. Their journal entries and discussions in class revealed that the project had given them an opportunity to feel like 'real' authors, rather than like novices learning to write (Phenix 1990, p. 60):

> This gave us a chance to feel like we are authors. (Jenny)
>
> I now see that all the books in the library take a lot of work and I respect the authors. (Leigh)
>
> When I look back at all my work, I feel really proud of myself, proud that I can actually sit down and write a good story. It makes me feel special. (Lindy)

The learners' reflections on the project also revealed that they felt empowered and inspired by this experience to continue writing stories for their own pleasure in the future (Phenix 1990, pp. 94–95, 124).

The learners' realization that they really could be authors was cemented by the knowledge that their stories would be published in a book and placed in the school library along with the work of professional authors (Zaragoza 1998, pp. 77, 83). Phenix explains how the publication of learners' written work reinforces their sense of ownership:

> Our students will develop as writers as they write for real purposes and real audiences . . . Pride in authorship is probably the greatest motivator there is when it comes to getting students to write and develop as writers. We have taken the first step in creating authors when we publish their work.
>
> (Phenix 1990, p. 60)

My interpretation of the Teen Stories curriculum experience as the evolution of a community of authors in my classroom has grown out of an exploration of my experiences of educational privilege. Through this interpretive work, I have become conscious that the teaching story that I wish to author in the future is one in which educational privilege is not understood as an advantage that is available only to a few, but rather as a sacred and vital civil right for each South African child. I have come to understand that my personal tension with the constraints of exclusive educational privilege has propelled me towards my teaching intention of facilitating inclusive, supportive and genuinely educative classroom curriculum experiences for every learner. I believe that the development of curriculum experiences, such as the Teen Stories project, that privilege the inclusion, affirmation and fruitful growth of every learner's self could give rise to the human interconnectedness, creativity and openness to ideas and experiences that is the basis of truly democratic schooling.

NOTES

1   Narrative inquiry is a qualitative research method that attempts to make sense of life as it is lived (Clandinin and Connelly 2000, p. 78). A narrative inquiry arises from experience, and the narrative inquirer allows experience to show the way (Clandinin and Connelly 2000, p. 188). According to Clandinin and Connelly (p. xiv), narrative inquiry is 'a dynamic process of living and telling stories, and reliving and retelling stories'.

2   This school is well resourced and its facilities are similar to those of nearby, formerly white, government schools. Owing to its independent status, the school receives very limited government funding and its fees are higher than the local government schools. Nevertheless, the fees are lower than the majority of independent schools in the area. Most of the learners at the school come from upper middle-income homes. The medium of instruction at the school is English, but the learners' home languages include Afrikaans, Chinese, a variety

of European languages, and Zulu. While the majority of the learners are white, there are also black, coloured, Indian and Taiwanese children at the school. Unlike most of the independent schools in the area, this school does not have an academic entrance exam and accepts children with a range of learning needs. Because the school has a policy of inclusion, all children learn in 'mixed ability' classes.

3   To ensure confidentiality, I have used pseudonyms when quoting from my learners' journal entries. For clarity, I have corrected any spelling and punctuation errors that appeared in the original journal entries.

4   This is an extract from the teaching journal that I kept during the project.

5   Lana wrote every day about her difficulties with friendships and her lack of confidence in herself. In the end, she was the only one who did not complete a story. I came to understand that until her low self-esteem and all-engrossing social concerns were attended to, she would not be in a position to do creative work. I tried to respond to her journal entries with supportive comments and I met with her at break times to listen to her concerns. Although Lana did not finish writing a story, I felt that the project was useful to her because it brought her emotional problems to the fore and enabled me to recommend to her parents that she see an educational psychologist. For nine months following our project, she attended psychotherapy sessions, which helped to build her personal, social and academic confidence.

REFERENCES

Ainscow, M., 1999, *Understanding the Development of Inclusive Schools* (London: Falmer Press).

Clandinin, D.J. and Connelly, F.M., 2000, *Narrative Inquiry: Experience and Story in Qualitative Research* (San Francisco: Jossey-Bass).

Conle, C., 2000, Thesis as narrative or 'What is the inquiry in narrative inquiry?'. *Curriculum Inquiry*, 30(2), 189–214.

Connell, R.W., 1993, *Schools and Social Justice* (Philadelphia: Temple University Press).

Dewey, J., 1963, *Experience and Education* (New York: Collier Books). (First published in 1938.)

Goleman, D., 1996, *Emotional Intelligence* (London: Bloomsbury).

Gough, N., 2001, Learning from *Disgrace*: a troubling narrative for South African curriculum work. *Perspectives in Education*, 19(1), 107–26.

Gregory, C., 1990, *Childmade: Awakening Children to Creative Writing* (Barrytown, NY: Station Hill Press).

Haarhoff, D., 1998, *The Writer's Voice: A Workbook for Writers in Africa* (Halfway House: Zebra Press).

Phenix, J., 1990, *Teaching Writing: The Nuts and Bolts of Running a Day-to-Day Writing Program* (Markham, Ontario: Pembroke Publishers Ltd).

Ritchie, J.S. and Wilson, D.E., 2000, *Teacher Narrative as Critical Inquiry: Rewriting the Script* (New York: Teachers College Press).

Roosevelt, D., 1998, 'There this kid was, stranded in a car': reading the fictions of children as if they mattered. *Curriculum Inquiry*, 28(1), 81–111.

Zaragoza, N., 1998, Mentoring authorship in the elementary school classroom through the writing process. In Steinberg and Kincheloe (Eds) *Students as Researchers: Creating Characters that Matter* (London: Falmer Press), pp. 77–93.

Zaragoza, N. and Vaughn, S., 1995, Children teach us to teach writing. *The Reading Teacher*, **49**(1), 42–47.

Chapter 19

'White female teacher arrives in native community with trunk and cat'

Using self-study to investigate tales of traveling White teachers

Teresa Strong-Wilson

INTRODUCTION

'Were it not for those many experiences, would I now still feel wholly like an exile from my own culture?' (Wilson 2000, p. 1). This self-ascription of 'exile' appears in my autobiography about teaching in the First Nations community of 'Ravenwing.' ('Ravenwing' is a pseudonym). Why did the word 'exile' seem apropos? Was exile an experience? A feeling? Or did the actual experience have very little to do with the choice of words? Bloch (1998) explains that as a stylized version of events, a public story becomes accepted by others because it follows accepted conventions. My story falls into tales of the traveling teacher, especially about the ones who self-exile to remote places. In this paper, using self-study methodologies, I examine 'exile' in relation to experience as well as a story structure common to White teachers.

METHOD OF SELF-STUDY

Autobiographical narrative seems to come out of nowhere but of course that is not true. Virginia Woolf (1978a) testifies that in her own case, 'memory supplies what I had forgotten, so that it seems as if it were happening independently, though I am really making it happen' (p. 77). Woolf also says, however, that 'strong emotion must leave its trace' (p. 78). Autobiography, like ethnography, has a reputation of 'commitment to the actual' (Fischer 1986, p. 198), in which here 'the actual' means memories arising out of personal experience.

In teaching, especially beginning teaching, the strong sensation most frequently evoked is discomfort. Camus (2000) identifies the inception of consciousness with a feeling of weariness that 'has something sickening about it' (p. 19). Beginning teachers often feel overwhelmed within their first year, alternating between despair and hope. Camus (2000) echoes Heidegger's idea that anxiety 'is at the source of everything' (p. 19). Sensations do not have to be strong to become etched in memory but can become so through slow accumulation and persistent repetition, like Sartre's (1966) knowing how a green apple tastes: 'Who can distinguish the green apple from its tart gaiety?' (p. 8). Both kinds of sensations are associated with my memories of teaching and the experiences leading up to teaching.

CONTEXT I: EXPERIENCE

Family travel

I have strong memories of feeling, at home, in growing up, like 'the stranger in the living room' (Personal communication, Janice Simcoe, First Nations Coordinator, May 2002). However, the more I have thought about the role that travel has played in my family, the more difficult it has become to see as unique my feelings of being an outsider. All my life, I have heard as a departure from the norm the story of my parents' move from the West Coast to Eastern Canada. My mother grew up on the Coast. My father traveled sparingly. He was posted to Newfoundland in World War II and after the war he and a friend went on a backpacking trip into the Rocky Mountains. When I probed further, I found more travel stories.

My parents know very little about the circumstances of their parents' lives before they left Scotland and England, except that economic necessity drove them. These 'leaving home' stories (Taylor 1989, p. 39), in our small repertoire of family stories, tend to be eclipsed by more spectacular dramas, such as the scandalous tale of an uncle. He failed to meet his family at the appointed time when they got off the boat. To this day, no one knows what happened to him, although the conjecture is that he planned his disappearance. Perhaps, like Canadian immigrant author Frederick Philip Grove, he needed to erase one identity so as to invent a new one. My grandparents' silence also played its role in self-invention by willing forgetfulness: a new story/life created as if from the here and now, without antecedents.

I see my story as also belonging with other predominantly Canadian stories that invent against the background of the north as if against a blank slate: '[t]o write is, in some metaphoric sense, to go North. To go North is, in some metaphoric sense, to write. One goes North at that very point on the page where the word is in the process of extending itself onto the blankness of the page,' explains Canadian writer Kroetsch (1995, p. 14, cited in Hulan 2002, p. 149). Rather than escaping from a family narrative, my journey further entrenched it. I traveled North not once but twice. I taught in Aboriginal communities as from a blank page and then I wrote about those travels. My actual experiences complicate the narrative, though, such that, though the plot may seem destructive, the experience was not.

Oppositional lived perspectives and traitorous identities

'I love my family, but I do not always agree with their opinions,' says Tonia, a student teacher (Allen and Labbo 2001, p. 49). 'Race traitors' can 'destabilize their insider status by challenging and resisting the usual assumptions held by most White people' (Bailey, 2000 p. 288) and may feel ostracized as a result, but the experience of being an outsider is denied to Whites because of the privilege they enjoy in society. Building on Harding's (1991) work, Bailey (2000) distinguishes between two kinds of 'traitorous identity': as perspective and political position (p. 284). As perspective, traitorous identity is rooted in experience. As political position, it is a way of acting in the world by consciously seeking change. The stronger position, Bailey argues, is the political one. The experience of 'feeling' on the margins is not enough. Indeed, Bailey says, it is not an experience that Whites can claim, given their privileged status in society. I want to complicate Bailey's distinction between perspective and experience.

My childhood memories echo those of Maxine Greene (1995): 'Since I was a little child, I have known that all perspectives are contingent [and] that no one's picture is complete' (p. 82). I recall formulating the idea that knowledge that people claimed to know about others was suspect unless based on direct information. An oppositional perspective begins with such niggling doubts. In the last chapter of her book, early twentieth-century teacher Hannah Breece's firm belief that indigenous peoples need to be 'civilized' begins to unravel. She tells the story of a young Aboriginal man who showed extreme promise but died suddenly when a steamer was grounded during a storm. His death was accidental, but it leads Hannah to question the promise of a White man's education, within which 'happy outcomes seldom occurred' (Breece 1997, p. 189). She admits that 'this question had long bothered' her (p. 189). Thus begins a process of separation from the myth of Whites' indispensability to natives that had sustained her career: 'I finally reached the conclusion that native children and young people should be taught in their own settlements, in schools adapted to their own ways of life' (p. 189).

Self-doubt deeply informed my experiences in Ravenwing and guided which episodes rose to the top. Of the fourteen sections in my autobiography, only one occurs in the classroom. Most teacher narratives are set within the privileged spaces of school or classroom, separate from 'Nature' or the indigenous community. In my narrative, most episodes occur in doorways or on streets, outside the bandstore or within an elder's house, thus performing a 'decentering' (Narayan and Harding 2000) from the norm. The narrative was not tailored to perform these transgressions but arose out of experience, or that oppositional lived perspective in which I doubted second-hand information circulating in teacherage and school and set about drawing my own conclusions, but not without a struggle.

CONTEXT II: NARRATIVE

Teacher travel narratives

White teachers' travels to indigenous communities participate in a colonizing discourse; formal education is a civilizing force. In the first decade of the twentieth century, Hannah Breece traveled to several Northern communities in Alaska, remaining in each place only long enough for her teaching to take root. Once she was satisfied that the community had made progress, she accepted an invitation to teach elsewhere. Her mandate was not confined to the standard subjects but included instruction on cleanliness, proper diet, and appropriate social and religious behavior. The more inaccessible the community, the greater the challenge and the more attractive it was to Breece, who reasoned that while villages closer to civilization would receive its benefits, those further away relied on intrepid teachers like herself: 'the people out there by themselves, groping for the light, appealed to me' (Breece 1997, p. 56).

My autobiography likewise draws attention to remoteness as a factor in my decision of where to teach: 'Accounts of teachers journeying to outlying communities follow certain conventions. They begin with a trip through difficult terrain, a laborious route that entails more time and energy than "civilized" people would tolerate' (Wilson 2000, p. 1). Implicitly accepting that my services were needed, fresh out of teachers' college and in need of a job, I undertook the journey:

> There are only two ways of getting into Ravenwing: by air or water . . . I needed to get a teacher's trunk up the coast and couldn't have planned a quainter entry: 'White Female Teacher Arrives in Native Community with Trunk and Cat'. We decided to drive up Island to Edgeport and have it put on a barge.
>
> The highway after Salmonrun changes abruptly from loping, easy curves to sharp twists and turns. Past the sawmill, human 'civilization' simply vanishes; it recedes behind a wall of trees . . . When I say that human civilization recedes, my tongue frolics against my cheek. What I mean is an ideal of order and decorum: the cozy beds and breakfasts and restaurants and houses and towns that hug the Mystic Island highways and impart to it its faux Old World charm . . . This complacent presence changes dramatically after Salmonrun, loggers' country . . .
>
> People in Ravenwing know this stretch of road between Endurant and Salmonrun – over five hundred kilometers – intimately: every bend, every curve, every slope. It takes the same amount of time to travel from Salmonrun to Endurant as it takes to drive from Elizaville to Salmonrun . . . Endurant is spread out, luxuriating in an expansiveness of geography, although you get the sense that things are stretched too thin, that places

that could be closer are farther away just because there's space to fill. For new teachers in Ravenwing, this is civilization.

(Wilson 2000, pp. 2–4)

Economic necessity often provides the rationale for why White teachers travel to remote communities. Max Braithwaite's (2002) trek in the dead of winter to a remote farming community in Saskatchewan during the Depression was made necessary by his financial straits. Abbie Morgan Madenwald's (1992) autobiography of her and her husband's teaching in an Alaskan community in the early 1930s likewise begins with economic hard times: 'the couple's financial future looked bleak. When offered contracts as part of the U.S. government's program to send teachers to remote areas to educate, train, and offer medical aid to the Native population in Alaska Territory, they debated briefly, then eagerly signed' (Madenwald 1992, p. xxiii). Stephen Gilbert Brown (2000) admits to finding a 'direction' in life (p. 18) when he was guaranteed a job contingent on becoming a 'bush teacher' in the land of the 'undesirables' in a remote part of Alaska (p. 15). Phyllis Taylor (1955), who taught in Big Bar Creek for two years, Gerry Andrews (1985), who taught in a Metis settlement from 1923 to 1925, as well as Hannah Breece, are exceptions, philanthropically motivated experienced teachers filling vacated spaces because of the teachers who would not come, even for economic reasons. My own decision was a mix of both: the need for a job and wanting to teach in a First Nations community.

Teachers' travel autobiographies are a subspecies of a travel genre that Pratt (1992) traces back to the seventeenth century and fit into the survival genre exemplified by Defoe's (1985) *Robinson Crusoe*. The first travel narrative within Western literary tradition goes back to Homer's *Odyssey* and many, if not most, teacher narratives imitate its literary structure: a journey away from home and back again, with many adventures along the way. Precedents for teacher narratives also exist in the stories of Jesuit missionaries crafted to appeal to the home audience by embellishing the European hero's ordeals with salacious details (Perron 2000). In keeping with such traditions, the journey in teacher stories is only the tip of the tale. Like Crusoe, teacher protagonists expend considerable energy demarcating 'civilized' spaces from the surrounding wilderness. My description is scanty, but I nevertheless allude to this convention: 'One of the first things I did, after finding out where I was staying, was to traipse down to the store. I needed cleaning supplies and a mop' (Wilson 2000, p. 8). In registering her impressions of the Russian homes, with their starched linens and carefully tended gardens, Breece (1997) contrasts them with Aleutian homes depicted as hovels and recounts how she spruced up her living quarters and schoolhouse.

Female travel narratives

While mostly men wrote within the travel genre, using males as protagonists, Pratt (1992) identifies two kinds of writing that featured women: one written by male authors but with a female protagonist, the other with women as protagonists of their own travel stories. The first kind is exemplified by La Condamine's (1745) *Brief Narrative of Travels Through the Interior of South America*, in which he tells the story of Isabela Godin des Odonais, an upper-class Peruvian who, waiting in Peru for her husband to arrange passage to France, 'made a daring decision' to travel over the Andes and down the Amazon in her husband's footsteps (Pratt 1992, p. 21). Only Isabela survived the trip, 'wandering deliriously' until she reached the banks of the river and was rescued by 'indigenous canoeists' (p. 21). Pratt likens Isabela to a 'female Amazon' (p. 23).

In the second type of narrative, the '*exploratrices socials*' were women who, like their male counterparts, 'the capitalist vanguardists,' ventured alone into South America and wrote accounts of their travels, such as Flora Tristan's (1838) *Peregrinations of a Pariah* and Maria Graham Callcott's (1824) *Voyage to Brazil* and *Journal of a Residence in Chile* (Pratt 1992, p. 155). Pratt identifies both women's purposes as to 'collect and possess themselves' (p. 160). Maria Graham Callcott accompanied her husband to South America, but after he died on the way, Callcott decided to remain in Chile, living there for two years. Callcott's journal, claims Pratt, is now valued as a 'perceptive and sympathetic source on Chilean society and politics in the independence period' (p. 157). Tristan's title is especially striking in light of the prominence of exile in my travel story. Tristan travelled to Peru to claim an inheritance and gain financial independence but also experienced a 'political awakening' (p. 156). She returned to France as a social activist, writing on the subjects of workers' rights and women's emancipation. Tristan saw herself as a 'pariah' because of her unpopular political convictions, which had emerged from her 'brutal marital experiences' and witnessing Peru's political struggles (p. 156).

Like their male counterparts, both women constructed themselves as 'interactive seeker[s] of knowledge' (Pratt 1992, p. 163) who thrust themselves in the thick of things. Whereas the male vanguardists couched their accounts in linear plots ending in achievement and domination, the 'exploratresses' were engaged in 'quests for self-realization and fantasies of social harmony' (p. 168). One of the ways in which they expressed their fantasy was in documenting 'feminotopias' (p. 164), or those settings in which Tristan and Callcott perceived indigenous women asserting their autonomy in the company of other women. Tristan, for instance, noticed how women's mode of dressing enhanced rather than inhibited female movement; such practices enhanced her perception of an idealized world of 'female autonomy, empowerment, and pleasure' among the women of Lima (pp. 166–67).

Callcott documented a meeting among six women in a garden (namely, Edenic) setting; in which the women struck Callcott as imbued with a powerful, female Amazonian mystique.

Intimations of a feminotopia come through in 'Ravenwing' in my descriptions of Gran and Joan, both of whom symbolize powerful local repositories of knowledge:

> When you meet Gran, you realize that the comforting smell that fills the house comes from her. Scott Momaday, Kiowa storyteller, talks about his great-grandmother's smell: the smell of her ancient hands seeping into his young ones as they sit, hands clasped, him imbibing her ancestral words and particular essence. Feeling the memories. Originally, an essence was a distinctive smell. It's awkward bending over to hug Gran because she's sitting down. She grabs your two hands and squeezes them, all the while smiling and saying how happy she is to see you. In her firm tender grasp you feel her spirit plummeting into the depths of your soul and pulling it skyward. You feel utterly vulnerable and naked. It isn't the kind of vulnerability that makes you crumble into tears; no, if you were feeling emotional, her grasp would make you strong.
>
> (Wilson 2002, p. 86)

Joan is aligned with Raven, who is identified as a deep source of indigenous knowledge in my story: 'I see a woman with beautiful dark hair and fierce eyes . . . Her eyes are mischievous, glinting and knowing' (p. 9). I construe Joan's visit as the Ravenwing version of the Welcome Wagon: 'She comes with a gift. Blackberries . . . It is real early when she chooses to pay a social call. Maybe six in the morning. She pounds on my door' (p. 9). Joan's social visit, like my visits with Gran, contrast with tea parties remembered from my childhood, in which the world of women is depicted as an Austen-like parade of manners, with no promise of important knowledge to be gained:

> The adults, mostly women, sat in the living room . . . The men did not remain there long but, once their conversation on gentlemanly topics began – carpentry projects, basement renovations, sports – retired to the kitchen, basement or outside. My mother, slim and well-dressed, sat poised on the edges of chairs or couches, sipping her tea, while holding the saucer circumspectly so as to catch any wayward drops. (Don't make more work for the hostess: a legitimate form of female solidarity.) I, on the other hand, inelegant, in no *apparent* need of dessert, luxuriated in the tasty treats then retired to a corner with a Nancy Drew mystery.
>
> (Wilson 2000, pp. 5–6; emphasis in the original)

I slip away at the first opportunity to create 'a room of my own' in the world of books (Woolf, 1978b; Woolf's book is entitled *A Room of One's Own*). Ironically, the book depicts a female protagonist (Nancy Drew) constructed within a male world. Perhaps like Tristan and Callcott, history within a patriarchal culture is what motivates me to remember in 'Ravenwing' those powerful females.

The ideal of a feminotopia is played out in other female teacher autobiographies in different ways. Like Renaissance poet Edmund Spenser's Britomart, who is immune to sexual influence (unlike the Red Crosse Knighte, whom Acrasia successfully ensnares in her Bower of Delights), a sexless Hannah Breece exercises her influence in domestic spheres, 'civilizing' mothers and young women by showing them how to sew dresses and plant gardens. Abbie Morgan Madenwald establishes sisterly societies of sewing and crafts with young women she befriends and, like Hannah Breece, rescues young female students from undesirable marital alliances (Madenwald 1992). Sylvia Ashton-Warner's (1960) *Spinster*, an account of her teaching of Maori children, is scandalized by a love tryst with a younger teacher, but it is more her consciousness of herself as a spinster that creates an ironic perspective on the feminotopeia that she tries to establish in her Kindergarten class:

> No wonderful blue eyes follow me into the austerity of my thinking in the infant room . . . As ever, my mind in the pre-fab is sacrosanct, cloistering nothing other than my absorption in my teaching. The image that jostles forward and upward demanding my inner eye is one of an infant room that has achieved the organic order; a seed-bed where children grow and expand and bloom.
>
> (pp. 47–48)

If Ashton-Warner's story feels repressed, it is because, as the central female in the story, her desires (both erotic and creative) are controlled by her male surroundings, in which she symbolizes the aberrant female longing for fulfillment even while she denies it to her aging and spinsterly self.

In 'Ravenwing,' romance enters allusively, as oblique references to a 'Joseph' who (readers of my autobiography have told me) tantalizes with his elusive presence: 'There wasn't anything familiar to hang onto, beyond that fragile thread of a new friendship begun in the Endurant airport with a Native man wearing a Ravenwing sweatshirt' (Wilson 2000, p. 7). Viewed retrospectively, Joseph provided me with an insider point of view. Our intercultural marriage belonged within a colonizing tradition of Whites marrying Natives and particularly on British Columbia's coast, of Scots marrying Natives (my grandparents were Scottish) (Brown 1980; Stevenson 1999; van Kirk 1980). The information that Joseph whispers as if in my ear provided a valuable source of knowledge within which to create the 'domestic space' of my classroom (Grumet 1988). That the connection is erotic and not merely one of ethnographic friendship is left out of the official teacher narrative and explored in other narrative writings:

We spent a lot of time by the beach sitting on logs outside Nan's smoke-house talking into the dusk. Throwing rounded rocks into the water and watching them skip. Words of love disguised as information. 'See that island out there?' he points. His arm brushes my shoulder or a blade of my hair. Swift intake of breath. That swooning sensation. Then a refocus. I see the island out there.

(Wilson 2001)

Neither the romance nor the domestic space of the classroom is the focal point of my autobiographical narrative. This omission provides insight into which 'public narrative' was more important to tell. Like my female, White, and 'feminist' predecessors, I am drawn to powerful indigenous women. Pratt (1992) argues that privilege undoubtedly framed Callcott's and Tristan's encounters with South American society: 'both privilege their houses and above all their private rooms as refuges and sources of well-being' (p. 159). They can venture out, says Pratt (1992), because of the safety of these 'domestic' (p. 159) 'room-sized empire[s]' attended by servants (p. 160). Similarly, my own privileged space was afforded by my Whiteness.

'ERIN'S' STORY

In 'Ravenwing,' exile is a fiction that allows the narrator to create a space within which to write and reinvent herself ('feminotopia') as well as corresponds to a lived experience. Kamler (2001) documents how a writer's decisions represent craft; the more conscious the writer is of her craft, the better she can tailor the narrative. Elsewhere, I draw on Kamler's notion of 'relocation' to envision how I could have written the teacher autobiography differently (Wilson 2002). To rewrite the autobiography within a 'traitor stance' would mean selecting episodes that exemplified that stance, thus turning the story into a political allegory. As it stands, the story of my experiences that rose 'to the top' (Woolf 1978a, p. 77) has the shape of a romance, in Frye's (1976) sense of an idealization of experience. Rather than critiquing the shape of romance in teacher stories (Graham 1995), though, I want to ask why it is there.

Ravenwing could feel like home to me because the oppositional perspective that made me feel like an exile in my own culture allowed me to feel accepted in an indigenous community suspicious of White society but for their own reasons. Paradoxically, my experiences in Ravenwing allow me to make the return back to 'my own culture': 'Were it not for those many experiences, would I now still feel wholly like an exile from my own culture?' (Wilson 2000, p. 1). The word 'many' is deceptive, implying that it was the sheer number of Odyssean-like adventures (as Pratt's (1992) *exploratrice sociale*) that led to my journey back 'home.' However, the journey back, rather than ending the exile, continues it: 'As it turns out, I am still living out the reverberations of those experiences' (Wilson 2000, p. 1). Exile is the only possible stance for my participation in White society: 'I feel my estrangement most poignantly when, because of having been there, I can't find the words to say what I now can see' (Wilson 2000, p. 1). I have learned something through my experiences.

Estrangement began with a self-imposed exile and the construction of a narrative of an 'authentic' self (Taylor 1992) who needed to 'leave home' to construct that self (Taylor 1989, p. 39). In Ravenwing, I become even more of a stranger to myself, and this estrangement happens on the turf of Western culture. It happens within that privileged domain of literacy: the school. Feelings of estrangement force me to contend with the very myths that I thought I had extirpated or escaped from. My story of a fictional 'Erin' (namely, myself) distills that insight. Far from knowing all, Erin slips into a state of uncertainty, that experience of self-doubt that I said earlier characterized my experiences of being in Ravenwing, particularly as a beginning teacher.

> Today, because Erin is on duty, Laura, Erin's T.A., has to manage the day's question. One of two things can happen and Erin dreads both. Either something happens on the way into their seats: a major altercation breaks out between students, which needs to be dealt with immediately. A tense tone is then set for the rest of the morning. Or Laura is supremely successful at establishing order and decorum in the classroom, far more than Erin could ever hope for, and as she enters and Laura recedes to her corner, there is an almost audible sigh: Why can't Laura teach us? To which Erin inwardly adds the barely audible: Laura's Native, she's one of us. If Erin is unsteady on her feet, and her chagrin shows plainly, as through an untimely deep blush as she begins the morning's lesson, Mark, a little Machiavelli, will calculatingly blurt out, cloaked in a child's third-grade innocence, 'I wish Laura was teaching us.' Technically, he didn't say: I wish Erin was not. But that was the intent. And invariably, if such a thing was to happen, someone else would loudly echo that wish. And then the subtle misbehaviors would begin: the pencil tapping while she is speaking, interrupting, getting up without asking, calling out. The mornings, if they get off to the right start, can be blessedly free of trouble. It is on the horizon of the afternoons, when the day is wearing thin, that difficulties loom, imminent, predictable, even though their precise shape and dimensions never cease to take Erin aback. In the moment of shock and indecision, primeval human responses in her are triggered that no amount of teacher training could prepare her for.
>
> (Wilson 2002, p. 88)

The story could stop there. It could refuse romance. However, in the actual situation, I ('Erin') have two choices: to leave or stay. Staying involves creating a new narrative, and the autobiography articulates this: 'Maybe the only kind of living that really matters is the one that rises, Phoenix-like, from the ashes' (Wilson 2002, p. 86). If staying is hard work, leaving is unbearable, because life then becomes etched with defeat and the loss of an opportunity to explore the reason for those 'primeval' responses, which I later recog-nize in incoming White teachers: 'that figure of a desperado written into the carriage and stride of a teacher who has reached – or almost – the end of her rope' (Wilson 2000, p. 16). Coming back to Bailey's (2000) distinctions, experience creates the possibility of an oppositional stance and the narrative of the self-inventing, self-doubting White teacher.

CONCLUSION

What is the value of self-study to theory and practice in teacher education? Cole and Knowles (1995) have concluded that the benefit is private; by participating in self-study, the teacher (or teacher educator) becomes more rigorously self-reflective. My own contention is that such narratives have a public aspect and writers are responsible for exploring those dimensions. Those dimensions have to do with the cultural myths, assumptions, predispositions and stories that inform the particular details of a life, as well as the way in which a life is shaped once written down as a story. It consists in asking questions like: Why is my/this story written in this particular way? How is my story like/unlike those written by others? If the writing accurately depicts experience (or the memory of experience), the conventional narrative can be contradicted by paying attention to niggling doubts. Practicing and pre-service teachers need more opportunities to remember and probe the platitudes along with the doubts, which is where I see the most fruitful ground for self-study methodologies in teacher education.

Postscript

The cat is buried behind the teacherages on her favorite hill overlooking the pond.

REFERENCES

Allen, J. and Labbo, L., 2001, Giving it a second thought: making culturally engaged teaching culturally engaging. *Language Arts*, 79(1), 40–52.
Andrews, G., 1985, *Metis Outpost: Memoirs of the First Schoolmaster at the Metis Settlement of Kelly Lake, B.C. 1923–1925* (Victoria, BC: Amity Press).
Ashton-Warner, S., 1960, *Spinster: A Novel* (London: Secker & Warburg).
Bailey, A., 2000, Locating traitorous identities: toward a view of privilege-cognizant

white character. In Narayan and Harding (Eds) *Decentering the Center: Philosophy for a Multicultural, Postcolonial, and Feminist World* (Bloomington, IN: Indiana University Press), pp. 283–98.

Bloch, M., 1998, *How We Think They Think* (Boulder, CO: Westview Press).

Braithwaite, M., 2002, *Why Shoot the Teacher* (Toronto, ON: McClelland & Stewart). (Original work published in 1965.)

Breece, H., 1997, *A Schoolteacher in Old Alaska: The Story of Hannah Breece* (New York: Vintage Books).

Brown, J., 1980, *Strangers in Blood: Fur Trade Company Families in Indian Country* (Vancouver, BC: UBC Press).

Brown, S.G., 2000, *Words in the Wilderness: Critical Literacy in the Borderlands* (New York: State University of New York Press).

Camus, A., 2000, *The Myth of Sisyphus* (London: Penguin Books). (Original work published in 1942.)

Cole, A. and Knowles, G., 1995, Methods and issues in a life history approach to self-study. In Russell and Korthagen (Eds) *Teachers who Teach Teachers: Reflections on Teacher Education* (London: Falmer Press), pp. 130–54.

Defoe, D., 1985, *The Life and Adventures of Robinson Crusoe* (London: Penguin Books). (Originally published in 1719.)

Fischer, M.M.J., 1986 Ethnicity and the post-modern arts of memory. In Clifford and Marcus (Eds) *Writing Culture: The Poetics and Politics of Ethnography* (Berkeley, CA: University of California Press), pp. 194–233.

Frye, N., 1976, *The Secular Scripture: A Study of the Structure of Romance* (Cambridge, MA: Harvard University Press).

Graham, R., 1995, Stories of teaching as tragedy and romance: when experience becomes text. In McEwan and Egan (Eds) *Narrative in Teaching, Learning and Research* (New York: Teachers College, Columbia University Press), pp. 195–210.

Greene, M., 1995, *Releasing the Imagination* (San Francisco: Jossey-Bass).

Grumet, M., 1988, *Bitter Milk: Women and Teaching* (Amherst: University of Massachusetts Press).

Harding, S., 1991, *Whose Science? Whose Knowledge? Thinking from Women's Lives* (Ithaca, NY: Cornell University Press).

Hulan, R., 2002, *Northern Experience and the Myths of Canadian Culture* (Montreal: McGill-Queen's University Press).

Kamler, B., 2001, *Relocating the Personal: A Critical Writing Pedagogy* (New York: State University of New York Press).

Kroetsch, R., 1995, *A Likely Story: The Writing Life* (Red Deer, AB: Red Deer College).

Madenwald, A.M., 1992, *Arctic Schoolteacher, Kulukak, Alaska, 1931–1933* (Norman, OK: University of Oklahoma Press).

Narayan, U. and Harding, S., 2000, *Decentering the Center: Philosophy for a Multicultural, Postcolonial, and Feminist world* (Bloomington, IN: Indiana University Press).

Perron, P., 2000, Creating memory: the martyrdom of Isaac Jogues in the Jesuit relations (1642–47). In Schuerewegen (Ed.) *Mnemotechnologies, Texte et Memoire* (Toronto, ON: Les Editions Trintexte), pp. 211–42.

Pratt, M.L., 1992, *Imperial Eyes: Travel Writing and Transculturation* (London: Routledge).

Sartre, J.-P., 1966, *Literature and Existentialism* (Trans. Bernard Frechtman) (New York: Citadel Press).

Stevenson, W., 1999, Colonialism and first nations women in Canada. In Dua and Robertson (Eds) *Scratching the Surface: Canadian Anti-Racist Feminist Thought* (Toronto, ON: Women's Press), pp. 49–63.

Taylor, C., 1989, *Sources of the Self* (Cambridge, MA: Harvard University Press).

Taylor, C., 1992, *The Ethics of Authenticity* (Cambridge, MA: Harvard University Press).

Taylor, P., 1955, *Buckskin and Blackboard* (London: Darwen Finlayson).

Van Kirk, S., 1980, *Many Tender Ties: Women in Fur-Trade Society in Western Canada, 1670–1870* (Winnipeg, MA: Watson & Dwyer).

Wilson, T., 2000, Ravenwing: a white teacher's experiences of teaching and living within a first nations community. Unpublished manuscript, University of Victoria.

Wilson, T., 2001, Butterfly tree. Unpublished story.

Wilson, T., 2002, Excavation and relocation: landscapes of learning in a teacher's autobiography. *Journal of Curriculum Theorizing*, **18**(3), 75–88.

Woolf, V., 1978a, *Moments of Being* (London: Grafton Books).

Woolf, V., 1978b, *A Room of One's Own* (London: Granada). (Original work published in 1929.)

Chapter 20

Starting with the self

Reflexivity in studying women teachers' lives in development

Jackie Kirk

INTRODUCTION

In this chapter I describe how 'starting with oneself' provides a very appropriate point of departure for studying the lives of women teachers in development contexts.[1] Locating myself as a one-time, some-time teacher, I draw on approaches to teacher self-study, and feminist reflexivity in western contexts, and explore their value and their implications in a development context. I begin with a brief introduction to the position of women teachers within development discourses, followed by a discussion of the theoretical foundations of my approach. The focal point of the chapter is an example 'vignette' – this is a short storied text that I developed as a response to my experiences of researching with women teachers in Pakistan. I discuss briefly the issues highlighted in the text, and end with a consideration of the implications of the methodology for progress towards gender equality in education, and for teacher education in development.

The specifics of my chapter refer to self-study in the context of teacher research, rather than teacher education. However, there is considerable overlap in terms of theoretical principles and of methodology. This is especially the case as I conducted fieldwork within a teacher training institution in Pakistan. I sought to develop a research methodology that was of professional relevance to participants, and I hoped to be able to make policy and programming recommendations to institutions and organizations training and working with women teachers in development contexts.

In relation to technical, pedagogical skills, dominant discourses of educational development tend to assume gender-neutral teachers. At the same time, however, an argument is made for the recruitment of more women teachers, and in some contexts in particular (especially South Asia and Sub-Saharan Africa) women teachers are the subject of a certain amount of policy and programming attention. Recruiting and training women teachers is often a priority strategy for increasing girls' enrolment in schools and in encouraging them to complete their studies. Women teachers are seen as important role models for girls, encouraging them to continue with their education.

Especially in conservative and traditional communities, recruitment and training of women teachers is seen as a strategy to encourage more parents to send their girls to school, and to create more girl-friendly school environments. In contexts in which male teacher abuse of girls is rife, the recruitment of women teachers can also be a child-protection issue. However, there is little research that addresses social and power relations in schools, and gender issues as experienced by women in the profession. Nor is there much attention to the realities of the relationships between girls and women in schools.

The feminist research paradigm in which I situate my doctoral study on women teachers' lives in Pakistan[2] connects important dimensions of my lived experience of being a woman, a teacher, a researcher, with my desire to make a difference for women through my academic work. I can only start to understand the multiple subjectivities of other women teachers if I can relate them to my own. It is in this sense, then, that the self becomes a re/source for re/search (Schratz and Walker, with Schratz-Hadwich 1995). Taking such an approach to the study of women teachers in development is rich in possibility, but also in challenges. Although there are numerous empirical and statistical studies of living and working conditions for women teachers in different countries, and much published work around classroom practice and performance, there is very little related conceptual and methodological work. There is, however, concern about the extent to which projects for women tend to be under-theorized, and a call for stronger theoretical work on gender issues in education (see Stromquist 1994). Narrow perceptions and limited conceptual frameworks for thinking about women teachers feed into policy and teacher education processes in which their perspectives are not fully considered nor their experiences fully acknowledged. Transformation of gender roles and relations in societies requires more from the education sector than increased girls' enrolment in school. Yet in a context in which attention is focused on numbers of girls entering and completing school, more complex theorizing may be tricky to do.

A self-study approach is quite different from most technical project and program-oriented work with teachers in development contexts and is not necessarily seen as a relevant strategy for meeting international targets on increased student enrolment and retention.[3] I would argue, however, that starting with the self, reflecting on one's own teaching and other identities, and how these relate to the issues affecting teachers elsewhere, is a necessary point from which to begin to develop sensitive, relevant and appropriate interventions. Despite the increasing numbers of researchers, teacher educators, international consultants, and other non-local 'technical experts' participating in activities in education in development, their selves, their identities, positions and biographies have been quite under-theorized. In this study, power, position and pedagogy are addressed from a body-conscious perspective through the conceptual linkages between feminist theories of women's teaching lives, and gender and development perspectives. Scholars such as Madeleine Grumet (1988), Valerie Walkerdine (1990) and Carolyn Steedman (1987) use their own experiences of mothering, of teaching and of being a girl in school as prisms through which to critically analyze and reconceptualize educational theory and practice. It is in this tradition that I work from the self outwards to engage with other women teachers, to explore and possibly to reinvent educational theories and practice in development contexts. Also important is to reflect on the research processes used to develop such theories. Women teachers are addressed as both subject and object, and they, rather than the teaching techniques, materials and training they might need, are placed central to theories of gender, education and development.

INTRODUCING VIGNETTES

Reflexivity

Reflexivity serves as the pivot of the methodological framework that I use to connect self-study with the study of other women teachers, and in particular to better understand the ruling relations between researcher and researched. Reflexivity is a starting point for self-study, and a place from which relationships between the self and others can be explored. The notion of reflexivity that I use is necessarily multi-layered, drawing on foundations in feminist theory, teacher research, teacher education and feminist ethnography. It allows me to draw attention to, and theorize around, the marginal position of women teachers in development. It also enables me to discuss the position of a feminist researcher whose position is at times a powerful one, but at others also a marginal one. Reflection on these shifting positions, on their limitations and partiality as well as the insights they may afford, is an integral part of my approach.

In my own experience, the praxis of reflexivity 'in the field' includes a sustained attention to the positions in which I place myself and am placed by others, a listening to and acknowledging of inner voices, doubts and concerns as well as pleasures and pride, and a sensing of what my body is feeling. It implies a constant questioning of what I am doing and why. I start to probe each of these experiences and sensations, to ask: Why? From where? Founded on what? I start to theorize based on my own experiences. Field notes and journals serve as the critical, practical tool of reflexivity; they are the place in which to capture fleeting thoughts, questions, images and ideas, and the place from which to start when engaging in a longer analysis and theorizing of them. The tensions and contradictions as well as the pleasures generated by my research activities may, at times, have been frustrating. However, when probed further, these continuities *and* discontinuities, the smooth linkages and the dissonances between periphery and center, between self and other, and between theory and practice, become sources of insights and a spring-board for further investigation.

Writing vignettes as reflexive, feminist practice

> But to intermingle the utopian 'feminine' space (of religious and a-social aura, of 'ultimates') with an attracted loathing for the blush/red etc feminine with a rooted feminist lust for material social justice in the quirky voice of a person mainly gendered female – well this is approximately the practice.
>
> (DuPlessis 1990, p. 165)

In taking such a reflexive approach to the study, it became necessary for me to develop process and form for my writing that was in keeping with my research aims and would do justice to my findings. I needed: (a) to express and analyze the reflexivity of the study and the insights it was generating; (b) to evoke in the reader some sense of the embodied research experience of studying women teachers' lives in Pakistan and how I interpret this; and (c) to rewrite women's lived experience of teaching within and yet at the same time against an apparently apolitical terrain of masculine theorizing of education in development. Creating short, storied texts based on my experiences had the potential for fulfilling these needs, allowing me to present some of my data of 'woman teacherness' in as complete a way as possible, resisting the tendency that van Manen (1990) describes for much of educational research to 'pulverize life into minute abstracted fragments and particles that are of little use to practitioners' (p. 7). This would allow me to work with the 'indeterminate realities of producing knowledge' (Jipson and Paley 1997), and to focus on women's experiential knowledge. This is so often lost in the apparently genderless, but implicitly male theories of teaching, learning and researching. Developing vignettes around my research experience made it more possible to convey powerful, multi-faceted and multi-sensory representations of research data, analysis and interpretations. Spaces are created for a politicized questioning of current social relations, structures and systems, and for the interrogation of my own 'entanglement' (Clifford 1997) within these.

For feminist ethnographers, the traditional written text, as product of a feminist ethnography, is highly problematic (see Stacey 1991, for example). Such a text inevitably perpetuates asymmetrical power relations between researcher and researched. Writing can, however, become in itself a form of feminist practice through which the issues of gender-based inequalities, of the power dynamics and relationships that exist between and amongst males and females, and of the male bias of many cultural, professional and academic norms can be addressed. A feminist ethnographer may find forms of writing and representation that challenge traditional scholarly forms, such as poly-vocal texts, autobiography, film and installation, as have feminist scholars working in education. However, as DuPlessis (1990) points out, as academic/poet/mother/wife/daughter, etc., she is inevitably 'marked' by gender, and is therefore 'produced' as gendered through certain forms of language. In a reflexive, feminist study of women teachers in Pakistan, the multi-layered challenge becomes that of deconstructing the language through which both my research participants and myself are produced as women, as women teachers, as women researchers, as women in development. It is then this same language that has to be used to develop and present alternatives.

To construct vignettes, I used the data I had collected in my field notes and journals, in order to both confront and intersect with stories already created about women teachers (Bailey 1997). My short texts, constructed through multiple layers of reflexive and self-situated writing, can be seen as an alternative to the traditional stance of the impartial observer. From a feminist perspective they fragment the 'univocal authority' (Lather 1991) on education in development that is predominantly male. I rewrite my own and other women's bodies and voices into education in development in alternative ways to the limiting discourses of nurturing and caring and of practical gender needs. In so doing it becomes possible to some extent to decentre knowledge about women teachers, to reterritorialize it from a feminist standpoint, and to critically remap what is 'known' (Aronowitz and Giroux 1991).

The writing of vignettes is not only a product of the research, rather part of the method (van Manen 1990). I wrote and rewrote in order to think through and process the data I had collected, and to reflect on issues of language, position, power and authority. I completed evocative texts that aim to engage the reader and draw her into the experiences being explored. As part of the analytical process, in the rewriting of these texts I borrowed from the genre of fiction, most especially for its attention to language, sounds and rhythms, and its power to explore and then provoke emotional response. I aimed to make the events more meaningful for the reader through attention to a narrative structure and to what I know is the evocative power of the story. Bailey (1997) writes of the importance of telling her own stories of teaching as a way of making herself and other women teachers subjects rather than objects of history. In the particular moment in time and place in the world that I was doing my fieldwork, this was particularly significant. Being in Karachi on and immediately after 11 September 2001, working with women teachers either side of this landmark world event, I felt powerless and insignificant. In this context, the vignettes represent a repositioning of myself, and of the women teachers and the issues I am interested in, into world history.

The example vignette below relates my experience of a meeting with women teachers during my fieldwork in Karachi. It was a research activity, but an unplanned and somewhat 'ad hoc' one that takes place in the unusual setting of the hostel residence in which these women teachers (all involved in a two-year professional development program) are living. It is an activity that generates significant reflections on my own identities as woman, researcher, and teacher, as both 'similar and other'.

The vignette: On meeting with a group of women teachers

As I am leaving the residence, the comments are ringing in my ears, 'We really enjoyed that', 'Come again soon', 'We only just got started', 'It's really interesting', and 'I've never thought about those things before.' So this is what it really feels like, to be a feminist researcher. So this is what my research objective, to stimulate discussion amongst women teachers about gender and education that goes beyond issues of access and attainment, actually looks like in practice. It must have been a success as I was invited to go back and continue one evening the next week.

But it had all started a little uncertainly, with a casual arrangement for me to go over to the women's residence to lead an informal session relating to my research. On the AKU-IED bus in the mornings and evenings I had chatted with some of the female teachers/students, about where they came from and what they were doing, about their experiences of being women teachers in their own countries and contexts. We had talked about what I was doing – and when asked, why. The invitation for the evening session had emerged from these conversations.

Having set it up like this, my plan – on paper and in my head – was a very flexible one. It could have easily been a non-plan if needed. I was very unsure what to expect from what had been quite a casual arrangement, and I was reluctant to make it more formal. Would the women really want to 'do' things, or just to chat? Would it actually be a workshop-type activity or more of a social visit? I prepared so that I could follow the flow, having a number of activities that could be quite fun, engaging, interesting and provocative, yet nonetheless not too 'heavy'. I was more than aware that as students in an intensive program, they were overloaded with different assignments and other tasks, spending long days on campus with each other. Would alternative, woman teacher-centred theories of teaching and learning be of interest to them, or would they contradict what they had been studying on campus? Would my work be the last thing they wanted to engage with on a Saturday evening? Although there were sixteen women in the residence, I had no idea how many would come, or whether they would all stay throughout.

As I arrived, two women were upstairs on the balcony hanging out washing, but came rushing down to greet me. Other residents were apparently busy elsewhere, and I was shown into the large, empty lounge, with a TV in the corner, a large shabby sofa and chairs round the outside of the room. There was nothing much else apart from a coffee table. 'Great,' I think. 'A big space to work in, in the middle of the room.' Four other women came in to join us, and we started chatting about life in the city and in the residence, about the difficulties of being so far from home and family, about the different sacrifices that had been made to follow the professional development course. We talked about the food, about children left behind in other countries and in distant regions of Pakistan, about the workload of the professional development course. We talked about persuading the driver to stop to get roast chicken on the way back from campus. We talked about wearing shalwar kameez. Our chatting was at the same time completely about being woman teacher, yet nothing about being a woman teacher.

I started to need to steer the conversation a little. I felt I had to explain myself and be explicit about my presence in their space. With the manoeuvre into this, into the 'ice-breaker' I had planned, and into follow-up activities and discussion prompts, I risked a loss of momentum, a breaking of the flow and a restructuring of the relationships being built. But the alternative seemed somewhat wasteful of the opportunity presenting itself. Anyway, I was sensing an expectation that I would in some way lead.

Following my prompt, as a group we discussed things we like and dislike doing that are typical and atypical for women. We talked as women and not necessarily as teachers. Discussion of menstrual taboos and exclusions arose from one woman's comment that she disliked 'all the caution you have to use during your period', explaining the need to sit and walk carefully. For women from different cultures, the discussion, which is simultaneously personal, social and starting to be somewhat critical, is clearly of interest. We move on to discuss the less than adequate toilet facilities for women and girls in schools, a subject which allows me to pose further questions about feeling empowered and disempowered in the school setting. Now we are thinking and talking as women teachers. The examples given become stories in themselves; multiple stories of marginalization from decision-making power but also contradictory stories of alternative sources of strength and empowerment. The card a woman receives from a parent, the possibilities to take on new projects and learn different things with the students, taking collective action to raise money for a less fortunate colleague, all make different women feel good about their roles as teachers.

Although I am unsure of the right tone to be taking, and find it difficult to lead *and* to let go, the whole tone of the evening is much more relaxed – even, I dare to think, more authentic than might have been the case had we organized a workshop session on campus. I appreciate a setting away from the confines of the institution. Within the women-only domain of the residence, my participants are more relaxed in their dress. Head scarves and drapes are no longer required, and several women are lounging in kaftan-type house clothes, sitting round on the floor and up against the cushions. Having come directly from campus, my own more formal dress feels suddenly restrictive, uncomfortable and inappropriate. My scarf is constantly in the way and yet it seems somehow wrong to discard it totally. The small amount of white skin I am showing contrasts with the brown and black bodies I am surrounded by. Togetherness and complicity are feelings as fleeting as difference, distance and 'otherness'.

Consent forms inevitably impose a formality onto the situation and my uncertainty about how to lead the evening meant that I hadn't got them out or even talked about them when I first arrived. I didn't want to scare these women off, nor contrive a more formal session than they were really wanting, but once we started talking it became obvious that the ideas flying about, the comments being made and the questions raised were too interesting not to be captured somehow as data. In researcher mode I intervene to stop the flow for a second, to ask if I can take notes, and to ask for their consent for me to use the data. Consent forms could be left with them to complete next time. Perhaps this was not the best, 'text-book' example of how to conduct group research, but if ethical research means comfortable and mutually satisfying for all concerned, then maybe we were creating an alternative model. The expectation was nonetheless there that I would use the data. Why would I be there otherwise? Why would I want to occupy women's precious time if the discussions weren't for some purpose? I had been asserting the importance of women's stories and women's lives, so surely the discussions were very relevant data.

Sitting in the car on the way back to my hostel, I try to imagine what the participants would now be thinking. Would the discussion have continued amongst themselves? Would there be follow-up the following day? I also wonder how the women would talk about what we had been doing with their male colleagues on the bus and in class the next day. How would they describe it? (How would I describe it?) Would they have considered it a 'real' research activity? (Do I consider it a real research activity?) Would its location, timing and women-only focus only devalue it within the institutional setting and its more formal research paradigms? But does that matter anyway?

DISCUSSION

The vignette is a means for me to present and theorize the inherent trickiness of working with women teachers in a development context, and to work with the emotional, affective and academic demands it makes on me, the researcher. It allows me to address the tensions between my own identification with these women – as women and as teachers – and my 'otherness' from them. I make explicit my questioning of the extent to which their expectations and needs were met by an evening that clearly excited me and provided me with lots of interesting data. It was much harder to know how to prepare for such an activity, and to gauge an appropriate tone for the interaction than for a more formal interview of group activity. I acknowledge that my own position is somewhat destabilized by the uncertainty of the experience. Whilst I might feel more comfortable in a less formal setting, the unpredictability and insecurity it generates are also somewhat disturbing.

My research experience is clearly an embodied one, and through the vignette, I can present the physical-ness of relations of power, of positions, of sameness and otherness. As I reflect on my clothing, my skin colour, my own reproductivity (or lack of it) in relation to those of the women I work with, our bodies are positioned into the research. Rather than mere bodies to be placed into schools, I articulate a different perspective on women, girls and education. Here, women's bodies are sites of experience and knowledge that, although somewhat contradictory and changeable, are nonetheless pedagogically and theoretically valuable.

Within the vignette I can highlight the uncertainties, the ambiguities and the hesitancies I experience. I shift from 'knower' to novice and back again in a way which I think is common to the experience of women researchers, and yet which is rarely explicitly addressed in the context of education and development. I problematize my own identities and positions as I do those of other women, and draw attention to the 'lines of fault' (Smith 1987) that I experience. These 'lines of fault' are the ambiguities, the insecurities and the uncertainties that do not match with what I read about women teachers in development. However, when probed and explored, they can become the starting points for new theories, which can challenge the over-simplification of gender issues in education.

IN CONCLUSION

With the above example, I suggest that studying the self makes a very appropriate starting point for research with women teachers in development contexts. Reflexivity is a crucial tool for connecting self-study with study of 'the other', and with which the 'ineluctable embeddedness' (Smith 1987) of the researcher and researched (teacher and teacher educator; teacher and student) within a larger context can be probed and problematized. Reflexivity necessarily engages the self in critical exploration of experience, perceptions and positions; the insight gained into these can then be used as a starting point for engaging with others, and for starting to develop shared understandings of educational issues and strategies to address them. Critical, feminist reflexivity as methodology then requires alternative forms of analysis and writing which in itself can further the political objectives of the research.

As Mitchell and Weber (1999) point out, studying ourselves is a commitment to personal and social change, and so for me, writing and working with field notes and journal entries is the catalyst for change. Lather writes that 'strategically, reflexive practice is privileged as the site from where we can learn how to turn critical thought into emancipatory action' (1991, p. 13). It is in this spirit that I see the study as a critical step in a process towards further, future action. The self is a starting point for professional and academic development, the place from which to identify what it is I want and need to do, and the place from where I can start to do that better. I use a reflexive, feminist perspective that draws on self-study scholarship relating to women teachers in the West, but which is at the same time attentive to the challenges (possibilities and impossibilities) of reflexive ethnography. Attune to the tensions and contradictions inherent in the telling of other women's stories, it can provide a meaningful framework within which to locate and examine these complexities. It constitutes a move towards individual and social change.

Foregrounding such methods, process and personal story in relation to gender, education and development, however, draw attention to issues, questions and complexities which are rarely acknowledged. Crewe and Harrison's (1999) question, 'Whose development?' remains for the most part unasked in these contexts, where little attention is given to the personal engagement and position of the teacher trainer/consultant/evaluator or researcher. Although the research landscape of Pakistan is described as 'dominated by people counting numbers in one form or another' (Smith 1997, p. 247) and teacher education is also relatively traditional in content and form, women teachers' own 'starting from the self' can be a possible starting point from which to generate alternative perspectives of gender and education. Placing the lived experiences of women and girls in schools and out of schools at the center, mining the 'lines of fault' (Smith 1987) between policy and practice, intention and reality, further insights could be gained of the relational complexities of women working in schools.

NOTES

1 I use the term 'development context' to refer to particular locations in countries, regions and communities of the South, the developing, majority or Third World.
2 This work in progress is tentatively entitled 'Impossible Fictions: Reflexivity in Studying Women Teachers' Lives in Development Contexts'.
3 These are, most notably, Education For All (EFA) targets and the Millennium Development Goals (MDGs) of gender equality in education: EFA target 5: eliminating gender disparities in primary and secondary education by 2005, and

achieving gender equality in education by 2015. MDG 3: promote gender equality and empower women: eliminate gender disparity in primary and secondary education, preferably by 2005, and to all levels of education no later than 2015.

REFERENCES

Aronowitz, S. and Giroux, H., 1991, *Postmodern Education, Politics, Culture and Social Criticism* (Minneapolis: University of Minnesota Press).

Bailey, C., 1997, A place from which to speak: stories of memory, crisis and struggle from the preschool classroom. In Jipson and Paley (Eds) *Daredevil Research: Recreating Analytic Practice* (New York: Peter Lang), pp.137–60.

Clifford, J., 1997, *Routes: Travel and Translation in the Late Twentieth Century* (Cambridge, MA and London: Harvard University Press).

Crewe, E. and Harrison, E., 1999, *Whose Development?: An Ethnography of Aid* (London: Zed Books).

DuPlessis, R.B, 1990, *The Pink Guitar: Writing as Feminist Practice* (New York: Routledge).

Grumet, M., 1988, *Bitter Milk: Women and Teaching* (Amherst: University of Massachusetts Press).

Jipson, J. and Paley, N. (Eds), 1997, *Daredevil Research: Recreating Analytic Practice* (New York: Peter Lang).

Lather, P., 1991, *Getting Smart: Feminist Research and Pedagogy with/in the Postmodern* (New York: Routledge).

Mitchell, C. and Weber, S., 1999, *Reinventing Ourselves as Teachers: Beyond Nostalgia* (London: Falmer Press).

Schratz, M. and Walker, R. with Schratz-Hadwich, B., 1995, Collective memory-work: the self as a re/source for re/search. In Schratz and Walker (Eds) *Research as Social Change* (London and New York: Routledge).

Smith, D., 1987, *The Everyday World as Problematic* (Boston: Northeastern University Press).

Smith, R.L., 1997, Implementing qualitative research in Pakistan: international teamwork. In Crossley and Vulliamy (Eds) *Qualitative Research in Developing Countries: Current Perspectives* (New York and London: Garland Publishing), pp. 245–64.

Stacey, J., 1991, Can there be a feminist ethnography? In Gluck and Patai (Eds) *Women's Words: The Feminist Practice of Oral History* (London and New York: Routledge), pp. 111–19.

Steedman, C., 1987, Prisonhouses. In Lawn and Grace (Eds) *Teachers: The Culture and Politics of Work* (London: Falmer Press), p. 120.

Stromquist, N., 1994, Gender and basic education in international development cooperation, UNICEF Working Paper Series, New York: UNICEF.

Van Manen, J., 1990, *Researching Lived Experience: Human Science for an Active, Sensitive Pedagogy* (London, Ontario: The Althouse Press).

Walkerdine, V., 1990, *Schoolgirl Fictions* (New York and London: Verso).

Subject index

Aboriginal communities 219
action research 201
adult educator 142–53
apartheid 207
Arizona Group 61, 67, 199
artefacts 77, 112, 147
artful experiences 69–80
artistic forms of representation 40
art museums 61
arts-based methodology 14, 81–94,
    95–110
art that tells story 77–80
art therapy 38
autobiography 32, 96, 183–92, 218;
    autobiographical art 40
auto-ethnography 155
A Visit From the Old Mistress 63, 66

batik 88, 89, 90
biographer 29
bisexual 49
bricolage 114
bullying 34–46

Castle Conference 61
Centre for Arts Informed Research
    2
collaboration: co-mentoring 163;
    research 73
colonizing discourse 221
community of writers 206–17
confrontational pedagogy 175
course-work in self-study; drama
    sequence 124–8; EDF 3002 171–7;
    'Literacy, School and Community'
    course 114
critics: friends 60–2, 151, 152;
    reflection 131–41, 143, 144

development contexts 231–41
dialogue 134
dissertation writing 91; and self study
    184, 188
drama 123–30
drawings 34–46; bullying 37–44;
    gender and technology 39; germs 43;
    gym class 41; self-portraits 39

e-mail 200
embodied knowing 6, 34–46, 239;
    clothing and memory 38; dress
    stories 4; embodied praxis 40; glass
    tunics by Lyse Lemieux 3; shoes
    13–21
epiphanies 72
ethics 101, 159, 164, 238

feminists: lens 185, 191, 240; voices
    95
feminotopia 223–5
fiction 111–20
found poetry 95–110

gay and lesbian identity 49–57,
    193–205; as teachers 49
gender 15, 39, 66, 197, 232
girls: education 231; voices 101

HIV/AIDS 4, 5, 8
homophobia 56

Image and Identity Research Collective
    2

journal writing 54, 59, 126, 134,
    136, 138, 139, 176, 201; response
    187

leaving home stories 219
life histories 70, 78
life story 112
literary anthropology 111, 119;
    literature 81; poetry 81–94
lived experience 69–70
ludic reading 118

mapping 187
mathematics 137
memoire 8, 22–33, 187
memory work 13, 34–46, 69, 76, 96,
    112, 155, 220
mentoring 134, 138, 142, 149, 155,
    166
metaphors 13, 81–94
mural-making 49

narrative inquiry 6, 22–33, 133,
    206–17
Nelson-Atkins art museum 61
No Great Mischief 113, 115
Not Just Any Dress 21
Nova Scotia 111–20
novice researchers 154–67

oral history 74
outward gaze 4, 112

Pakistan teachers 231–41
Participatory Action Research
    163
partnership: support group 158;
    research partnership 71, 73
pedagogy of reinvention 161
performance 3, 15–20, 195
performativity 195
Personal Narratives Group 95
phenomenological lens 56
photography 3, 16, 50, 75, 117, 118,
    187
poetic self-study 67, 87, 95–110
poetry protocol 108
pre-service teachers 83, 123; value of
    168
protocol writing 72

queer studies 54, 193–205

reading literature 114
reflection 78, 79, 80, 123, 125,
    127, 143, 177; different from
    self-study 131, reflection in action

135; reflection-on-action 135;
    reflexivity 233
Reinventing Ourselves as Teachers 2,
    16
remembering 184, 228
research maps 162
romance 226, 227
rural life 111–20

Saudi Arabia 186
school days 104–6
self-reflexive artistic dialogue: in
    relation to literacy 66; through
    imaginary letters 66; with Winslow
    Homer 61–66
self-study: emancipatory 197; mini
    self-studies 42–3; 'othered' 194;
    self-study guide 154–67;
    vulnerability 183–92; with youth
    143
selves: rural selves 111; textual selves
    113
September 11 235
seventh moment 95
sexuality and identity 51
South Africa 206–17
Spinster 225
S-STEP 2, 4, 194
staging 66, 111
stakeholders 160
starting with ourselves 7, 231, 232,
    240
student teacher supervision 132
Studying Teacher Education 2

Taking Sunflower to Teacher 63,
    64
teacher educator 58–68, 70, 128–9,
    168–80
teacher development 81; and change
    84
teacher identity 113
teacher research 154–67, 231–41; living
    research 85; teacher participant 212
team teaching 174
Teen Story Project 206–17
*That's Funny You Don't Look Like a
    Teacher* 2
The Cotton Pickers 63, 65
The Country School 63
travelling 118, 191, 218–30; teachers'
    travel autobiographies 223
triangulation 61

Van Gogh 13, 14, 20
video 3, 16, 151
vignettes 234, 235
visual texts 8, 50, 75

When the Shoe Doesn't Fit: Death of a Salesman 17

white-ness 7, 208, 218–30
Winslow Homer paintings 58–68
women teachers 71, 114, 183–192, 231–41
working with youth 142 ff, 206–17

Author index

Aronowitz, S. and Giroux, H. 235
Ashton-Warner, S. 225

Bailey, A. 220
Bailey, C. 235
Barbieri, M. 103
Barone, T.E. and Eisner, E. 164
Barthes, R. 28, 29, 30, 31, 32, 114, 117
Belenky, M.F. et al. 103
Benjamin, S.G.W. 62
Berger, L. 95, 97
Bergson, H. 88, 91
Berry, A. and Loughran, J.J. 133, 134,
    171, 176
Bornstein, K. 193, 200
Brookfield, S.D. 169
Bullough, R.V. and Pinnegar, S. 104
Butler, J. 193, 195
Byatt, A.S. 81

Cherland, M. 66
Clandinin, J. and Connelly, M. 58,
    133
Clifford, J. 234
Cochran-Smith, M. and Lytle, S. 58
Cole, A.L. 73
Cole, A.L. and Knowles, J.G. 71, 73,
    74, 143, 228
Cole, A. and McIntyre, M. 195
Conle, C. 206
Conle, C. et al. 133, 134
Connell, R.W. 209, 213

De la Huerta, C. 196, 197
Denzin, N.K. 61, 72
Dewey, J. 16, 83, 208
Diamond, C.T.P. and Mullen, C.A.
    82
Dinkelman, T. 147, 148, 170, 171

Donmoyer, R. 96
Drabble, M. 83
DuPlessis, R.B. 234, 235

Eisner, E.W. 36, 37, 40, 41, 58, 91, 96
Ellis, C. and Berger, L. 50
Ellis, C. and Bochner, A. 50
Ely, M. et al. 50, 192

Foucault, M. 113
Freire, P. 93, 127

Geertz, C. 184
Gibbson, R. 146, 147, 148
Giroux, H. 58
Gough, N. 210
Greene, M. 85, 92, 152, 220
Grimmett, P.P. 177
Grumet, M.R. 83, 186, 225, 233
Guilfoyle, K. 134
Guilfoyle, K. et al. 175

Hamilton, M.L. 79
Hamilton, M.L. and LaBoskey, V. 59,
    61
Hamilton, M.L. and Pinnegar, S. 59
Harding, S. 220
Hargreaves, A. 163
Hargreaves, A. and Fullan, M. 166
Haug, F. 110
Heaney, S. 81
Hussey, C. 67, 101

Irigaray, L. 114
Iser, W. 111, 120

Jipson, J. and Paley, N. 234

Kirsch, G. 100

Lakoff, G. and Johnson, M. 85
Lather, P. 235
Lincoln, Y.S. 164
Lincoln, Y.S. and Denzin, N.K. 95
Lincoln, Y.S. and Guba, E.G. 75
Lomax, P. *et al.* 133
Loughran, J.J. *et al.* 2
Loughran, J. and Northfield, J. 131, 169

McNiff, S. 34, 36, 37
Mitchell, C. 16, 66
Mitchell, C. and Reid-Walsh, J. 4
Mitchell, C. and Weber, S. 4, 5, 6, 38, 79, 151, 155, 156, 163, 164, 183, 240
Moi, T. 113
Mullen, C.A. 157
Mullen, C.A. and Lick, D.W. 158, 159, 163
Munby, H. 169

Narayan, U. and Harding, S. 220
Neilsen, L. 116
Nell, V. 120
Noddings, N. 175

Oakley, A. 5
Olsen, T. 187

Peters, M. and Lankshear, C. 162
Pratt, M.L. 223

Richardson, L. 84, 95, 96, 97, 104

Rose, J. 119
Russell, T. 174

Said, E.W. 192
Schön, D. 135, 169
Schratz, M. and Walker, R. 232, 241
Sedgwick, E. 199
Smith, R.L. 239
Stacey, J. 234
Steedman, C. 233
Steele, V. 15
Stromquist, N. 232

Taylor, C. 219
Tidwell, D. 174

Upitis, R. and Russell, T. 200

Van Halen-Faber, C. and Diamond, C.T.P. 83
Van Manen, M. 5, 37, 44, 69, 72, 173, 234, 235

Walkerdine, V. 233
Weber, S. and Mitchell, C. 2, 3, 35, 37, 38, 39, 195
Whitehead, J. 188
Williams, R. 114
Williams, S.J. and Bendelow, G. 35, 41, 42
Woolf, V. 218, 224

Zeichner, K.M. 58
Zeichner, K. 194